WOMEN
EDITING
MODERNISM

WOMEN EDITING MODERNISM

"Little" Magazines & Literary History

JAYNE E. MAREK

THE UNIVERSITY PRESS OF KENTUCKY

Copyright © 1995 by The University Press of Kentucky

Scholarly publisher for the Commonwealth,
serving Bellarmine College, Berea College, Centre
College of Kentucky, Eastern Kentucky University,
The Filson Club, Georgetown College, Kentucky
Historical Society, Kentucky State University,
Morehead State University, Murray State University,
Northern Kentucky University, Transylvania University,
University of Kentucky, University of Louisville,
and Western Kentucky University.

Editorial and Sales Offices: Lexington, Kentucky 40508-4008

Library of Congress Cataloging-in-Publication Data
Marek, Jayne E., 1954-
    Women Editing Modernism : "little" magazines and literary history
/ Jayne E. Marek
        p.   cm.
    Includes bibliographical references and index.
    ISBN 0-8131-1937-5 (alk. paper). — ISBN 0-8131-0854-3 (alk.
paper)
        1. American literature—20th century—History and criticism.
    2. Modernism (Literature)—United States.   3. Women editors—United
    States.   4. English literature—20th century—History and criticism.
    5. Women editors—Great Britain.   6. Literature, Experimental—
    History and criticism.   7. Literature publishing—History—20th
    century.   8. Modernism (Literature)—Great Britain.   9. Little
    magazines—History.   10. Avant-garde (Aesthetics)   I. Title.
    PS228.M63M37   1995
    810.9'1—dc20   95-14890

This book is printed on acid-free recycled paper meeting
the requirements of the American National Standard
for Permanence of Paper for Printed Library Materials.

To my parents,
David and Lorraine Marcum Menich

CONTENTS

ACKNOWLEDGMENTS

The massive amount of research necessary even to begin to address this topic has required me to visit a score of libraries, contact dozens of people, and refer to hundreds of documents. In addition, as any scholar knows, this research has often required that I ask more than professional expertise from those I met on my travels; I have been the beneficiary of gifts, insights, meals, housing, transportation, and practical help with problems having to do with hunting down obscure information, finding my way around in new places, and struggling with the ever-changing materials of word processing. At the very least, my investigations into the lives and works of the modernist women I discuss have shown me that such pragmatic connections are the backbone of any sizeable accomplishment, as well as one of its chief pleasures.

Accordingly, I would like to begin with personal thanks to a number of persons whose assistance and goodwill have helped my research along: my husband, Joe; my parents, Lorraine and David Menich; my sister, Gayle Roehm; past and present personnel at *Poetry* magazine, especially Helen Klaviter; and the director of my dissertation, professor Cyrena N. Pondrom of the University of Wisconsin at Madison. Another group of people I would like to thank includes those whom I have met or corresponded with in the course of my research, whose knowledge and consideration have greatly abetted my work: Holly Baggett, Chris Baird, Eileen Cahill, Alice Clark, Elizabeth Cleary, Lori N. Curtis, Dale Davis, Nancy Watson Dean, Michelle Dorgan, Ken Dunmire, Elizabeth Dunn, Rachel Blau DuPlessis, Evelyn Feldman, Susan Stanford Friedman, Connie Hale, Diana Haskell,

Cathy Henderson, Andrea Inselmann, Chris Kellett, Margaret Kulis, Sally Leach, Paula Y. Lee, Laura Lewis, Melanie Lewis, Jane Lidderdale, Stanley I. Mallach, L. Rebecca Johnson Melvin, Ellen Murphy, Tabitha Palmer, Susan Noyes Platt, Nancy Romalov, Jill Rosenschild, Daniel R. Schwarz, Bonnie Kime Scott, Margaret Sherry, Liz Weisberg, and Max Yela. I am also pleased to thank Mrs. Edwin S. Fetcher, grandniece of Harriet Monroe, and Mrs. Perdita Schaffner for their encouragement and generosity.

I would also like to thank the Harry Ransom Humanities Research Center of the University of Texas at Austin, the Board of Regents of Pacific Lutheran University, and the Graduate School of the University of Wisconsin at Madison for funding portions of my research through grants.

For permission to quote from unpublished and published materials in this study, I am grateful to many literary executors and libraries. Unpublished letters of Marianne Moore are used by permission of Marianne Craig Moore, Literary Executor for the Estate of Marianne Moore; all rights reserved. Previously unpublished material by H.D. (Hilda Doolittle), Copyright © 1995 by Perdita Schaffner, is used by permission of New Directions Publishing Corporation, agents. Previously unpublished material by Ezra Pound, Copyright © 1995 by the Trustees of the Ezra Pound Literary Property Trust, is used by permission of New Directions Publishing Corporation, agents. Grateful acknowledgment is also given to New Directions Publishing Corporation and Faber and Faber Ltd. for permission to quote from the following copyrighted works of Ezra Pound: *The Cantos* (Copyright © 1934, 1937, 1940, 1948, 1956, 1959, 1962, 1963, 1966, and 1968 by Ezra Pound); *Pound/Ford* (Copyright © 1971, 1972, 1973, 1982 by the Trustees of the Ezra Pound Literary Property Trust); *Pound/Joyce* (Copyright © 1967 by Ezra Pound); *Pound/Lewis* (Copyright © 1985 by the Trustees of the Ezra Pound Literary Property Trust); *Pound/ The Little Review* (Copyright © 1988 by the Trustees of the Ezra Pound Literary Property Trust); *Selected Letters 1907-1941* (Copyright © 1950 by Ezra Pound); *The Letters of Ezra Pound to Alice Corbin Henderson* (Copyright © 1993 by the University of Texas Press); and *Ezra Pound's Poetry and Prose: Contributions to Periodicals* (Copyright © 1991 by the Trustees of the Ezra Pound Literary Property Trust). Unpublished letters of J. Sibley Watson are used by permission of the Literary Executor for the Estate of Dr. James Sibley Watson, Jr: The Sigma Foundation, Inc. Unpublished letters of Scofield Thayer are used by permission of Frederic B. Ingraham, Literary Executor for the Estate of Scofield Thayer. Unpublished letters of Harriet Monroe are used by permission of Ann Monroe, Literary Executor for the Estate of Harriet Monroe. Unpublished letters by Richard Aldington, H.D., and Ezra Pound are used by permission of the Houghton Library, Harvard University. Unpublished letters by Harriet Monroe and Alice Corbin Henderson are used by permission of the Harry Ransom Humanities Research Center, the University of Texas at Austin. Unpublished letters by H.D., Marianne Moore, Scofield Thayer, and J. Sibley Watson in the Marianne Moore Papers are used by permission of the Rosenbach Museum and Library, Philadelphia. Unpublished letters by Bryher, H.D., and Kenneth Macpherson are used by permission of Perdita Schaffner. Unpublished letters by Bryher, H.D., Dorothy Elise de Pollier, Alyse Gregory, Jane Heap, Kenneth Macpherson, Marianne Moore, Scofield Thayer, and J. Sibley Watson are used by permission of the Yale Collection of American Literature, Beinecke Rare Book and Manuscript Library, Yale University. Unpublished letters by Alice Corbin Henderson are used by permission of the Department of Special Collections, University of Chicago Library, and by permission of the Estate of Alice Corbin Henderson. Unpublished letters by Jane Heap are used by permission of Karen L. Clark.

Versions of portions of chapters 2, 4, and 5 have appeared previously: "Alice Corbin Henderson, Harriet Monroe, and *Poetry*'s Early Years" in *Illinois Writers Review* 7.2 (1988): 16-22; "Bryher and *Close Up*, 1927-1933" in *H.D. Newsletter* 3.2 (1990): 27-37; and "Marianne Moore's Editorship of *The Dial*," in *Sagetrieb* 11.1-2 (1992): 181-205. An earlier version of this study, "'I Know Why I Say What I Do Say': Women Editors of 'Little' Magazines, 1912-1933," was presented as my dissertation to the University of Wisconsin at Madison in 1991.

I am also grateful to the following libraries whose collections I consulted: the British Library; the Library of University College, London; the Library of Congress; the Golda Meir Library of the University of Wisconsin at Milwaukee; the Bibliothèque Nationale; the Bibliothèque Jacques Doucet; the Suzzallo Library of the University of Washington; the Newberry Library; and the Memorial Library of the University of Wisconsin at Madison.

1 MAKING THEIR WAYS

Women Editors
of "Little" Magazines

It is some kind of commentary on the [modern] period that Joyce's work and acclaim should have been fostered mainly by high-minded ladies, rather than by men. Ezra first brought him to Miss Weaver's attention, but it was she who then supported him. The *Little Review*, Sylvia Beach, and Harriet Weaver brought Joyce into print.
—Robert McAlmon, *Being Geniuses Together*

This book so far may have given the impression that I have had no diffi-culty in making myself, that I sprang like a warrior out of the earth. If so, I have been unjust to my effort. . . . The causes I have fought for have invariably been causes that should have been gained by a delicate suggestion. Since they never were, I made myself into a fighter. . . . I remember periods when I have been so besieged that I had to determine on a victory a day in order to be sure of surviving.
—Margaret Anderson, *My Thirty Years' War*

These passages, quoted from two publishers who were closely associated with the foremost innovators in modernist literature, give a sense of con-text for discussing women's contributions to the development of modern literature, particularly in terms of publishing. In any such discussion one ought to bear in mind the climate of opinion suggested by these quota-tions. McAlmon's comment implicitly relies on masculinist assumptions and privileges—he characterizes women as "high-minded" and worth acknowledgment because of their promotion of Joyce's writings, although his tone carries a distinct note of regret, or surprise, that women's support was integral to Joyce's success. In the second passage, Anderson expresses her sense of constant struggle not only for acceptance and "victory" but also for bare recognition of what she was trying to do; she expresses, in short, her feeling of being limited by social attitudes and prescribed roles. If one looks past the habitual flamboyance of both Anderson's and McAlmon's writings, one may see in these quotations the indications of substantial differences between the experiences of male and female modernists. Such differences come as no surprise to scholars aware of the nature of women's history or the much higher proportion of attention that has been given to male modernists. Men, as had been usual, operated from an assumption of power and capability, looking among themselves for the important work of the new century; women, also as usual, faced exhausting struggles even to achieve passing notice. For readers who take seriously Anderson's work as an editor of the *Little Review*, or the work of dozens of other women connected with modernist publishing, it is clear that women had far more to do with the support and evolution of modernism than has been generally acknowledged. The skein of women's influence that I shall address in this book concerns the contributions made by some of the women who edited "little" literary and arts magazines.

The dynamic history of modernist publishing is embodied in the trajectories and vicissitudes of such little magazines. Many young writers, charged with the excitement of ideas and artistic perspectives that had been developing in Europe, could find neither a sympathetic audience nor a market among the generally conservative publishers of the day. Granted, the aesthetic risks of publishing experimental materials were underscored by obscenity laws that could—and did—censor publications and ruin businesses. As a consequence, scores of small journals sprang up, usually fueled more by energy than by funds or knowledge of the exigencies of publication. Nevertheless, these magazines created vigorous new connections between readers and writers who wanted to foster experimentation and challenge aesthetic traditions. George Bornstein notes a strong connection between the literature in and the editing of such new venues: "Both their astute sense of literary politics and their respect for documentary transmission led the major modernists to enmesh themselves in a wide range of editorial activities. They saw clearly that editors set the field of literary study, both by deciding what works came to the public and by determining the form in which those works appeared."[1]

Modern little magazines, as Frederick J. Hoffman, Charles Allen, and Carolyn F. Ulrich, authors of *The Little Magazine: A History and a Bibliography*, describe them, were "designed to print artistic work which for reasons of commercial expediency [was] not acceptable to the money-minded periodicals or presses," which appealed to "a limited group of intelligent readers," and which expressed a "spirit of conscientious revolt against the guardians of public taste" (2-4). These iconoclastic publications—deliberately violating accepted principles of publishing and commercial success—afforded a particularly pertinent venue for the avant garde work that few established magazines were willing to print.[2] The precarious and idiosyncratic nature of such alternative magazines meant that a good portion of the contents was acquired through word of mouth among circles of experimental writers and was often borne on the currents of internecine squabbles, strong personal enthusiasms, and plays for power and influence. The personalities of editors, like those of the writers and artists who opened the doors of experimentation, became central to the dynamics of modernist publishing. Considering the cultural constraints upon women at that time, it is therefore particularly significant that the editors of many of the most important avant garde journals were women.

One might not at first expect this to be true. Very few literary histories treat women editors seriously. Modern historians have concentrated on the works of men, for the most part, and the act of editing itself has drawn attention mostly in terms of what happened when Ezra Pound met T. S. Eliot's draft of "The Waste Land" or when James Joyce added huge quantities of text to successive galleys of *Ulysses*. The women editors who are mentioned in such influential works as Malcolm Bradbury and James McFarlane's *Modernism* (1976) generally appear as adjuncts or foils to the men whose works they printed. As Bonnie Kime Scott notes in the introduction to her book *The Gender of Modernism* (1990), "Typically, both the authors of original manifestos and the literary historians of modernism took as their norm a small set of its male participants, who were quoted, anthologized, taught, and consecrated as geniuses. Much of what even these select men had to say about the crisis in gender identification that underlies much of modernist literature was left out or read from a limited perspective. Women writers were often deemed old-fashioned or of merely anecdotal interest" (2). As a result, Scott notes, "Modernism as we were taught it . . . was perhaps halfway to truth. It was unconsciously gendered masculine" (2). Scott's words reinforce the observations of a number of recent studies that note that in histories, biographies, compilations, critical commentaries, and memoirs, women's contributions and reputations have rarely been treated with the same depth and discernment used for men's work, which was assumed to be "universal" in scope—an assumption that affects many critical histories to this day.[3]

No compelling argument upholds such exclusion. In terms of women editors alone, for instance, most readers interested in the modernist era know that small magazines were extremely important in bringing the new literature to its public—witness the central roles played by *Poetry*, edited by Harriet Monroe and her associates, and the *Little Review*, edited by Margaret Anderson and Jane Heap. As the passage quoted from McAlmon indicates, the appearance of *Ulysses* itself depended upon the discernment and tenacity of various women, Heap and Anderson among them. Further investigation uncovers the names of a striking number of women editors active during the rise and flowering of modernism, including Monroe, Anderson, Heap, Kay Boyle, Bryher (Winifred Ellerman), Emily Clark, Caresse Crosby, Nancy Cunard, H.D. (Hilda Doolittle), Jessie Fauset, Florence Gilliam, Alice Corbin Henderson, Maria Jolas, Amy Lowell, Katherine Mansfield, Marianne Moore, Lola Ridge, Laura Riding, May Sinclair, Harriet Shaw Weaver, Rebecca West, and Virginia Woolf. The work of these women editors was extremely varied and highly influential; the incongruous paucity of scholarship about many of these women raises important issues for theorists of modernism who are willing to deconstruct the assumptions characterized by McAlmon's statements and explore the hardships and strengths characterized by Anderson's. What remains obscured in literary history that will be uncovered once women's contributions to "gatekeeping" as well as to creative work are taken seriously?

Since women's experiences, in literary as in other milieus, have differed considerably from those of men, women's writings often reflect this disparity through theme, writing style, and imagery.[4] The pervasive nature of such differences shows the need to continue studying implications of gender bias in the history and operations of literary production, criticism, and evaluation. In some cases, the poetry or fiction women wrote has received far more attention than their editorial and critical work; in other cases, women's editorial contributions have been overlooked, denigrated, or even attributed to men. Any assessment of the nature of modernism that aims to provide a sufficient overview, however, must address how women's writing, criticism, and publishing affected literary history, and how the roles these women chose had distinctive effects on what they accomplished. Such study seems especially appropriate to the modernist era, with its literature expressing considerable anxiety over the upheavals that characterized the early twentieth century.

Modernist literary experimentation arose from many aspects of life that were affected by a strong contemporary sense of cultural flux. Pertinent historical pressures of the time included the First World War, the residues of works by Darwin, Marx, and Freud, immense technological innovation, and archaeological and philological discoveries that modified ideas of human history—a set of pressures that culminated in the "disestablishing of communal reality and conventional notions of causality . . . [and] the destruction of traditional notions of the wholeness of individual character. . . . [In modernism] all realities [had] become subjective fictions."[5] Reflecting on these momentous changes, modernist writers and artists attempted to express the flux of reality by dispensing with conventional modes of depiction and by experimenting instead with abrupt and unusual juxtapositions, sensory immediacy, linguistic play, and combinations of prosaic subject matter with idiosyncratic and esoteric allusions, all of which radically challenged aesthetic conventions.

Not surprisingly, the many aspects of modernist development have given rise to an impressive—and confusing—range of interpretations. Standard histories of modernism, particularly those predicated upon New Criticism, are currently being revised, although for the most part scholars still orient their studies toward literary and critical works written by men. Such an approach may express itself in the form of theoretical positions that do not include attention to women's history, or in a "humanism" that claims to include women's history and feminist theory but that in fact subsumes them, once again, into a presumably "universal" position.

In one discussion, for instance, historian Albert Gelpi finds that modernism, like the Enlightenment and Romanticism, was a response to "the rising sense of threat and confusion at every level of life in the West, religious and psychological, philosophic and political: a sense of crisis."[6] This crisis developed from the decay of the Romantic notion of "the individual's intrinsic capacity to perceive and participate in the organic interrelatedness of all forms of natural life and . . . to intuit [through the imagination] the metaphysical reality from which that natural harmony proceeds" (3). Gelpi believes this decay turned into a skeptical modernism, of which the salient characteristics were "complexity and abstraction, sophisticated technical invention and spatialized form, the conception of the artist as at once supremely self-conscious and supremely impersonal" (5). The dualism of such paradoxical constructions reinscribes a good many of the qualities it seems to question, most obviously in the familiar notion that modernist dissonances expressing "crisis" necessarily undergirded a drive toward an encompassing consonance. It is also apparent that this sort of critical language itself reflects the values of a masculinist viewpoint that reinforces hierarchy.

Another way in which dualism tends to be reinscribed in conservative literary histories concerns the "break with the past" that many critics see as essential to the modernist agenda, as if the artistic expressions of the twentieth century were an abrupt and complete change from earlier traditions. In discerning and interpreting such a break, Michael Levenson decides, for instance, that the emphasis he sees on "two-ness" in the pronouncements of Eliot, Pound, Ford, and Hulme indicates a desire for "thorough historical discontinuity" (ix), which would obviously invest these men's works with pivotal significance in the development of modern thought. One kind of radical discontinuity, however, is absent from Levenson's own "genealogy" of modernism; this book, too, concentrates on the work of a few—mostly very familiar—male writers, despite its overt language of reproduction that might at least suggest the presence of women. Of course no single book can do justice to the huge range of writers and artists who might be included in a discussion of modernism, but it is particularly ironic, given Levenson's refusal even to acknowledge the influence of such women as Dorothy Richardson, Gertrude Stein, and H.D., that he writes, "Part of the difficulty of modernism is that it has suppressed its origins" (xi). Indeed.

The problems occasioned by ignoring or suppressing women's contributions must be taken seriously, since the effects infiltrate every aspect of history-making and canonization. One instance of such a "filtering" effect, as Shari Benstock terms it in *Women of the Left Bank* (27), can be found in the language of the following scenario from Hoffman, Allen, and Ulrich's *The Little Magazine: A History and a Bibliography*, in which the authors note that little reviews often served as the key to recognition for beginning or experimental writers:

One may speak casually of an Ernest Hemingway's receiving his first half-dozen publications in little magazines and thereby gaining a reputation. . . . But let us be more specific. Hemingway publishes his first story in *The Double Dealer* in 1922. Assume that the editor and a few other people read this story and like it. These people talk enthusiastically of the story and perhaps twice as many read the next Hemingway offering. Soon many admirers are talking—a snowball is rolling in the advance guard. A half-dozen little magazines are printing Hemingway stories and he has several thousand readers. An obscure, noncommercial press in Paris publishes his first thin volume, *Three Stories and Ten Poems*. The snowball rolls into the Scribner's office. Finally in 1926 comes *The Sun Also Rises*. A writer has been started on the road to success—by the little magazines and their readers. [14]

One might well add, "and by their editors and sponsors." If the appearance of *Three Stories and Ten Poems* in 1923 helped Hemingway's "snowball" to gain crucial momentum (or at least to bring him to Contact Editions' affiliation with Three Mountains Press, which printed his *In Our Time* a year later), then thanks in good measure can be laid not only at publisher Robert McAlmon's door but also at the door of his wife, Bryher, whose funds and connections helped provide for the success of Contact Editions.[7] After two brief publications in *The Double Dealer*, Hemingway's next appearances were in *Poetry*, with poems and bits of literary gossip that were to become characteristic, and in the *Little Review*, with six stories that later appeared in *In Our Time* and the poem "They All Made

Peace—What Is Peace?"[8] Clearly, the discernment of the women who edited little magazines and supported small publishing concerns proved essential to the "snowballing" of Hemingway's reputation.

The Little Magazine: A History and a Bibliography (1947) remains the best general introduction to the role that small magazines played in the early twentieth century, but its tendency to highlight the works of men reflects an approach that many literary histories have used. This tone particularly affects interpretations of the psychological politics behind the creation and promotion of avant garde work. If men have been expected to be bold or experimental, and women have been expected to be emotional or compliant, then post hoc discussions of the bravado that is obvious in much modernist writing will be pitched a certain way. For instance, Hoffman, Allen, and Ulrich choose to characterize Ezra Pound as "truly the 'personality as poet,'" a man whose "critical remarks are characterized by spasmodic penetration, an arbitrary and cocksure forthrightness, and an obstinate refusal to brook what he considered untimely or petty opposition," and who thereby became "one of the most effective sponsors of experimental literature in our century" (21). Their assessment of the *Little Review* notes some of the same energy and individuality but gives these qualities a distinctly different spin; the *Little Review* is characterized as a "personal" magazine that reflected Margaret Anderson's "breathless racing with life" from interest to interest (20): "It was an exciting magazine, quixotic, sometimes immature, but always radiating the blue sparks of highly charged feeling. Many were the stars that danced before Margaret Anderson's impulsive vision. . . . Inevitably, there was to come a time when she could glimpse no further horizon" (52). The style of Anderson's magazine is equated with her personality and dismissed as a limitation, and Anderson's successes in dealing with "opposition"—most notably in her and Jane Heap's attempts to publish as much of *Ulysses* as they could in the face of legal and economic sanctions—are given little credit even during the more extended discussion of the magazine found in the book. Also, Anderson is often discussed as if she stood alone in her editorship, although readers of the magazine find abundant evidence of Heap's contributions made in her own particular style. In general, the terms applied to Anderson carry heavy connotations of emotionalism, immaturity, and frivolity, which have often been used to dismiss women and their achievements, whereas Pound's strong personality quirks are treated as an important component of the era's powerful experimental urge.

Through such selective discussion of their topics, these and other literary historians often decide, for example, that Pound "took over" or managed literary magazines more ably than the actual editors, and in a broader sense base their discussions on an assumption that only men's literary work merits critical attention. Discussions of women's work are usually predicated upon the work of associated men, or upon the assumption that women's accomplishments occurred in spite of their personalities rather than because of them. Some historians, sharing the viewpoint of many male modernists, see women's literary magazines as "vessels" that carried the "creations" of male writers—an extension of the belief that women's importance rests in "serving men," a figure of speech carrying a negative sexual charge. Such attention skews and reduces the complexity that these historians claim for modernism, even as it marks the prevailing attitudes within which literary women had to work.

Fortunately, some recent scholarship has begun to correct the neglect and misunderstanding that has resulted from a masculine orientation in scholarship and criticism. When scholars decide to evade certain masculinist assumptions by returning to original data, there is much to discover. Women's influence in literary publishing has been persistent even if not immediately apparent. First books by Ernest Hemingway, Marianne Moore, Samuel Beckett, and William Carlos Williams, for instance, appeared as a result of publishing ventures managed or paid for by Bryher, Harriet Shaw Weaver, and Nancy Cunard, while other women, including Caresse Crosby and Maria Jolas, actively arranged for publication of work by Gertrude Stein, James Joyce, and D. H. Lawrence. The extensive influence even of acknowledged little reviews sometimes comes as a surprise. Perhaps the most important example is the English periodical the *New Freewoman*. Under its former identity (the *Freewoman*, started in 1911 by Dora Marsden), the paper had pursued social issues, particularly feminist and suffragist concerns; after an eight-month hiatus resulting from the publisher's bankruptcy and a distributor's boycott, the fortnightly was refunded through the initiative of Harriet Shaw Weaver, who had answered Marsden's call for assistance in the last issue of the *Freewoman* and had become a good friend, interested in supporting Marsden's socialist, feminist, and individualist ideas. In 1913 the periodical's title became the *New Freewoman*, with Rebecca West, who had both contributed to and raised funds for the paper, as assistant editor, and the paper began to print more poetry and fiction. Les Garner notes that West worked tirelessly for the paper and served as a link to the public "Discussion Circles" it had spawned (93). After a few months, she secured the additional services of Ezra Pound as literary editor, although his demanding nature was one reason she decided to resign in October 1913, with the assistant editorship going to Richard Aldington.[9]

But the magazine's most influential era lay ahead, when the *New Freewoman* became the *Egoist* in 1914, with Weaver as editor and Aldington as literary editor, a position that passed to H.D. during 1916 and then to T. S. Eliot in 1917.[10] Gillian Hanscombe and Virginia Smyers note that, under Weaver, "*The Egoist* became clearly a literary periodical" (178); Marsden had effectively withdrawn due to strain and a desire to spend more time with her own writing. The *Egoist* printed the much-discussed "Imagist number" in 1915, as well as many serializations, particularly James Joyce's *Portrait of the Artist as a Young Man* and portions of *Ulysses*. Its literary reviews provided early critical notice for H.D., Ford Madox Ford, Joyce, Wyndham Lewis, Amy Lowell, Marianne Moore, Pound, Dorothy Richardson, and many other emerging figures. In addition, Weaver developed the Egoist Press in order to publish *Portrait of the Artist* in book form, since no other publisher would do it; some extremely important by-products of the Egoist Press's existence included books by Richard Aldington, Jean Cocteau, H.D., T. S. Eliot, Moore, and Pound.[11] Weaver's propitious decision to become editor despite her inexperience not only led to the printing of significant modern writing but also served private purposes: it allowed her to provide a steady outlet for her friend Marsden's philosophical writings, it kept Marsden independent from Pound's antagonism, and it allowed Weaver to expand her skills and knowledge in new directions while still consulting with her friend through frequent correspondence (Garner 133, 135). Marsden and Weaver's cooperation in running the *New Freewoman* and in consulting about the *Egoist* served their ambitions in mutually satisfactory ways.

At almost the same time as the *New Freewoman*, *Poetry: A Magazine of Verse* appeared in Chicago under the editorship of Harriet Monroe and her first coeditor, Alice Corbin Henderson. *Poetry* presented in its early years an astonishing gallery of new poetry by H.D., T. S. Eliot, Marianne Moore, Ezra Pound, Carl Sandburg, Wallace Stevens, and William Carlos Williams, among others. Although, as Ellen Williams points out, retrospect causes us to expect more from the first issues than they actually contained, the impact of that magazine upon the literary community was immediate (31-33). *Poetry* served as a forum for debate about the Imagists, free verse, international versus national identity in art, and the role of the artist's audience—all issues of considerable importance for the development of modern aesthetic ideas. The early editorial dynamics of *Poetry* included not only Monroe and Ezra Pound, as is usually pointed out, but also Henderson, who assisted Monroe during the first crucial years of the magazine's existence. The relationship between Monroe and Henderson altered and sharpened *Poetry*'s editorial policies. Henderson, for example, mediated between Monroe and Pound, discovered and promoted such figures as Sandburg, Edgar Lee Masters, and Sherwood Anderson, and engaged in vigorous defense of vers libre. Henderson and Monroe's interactions, like those of Weaver and Marsden at the *New Freewoman*, demonstrate the kind of cooperative work often found in women's editorial activities, which when viewed in the aggregate suggest that women's community was integral to the development of modern critical sensibility.

In addition to the pioneering work done in *Poetry* and the *Egoist*, numerous other periodicals that were edited, produced, or funded by women provided space and encouragement for new ideas. Among these, two of the most important are the *Little Review*, edited by Margaret Anderson and Jane Heap, and the *Dial*, under Marianne Moore's editorship from 1925 to 1929. The *Little Review*, founded in Chicago in 1914, carried sections of Joyce's *Ulysses* (later published in its entirety by Sylvia Beach in Paris), and pieces by Djuna Barnes, Mary Butts, H.D., Eliot, Moore, Pound, and Richardson; it also served, under Jane Heap's guidance especially in the 1920s, to introduce many avant garde visual artists and theorists. The *Dial*, which had already demonstrated a bold modern vision by printing Eliot's "The Waste Land" and work by E. E. Cummings, came under Moore's hand in 1925; she solicited and secured work from such important writers as D. H. Lawrence, Pound, and Gertrude Stein.[12]

Other women such as Ethel Moorhead and Kay Boyle (*This Quarter*), Katherine Mansfield (*Rhythm*, the *Blue Review*, the *Signature*), Florence Gilliam (*Gargoyle*), and Maria Jolas (*transition*) helped to edit and produce small magazines that extended the influence and scope of avant garde art and writing. Women were drawn to work in and support other kinds of publishing as well, most notably through independent publishing concerns founded or operated by Sylvia Beach (Shakespeare and Company), Gertrude Stein (Plain Editions), Nancy Cunard (The Hours Press), Caresse Crosby (Éditions Narcisse, At the Sign of the Sundial, and Black Sun Press), and Wyn Henderson (Aquila Press), or through financial "patronage" of fine presses by such women as Barbara Harrison (Harrison Press), Helena Rubinstein (who staked her husband, Edward Titus, for At the Sign of the Black Manikin Press), Harriet Shaw Weaver (The Egoist Press), and Annie Winifred Ellerman—known as Bryher—whose funds helped support a number of avant garde presses in England and Europe, as discussed in chapter 4. Whatever list one might compile of the "masterpieces" of the early twentieth century, it will include a high proportion of pieces for which women provided the forum for first publication, the impetus, the monetary support, or the initial critical reception, which was extremely important because so much experimental writing was going on. The more one looks, the more evidence one finds that, but for women's foresight and resourcefulness, much important modernist literature, art, and criticism might never have been printed.

As a result of this pervasive influence, it is imperative to learn more about what these women did, and how and why they chose to pursue their particular paths. A few books do address the roles of women as catalysts of literary modernism, and often decide that the connections between literary production and "authority" were addressed differently by female and male writers.[13] In their readings of modernist works, these scholars find a general sense of sexual anxiety or misogyny in many of the male writers, while they find in female writers a new sense of purpose as well as some confusion over the variety of roles that were becoming available to women at the time. These scholars also question the outspoken masculinism of certain literary men that has often been characterized as the sort of rebelliousness necessary for dismantling outmoded sensibilities in the early twentieth century. Sandra M. Gilbert and Susan Gubar, for instance, link the assumption of an intrinsic male rebelliousness to a misogynistic egotism, or fear, that refused to accept or to credit women as real contributors within the literary world.[14] Cheryl Walker points out the extreme condescension expressed later in John Crowe Ransom's 1937 essay "The Poet as Woman," in which Ransom not only dismisses the work of women poets but also "refuses to acknowledge the role of culture in shaping his own views" (5). The treatment of "women poets" as an undifferentiated mass, which Walker sees as a legacy of the popular "nightingale tradition" in nineteenth-century women's poetry, reflects the ways in which twentieth-century male critics have ignored the many different ways in which women have pursued their art (2, 7).

As may be surmised, women's methods for dealing with the male-oriented literary establishment varied widely according to individual circumstances and temperament. Studying the contributions of literary women, therefore, should not be expected to result in neat sets of reactions centered on imposed roles and prescribed behaviors. The assumption of reaction, which informs several recent studies of modernist women's work, provides one initial means of approach, although in a reductive way that can distort readings of texts. Women's work did not simply form "the underside" of modernism, as Shari Benstock suggests, or one side of a "battle of the sexes" in which women provided the "female half of the dialogue" expressing a sense of "feminine mimicry," as Sandra M. Gilbert and Susan Gubar propose.[15] Nor is it fully satisfying to decide that women who were "inheritors" of their literary and social worlds necessarily felt that they were also "outsiders," as Hanscombe and Smyers suggest.[16] Marianne DeKoven's assumption that female and male modernists reacted in two different ways to visions of social change imposes a gender-based dialectic (4), which, like the other dualistic approaches, can easily obscure the personal motivations and accomplishments of individuals and coteries.

These critics' stances are limited in presuming that women's lives and art developed only in reaction to the constrictions of prevailing social modes. Modernist women did not necessarily consider gender to be an analytic category, as scholars now do, and it is misleading to assume that a "sex war" necessarily pitted women against men in bruising struggle, or that women's achievements represent the "underside" of a modernism that must first be understood in terms of men's work and ideas. The varied nature of women's experiences, clearly, cannot be adequately theorized within such reductive pronouncements despite the cultural paradigms such pronouncements represent. The very nature of theorizing presumes the existence of commonalities as well as a privileged position that may well be unsuitable for approaching certain texts.[17]

One persistent conundrum in literary theorizing that is bolstered by feminist and new historical approaches remains the question of what to do with gender without necessarily falling into dualism. It is true that cultural language, especially earlier in the century, has made use of dualistic imagery, which offers a persuasive model to scholars returning to historical materials. From the standpoint of the current critical climate, however, dualism must be reconsidered at least in terms of the proposals of French theorists. If women are assumed to constitute or to see themselves in terms of being half of a dualism, or as some form of "Other," French feminist theories offer an obvious choice for critics trying to illuminate some of the political and psychoanalytic resemblances between literary history and women's experiences in patriarchal society. Anne Rosalind Jones notes that "French theorizing of the feminine emphasizes the extent to which the masculine subject has relegated women to the negative pole of his hierarchies, associating her with all the categories of 'not-man' that shore up his claim to centrality and his right to power," a view based upon Lacan's reading of Freud.[18] Since in Lacan's view an individual's sense of self is shifting and fictionalized according to internalization of others' views, with the symbol-pronoun "I" designating entry into public discourse through identification with the "Father," the position of women is negated; woman can "enter into the symbolic life of the unconscious only to the extent that she internalizes male desire . . . [if] she imagines herself as men imagine her" (Jones 83). Therefore Lacan's view places woman as either a male-determined fiction or a silent figure. Jones notes that French feminists' deconstruction of male-authored texts reveals "the suppression of whatever stands outside masculine norms," which may take the form of treating women as "separate, manipulable body parts" or a "surrealist view of women as childish, close to nature and irrational" (98). This oppression of women gives rise to the *différence* of women's writing, as described variously by Luce Irigaray, Monique Wittig, Hélène Cixous, and Julia Kristeva, characterized as taking a multitude of antirational and unconventional forms that are incomprehensible to readers schooled according to patriarchal traditions.[19]

Among these theorists, Luce Irigaray has been especially influential. Like many French feminists, Irigaray retains a dualistic division between "male" and "female" as a residue of psychoanalytic theory, but her approach is nevertheless useful because she refuses to place restrictions on the experiences of women or on the concept of "woman." Whereas Hélène Cixous in her well-known essay "The Laugh of the Medusa" imagines an anti-authoritarian reversal of what "woman" has meant in patriarchal ideology, Irigaray predicates her assessment of women's place upon the idea that "woman" embodies a multiplicity that cannot be understood in terms of patriarchal culture. Specifically, she uses the sexuality of the female body as an emblem for women's integrative experiences of life. The multiple and mutable forms of women's sex organs, Irigaray decides, cannot be defined within a "culture claiming to count everything, to number everything by units, to inventory everything as individualities. . . . *woman has sex organs more or less everywhere. . . . the geography of her pleasure is* far more diversified, more multiple in its differences, more complex, more subtle, than is commonly imagined—in an imaginary rather too narrowly focused on sameness" ("This Sex Which Is Not One" 26-28). In this sense a woman eludes definition and expresses herself in the same multivalent ways she experiences the world. In order to comprehend what "the female" can be, Irigaray writes that one "would have to listen with another ear, as if hearing *an 'other meaning' always in the process of weaving itself, of embracing itself with words, but also of getting rid of words in order not to become fixed, congealed in them.* For if 'she' says something, it is not, it is already no longer, identical with what she means. . . . [A woman] enters into a ceaseless exchange of herself with the other" (29, 31).

   If modernist literature is indeed characterized by its "subjective fictions" of reality, then French feminist thought not only illuminates women's language but also offers an approach for theorizing about the ways modernist subjectivity may have provoked, as well as expressed, masculine anxieties. Certainly modernism proper, like women's experimental writings, necessarily undermined a definitive worldview; to define modernism as multifarious, diffuse, and self-conscious suggests that there may be important connections between modernist innovations and qualities that have often been seen as "female" attributes. Particular aspects of modernism might serve as metaphorical equivalents to contemporary theories of women's psychology proposed, for instance, by Nancy Chodorow, Mary Belenky et al., and Carol Gilligan.[20] The so-called "break with the past" that modernism supposedly enacts might even be seen as a metaphorical equivalent of masculine anxiety, reducing the complexities of cultural developments to a coded phrase expressing loss and disjunction and creating an antagonistic "other." It is this oppositional construction of the "other" that some feminist models reject, preferring to theorize women's lives and writings in more inclusive or loosely structured ways in order at least to suggest the diversity of female experience, adapting and selecting from different critical approaches in the process.[21]

   Bakhtinian dialogics, a theoretical model that has proven useful in postmodern considerations of polyvocality and of resistance to various forms of literary authority, has offered an appealing structure for feminist adaptation. In its original form, dialogics neglects to consider the function of gender. To create feminist dialogics, then, theorists must include gender in analyzing the "position" of women's responses. These can express resistance "when women negotiate, manipulate, and . . . subvert systems of domination they encounter" (Bauer and McKinstry 3), including the so-called objectivity or rationality that masculinist discourse has claimed. In the case of modernist women editors, it is clear from public and private evidence that these women were engaged in negotiation with, and manipulation of, systems of literary authority on a number of levels—the *Little Review*'s "Reader Critic" section is perhaps the most visible example. Feminist dialogic theory is concerned with gender-based redefinitions of the "answers" that Bakhtin claimed were necessarily part of the context of an utterance and that created meaning in dialogue. Whereas Bakhtin posited a "double-voicedness" ("dialogism"), however, many feminists prefer to see "multi-voicedness" or polyvocality in the ways women express themselves in language. The real question of Bakhtin's usefulness for feminist theories lies in whether a critic believes Bakhtin finally deconstructs dualism by imagining endless dialogic exchanges— through a continual modification of the speakers' contexts of meaning— or believes that dialogics reinscribes dualism in a way that continues to force women to create space for themselves as "Other," or indeed as "others."

In part, the several strategies included in this study offer a small taste of the variety of ways women have found to express themselves and shape their experiences—a variety that critical theories have only begun to address. While dualistic as well as masculinist approaches tend to obscure women's work, and although the dualism within French feminist theory provides space for women's experiences, a more open attitude is needed in order to treat fairly the variety of, and within, these materials. Michel Foucault's example of using a number of social, political, and economic aspects to rethink historical approaches as well as history "itself" demonstrates the necessity of awareness about one's own critical positionality— especially as regards power relations—which many feminist critics have found to be a crucial tool. One of the benefits of contemporary feminist theories, in fact, is that they encourage critics to see a far broader range in the expressions and effects of women's literary voices. Seeing constructions of "the other" in terms of women's collaborative writing and editing, for instance, radically revises the oppositional assumptions inherent to the term; if an "other" is a friendly and knowledgeable coworker— indeed, if "the other's" work can scarcely be distinguished from one's own—the meaning of "otherness" can become as fluid as perceptions of self.

At the very least, women editors and publishers took a variety of paths in pursuing their ambitions within a society oriented toward the work of men. It is true that a number of women who saw male dominance in literary matters acceded to it and refused to take credit for their own accomplishments; sometimes women accepted the expectation that their work was "in the service of literature" and that they should encourage the men with whom they were connected, act as mediators and comforters, and efface their own ambitions. Sylvia Beach, Harriet Monroe, Harriet Shaw Weaver, Maria Jolas, and Marianne Moore, for instance, at various points played down their own contributions and innovations, giving credit instead to the men with whom they were associated. Hanscombe and Smyers note that Katherine Mansfield "had to encourage [John Middleton] Murry, rather than he her work, even when she was terminally ill" (245). H.D., during her early years in London while she was still closely associated with Pound, expressed uncertainty about her own abilities in her letters, even though she also helped to arrange the Imagist anthologies through solicitation, encouragement, and mediation among a group of writers.[22] The apparent internalization of "female" roles—which Mina Loy sarcastically characterized as "Parasitism, Prostitution, or Negation"[23]—seems to have carried with it some degree of reluctance to assert women's own abilities, a self-censorship that could go so far as silence.

Other women, including some of those who at times acceded to men, found more proactive ways to define their positions within the literary world, although usually at a cost. Women who did assert themselves, or who openly flouted male expectations, such as Margaret Anderson, Jane Heap, Gertrude Stein, and Nancy Cunard, have generally been characterized as intimidating, pushy, or flighty, and as having made their contributions in spite of themselves. Considering these women's extraordinary accomplishments, however, it is clear that traditional expectations did not prevent them from working or creating new lifestyles for themselves. Many of these women, in resisting patriarchal restrictions, also rejected traditional sexual roles, including motherhood and heterosexual marriage; others, for instance Nancy Cunard, Jane Heap, and Margaret Anderson, ironically manipulated the stereotypes attached to women's appearance. Of the few modernists who were mothers, some, like H.D. and Mary Butts, let their children be raised by other people. Of those who married, several—including H.D., Bryher, Dorothy Richardson, Katherine Mansfield, and Djuna Barnes—also maintained lesbian attachments that were more enduring than their marriages with men. Benstock suggests that lesbians often enjoyed much more freedom in choice and lifestyle than did women in heterosexual relationships; they could distribute their time and inheritances as they chose, and they had access to a distinct female subculture that provided a strong base for community (9). Even those women who never married and had no obvious lesbian relationships were often criticized for their failure to follow a traditional lifestyle, even though men's personal attachments did not occasion such comments. "Unattachment is, after all," note Hanscombe and Smyers, "as subversive of social expectation [for women] as is lesbianism" (246).

Such rejection of social conventions reflects a deep dissatisfaction with, or disbelief in, "male consciousness" or traditional authoritarian structures. Dorothy Richardson and Mina Loy spoke out specifically against using men as any yardstick by which to discuss women's ideas and concerns; Gertrude Stein deliberately subverted the authority of language linked with male cultural authority; Bryher protested against the restrictions placed upon young women by the English educational system. Women's frequent rejection of conventional lifestyles and of conventional literary forms, their sense of obligation to literature and their indirect as well as direct support of it, their rejection of "male consciousness" and concomitant development of female-centered systems of support—these are crucial aspects of women's experiences during the modernist era. A close examination of women's aims during the growth and maturity of modernism reveals the deeply radical nature of much of their work, breaking the "sentence" and the "sequence" of traditional language and literature the better to allow for women's experiences (DuPlessis, *Writing Beyond the Ending* x, 32).

Literary historians and theorists with a traditional orientation have treated these women as if they were anomalous—or anonymous—in the processes of canonical choice, rather than seeking out their real function as powerful and influential arbiters of modern aesthetic views. Additionally, history has neglected the cooperative work often found in women's editorial operations, a teamwork less common in men's, perhaps due to cultural training that "the other" was a threatening presence. Collaborative female relationships indicate that feelings of community between women, described by Hanscombe and Smyers as vitally important to the actual writing and production of literature, were integral to the development of modern sensibilities in other ways as well.

Modernism therefore designates not only a literary phenomenon but also a period in which women were developing alternative ways of thinking and living their lives. By upending conventions, modernist women developed their literary tastes and their lives in ways that were not necessarily predicated upon the prerogatives of men. If women participated in silencing themselves, the silence often served as a diversion so that they could work without attracting censure. If women served as mediators, the mediation need not be seen as acquiescent compromise but as a token of connection and interaction. If women openly defied tradition, this defiance may be viewed as protest through which viable new definitions of culture could arise. The possibilities of such critical reinterpretations prove the importance of reexamining modernism from the points of view of women who enacted some of its most radical tenets. New approaches to gender issues in modernism will allow critics to understand women's contributions with much more sensitivity to complexity. Whether a critic chooses to examine the "cultural poetics" of disparate material texts in the manner of new historicists, adopt a technological metaphor for diversity as proposed by Laurie Finke, or analyze the psychological or philosophical possibilities of feminist epistemologies, what is needed is a flexible framework that can accommodate as many versions of literary creativity as there are writers—and the certainty of change within critical approaches as well.[24] My purpose is not to sketch a theory around literary data but to write a portion of women's history, as part of new historical reassessments of cultural data that affirm women's involvements in the development of modernism, a project upon which future theorists can draw.

In this study, I will recover and examine the roles seven white American and English women played in editing and producing highly influential literary magazines during the modernist era. Also, with an eye toward revising some existing sex-biased assumptions about these women's work, I will consider how these women responded to the difficulties placed before them by the male-oriented literary establishment. Both actions—of recovery and of revision—are necessary in order to restore the achievements of these women and to evaluate the overall importance of their contributions to modernist literature. Additionally, I must note that in this book I have not addressed the experiences of women of color, particularly the African-American women editors—such as Carrie Clifford, Jessie Fauset, Nora Douglas Holt, Pauline Hopkins, Paulette and Jeanne Nardal, and Dorothy West—who contributed enormously to the cultural climate that eventually fostered the Harlem Renaissance. My context, deriving as it does from a few white women of a certain social class, is not appropriate to a broader discussion of issues of race and ethnicity as they relate to modernist publication; the power relations faced by women of color in publishing show significant features of their own. There exists a great need to locate the texts of underrepresented writers and editors so as to explore further aspects of the history of modernist development. Here again my work is intended to advance critical discussion onto ground upon which later studies can build.

The two chapters following will examine in detail the crucial editorial interactions between Harriet Monroe and Alice Corbin Henderson of *Poetry* and between Margaret Anderson and Jane Heap of the *Little Review*. The fourth chapter will take up H.D. and Bryher's editorial and aesthetic interests, focusing on the Imagist anthologies of 1914-16, the *Egoist*, and *Close Up*, the film magazine founded by Bryher and Kenneth Macpherson in 1927. Collaboration and community serve as recurrent themes in examining the work of these women and others; as another chapter will illustrate, even Marianne Moore, editing the *Dial* from 1925 to 1929, created a fiction of working in concert with Scofield Thayer and J. Sibley Watson, although not quite in the way suggested by the standard *Dial* histories. After these four chapters concentrating on women's work in some of modernism's most influential little magazines, one chapter will reassess Pound's interactions with these women.

The neglect of women's critical literary work finds its paradigmatic expression in the opinions of Ezra Pound. What opinion exists about women editors has been shaped to a considerable extent by Pound, whose influence over current perceptions of twentieth-century literature is as pervasive as his pronouncements are idiosyncratic. As a catalyst of modernism, and as a figure integrally involved with the editorial dealings of many of the most important literary magazines, Pound necessarily serves as one of the focal points of this study. His responses to women editors and writers are problematic, since even as he depended upon some to provide outlets for his literary promotions, he fought with them and derided their tastes and accomplishments with language that is noticeably gender-inflected. Even as he drew upon the friendship and artistic sensitivity of H.D., he presented her with a sore trial during the Imagist years in London; his work as "foreign correspondent" for *Poetry* and the *Little Review* included bullying letters and the vainglorious assumption of his right to make policy; his acrimonious disagreements with Amy Lowell over the Imagist anthologies are popularly known. Although his relationships with other writers and publishers often display similar problems, the misogyny displayed by Pound and other people helped to create the intertexts in which these women's work took place.

The afterword to this book briefly notes some ways in which further reassessments might proceed, although my purpose clearly is not to deduce or propose a new theory of modernism but to discuss women's accomplishments that have heretofore been misrepresented or ignored. In light of the current critical climate, which has allowed many values and judgments that were formerly rigid and exclusive to be questioned, it seems crucial to continue to interweave awareness of evolving critical and theoretical approaches with solidly grounded historical research. Finding out about these women editors has been a great pleasure; so too is the hope of assuring that they, and scores of other women, secure a prominent place in the continuing development of the history of modernist literature.

2 BEGINNING IN CHICAGO

Harriet Monroe,
Alice Corbin Henderson,
and *Poetry*

Poetry, A Magazine of Verse, founded by Harriet Monroe in 1912, is one of the best-known of the little magazines that ushered in the gathering energies of modernism in English-language literature.[1] *Poetry* introduced and printed nearly every major figure in twentieth-century poetry and served as a forum for critical debate on a number of fundamental aesthetic issues. In its pages were waged the debates—over such topics as vers libre, Imagism, artistic elitism, the role of audience, American literary identity, and the value of regional writing—that engaged many literary figures besides Monroe and her first coeditor, Alice Corbin Henderson. Even though the rush of novel and challenging work slowed after the first several years, *Poetry*'s place in literary history is secure, not only for its pathbreaking early years but also for its sheer tenacity and broad-ranging interests, qualities in which the magazine reflects its editors.

Monroe and Henderson's daily interactions over matters profound and mundane served as the most important basis for *Poetry*'s editorial processes. Especially during the crucial early years, when the magazine had to establish itself and gain credibility for the new poetry it was printing, Monroe and Henderson tested ideas on each other, shared their discoveries, argued over submissions, commiserated over criticisms, and struggled to make ends meet for the magazine that had promised to be a paying forum for "the best new work" of many kinds of poets. Henderson shared *Poetry*'s first office with Monroe from late 1912 through mid-1916, when she moved to New Mexico because of ill health; after that time, however,

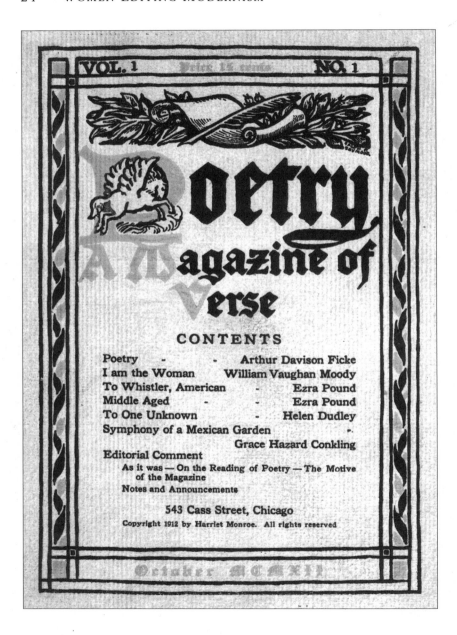

VOL. 1   Price 15 cents   NO. 1

Poetry
Magazine of Verse

CONTENTS

543 Cass Street, Chicago

October MCMXII

she stayed in touch with Monroe and with other important literary figures through regular correspondence. Numerous editorial and critical comments by both "H.M." and "A.C.H." in *Poetry* set many of the critical parameters within which the magazine operated and engaged *Poetry*'s supporters, rivals, and critics in important debate; as well, the two women's collaboration on the popular anthology *The New Poetry* helped to define the parameters of contemporary achievement.

Poetry's prominence in modern literary history has not, however, prevented a few distortions from arising. First, Henderson's contributions have often been overlooked, despite passages in Monroe's autobiography (*A Poet's Life*) that suggest Henderson's critical faculties as well as her assistance in production were vital to *Poetry*'s development; Pound's *Letters*, in fact, testify to his editorial dealings with Henderson and his respect for her.[2] Henderson's neglected (indeed, nearly invisible) position reflects the fate of many literary women who were "second in command." As well, the interactive nature of *Poetry*'s editorial processes has received little attention, although it clearly affected what appeared in the magazine and what subsequently formed one basis for modernist literary history. Henderson helped Monroe to succeed, but the value of the two women's collaboration, as well as of Henderson's own acumen, skills, taste, and determination, has gone unexamined.

Also, Monroe's own work for *Poetry* has usually been characterized on the basis of her interactions with Ezra Pound, who served as foreign correspondent during 1912-1917 and continued to offer his submissions and suggestions for many years. Most discussions of editorial give-and-take at *Poetry* have focused on Pound's disagreements with Monroe and have tended to show Monroe in an unfavorable light. It is true that Pound's contributions to the magazine were extremely useful; as Ellen Williams has noted, his presence and connections in London gave Monroe and Henderson the chance to read work by writers whom *Poetry* would not otherwise have been able to reach (287-88). In this case, however, the figure of Pound has not only overshadowed Monroe's far longer and more immediate tenure with *Poetry*, but has actually pitched discussion against Monroe on the grounds of personal characteristics. The denigration and dismissal of Monroe throughout much of modern literary history constitutes a telling example of the fate of many women; reexamining her contributions to that history requires a change of perspective that allows her to be seen on her own terms.

The temptation to view the expansive variety of modernist literary history through the single lens of Pound's involvement is addressed in a later chapter. This attitude betrays an orientation toward men's activities—particularly those of such strongly vocal men as Pound—that has skewed assessments of modernist literature away from acknowledging the nature and extent of women's accomplishments. In this case, it is pertinent to note that even those commentators who do place value on Henderson's work for *Poetry*, or profess to weigh Monroe's, very often incorporate this attitude.

Some commentators have at least briefly noted Henderson's influence on the magazine, or the two editors' interactions. In their important introduction to literary magazines, the editors of *The Little Magazine: A History and a Bibliography* (1947), Frederick J. Hoffman, Charles Allen, and Carolyn F. Ulrich, write:

Harriet Monroe's editorship was at first prompted by a desire to give all poets a hearing. Through the influence of Ezra Pound, who in 1912 became her foreign correspondent, she turned her attention to the new poets and to the championship of new verse forms. Her courage helped to save the magazine from occasional financial depression; her intelligent judgment, and that of her first assistant editor, Alice Corbin Henderson, gave it a consistently high rate of creditable performance. The most exciting years of *Poetry* were the first ones, 1912-1917, when the debate over free verse and imagism seemed vital. [241-42]

Henderson's contributions are acknowledged, and yet the exact nature of her work for the magazine during its "most exciting years" is simply ignored, while Monroe is portrayed as having achieved what she did through the "influence" of Pound, despite her own "intelligent judgment."[3] Many other studies follow this pattern—which seems to be based on Pound's own self-congratulatory comments in such articles as "Small Magazines"—of validating Pound's point of view at Monroe's expense. Since Monroe's and Pound's interests and aims differed, it is unfair to use Pound as an instrument for criticizing Monroe's tastes, particularly when Henderson's contributions are not elucidated. While Pound saw *Poetry* as a forum for important work, one should also remember the obvious fact that Monroe and Henderson—and scores of other people—did too.

Ellen Williams's *Harriet Monroe and the Poetry Renaissance: The First Ten Years of* Poetry, *1912-1922* (1977) remains the only major study of the magazine and its founder, providing a close examination of editorial policy during the early years of *Poetry* by concentrating on the figures of Monroe, Pound, and William Carlos Williams. The author consistently refers to Henderson's role on the magazine but does not specify what that role entailed despite concentrating on *Poetry*'s first five "exciting" years. Only in a single chapter covering the period of late 1917 through 1922 does Ellen Williams spend several pages discussing Henderson's influence with Monroe and interactions with Pound. While this scholar suggests that some poets found Henderson a sympathetic figure, as opposed to the "forbidding" figure of Monroe, she also finds Henderson's enthusiasm for "middle-western regionalism," her distrust of the *Others* poets, and her contempt for Amy Lowell to be less than admirable aspects. Ellen Williams concludes, "It seems quite reasonable to argue that Harriet Monroe was a better editor when she had Mrs. Henderson, with her sharp and immediate reactions, her keen sense for what worked in individual poems, at her side in the Chicago office. . . . There was not a comparably sensitive or stimulating literary intelligence among the circle of people who worked for *Poetry*" (230). While Ellen Williams acknowledges that the two women made a good editorial team, she prefers to assign responsibility generally to Monroe because the two women worked so closely that "editorial policy" cannot be definitely attributed to one or the other. In the absence of much archival evidence such a decision may be expedient, but it oversimplifies the involved processes by which magazines are put together and by which editorial policies work. As well, limiting and conflating both editors' contributions in this manner erases the importance of collaboration and subsumes one woman's work into someone else's. The cumulative effect of making Henderson nearly invisible and Monroe a foil for Pound fits into a familiar pattern of the way female experiences have been treated in literary history.

Some of Ellen Williams's conclusions must be reconsidered when one reexamines the evidence in *Poetry* and in correspondence. For instance, her suggestion that *Poetry* was limited by a "regional" bent in its editors' preferences is problematic (230). The term "regional," as applied to Henderson, apparently indicates that she favored the work of Vachel Lindsay, Edgar Lee Masters, Carl Sandburg, and (occasionally) Sherwood Anderson; it may also be meant to include Henderson's enthusiasm for the "cowboy poets," the Native American, and the Hispanic-American poets whose oral literatures drew Henderson's interest after her move to the Southwest. It is not true, however, that Henderson preferred these writers over William Carlos Williams and Wallace Stevens, or that she recommended excessive amounts of their work, or that Monroe herself did not like Lindsay, Masters, and Sandburg. Monroe sometimes wrote warm reviews of Lindsay's poetry and sometimes rejected it (as with "The Tiger Tree") as needing "ruthless pruning."[4] Henderson and Monroe did disagree over the amount of such work that went into *Poetry*, but while Henderson did recommend batches of such work at times, she never recommended a preponderance of any. Her sponsorship of American ethnic literatures, in fact, was an impressive innovation that underscores *Poetry*'s importance. As well, exchanges during the time that Monroe and Henderson were assembling the second edition of *The New Poetry* show Henderson strongly supporting exempla of nineteenth-century poetry that showed a modern "spirit" as well as sections by established and new twentieth-century poets, particularly Wallace Stevens; her recommendations reveal that she read widely.[5]

Equally, Monroe's own admiration was sometimes drawn by "regional" writers outside the Midwest, for instance, DuBois Heyward of South Carolina. Monroe thought that accusations of midwestern preferentialism often came from easterners accustomed to dominating the world of letters, and she felt it important that her magazine include a variety of poets from different regions: "As for our 'obsession' about the Middle-West," Monroe wrote to Henderson, "it's a natural reaction to the eastern exclusion of this region and its own self-distrust. But I will try not to over-stress locale. I am not afraid that we won't keep up, in our specialty, with other magazines present or future."[6] Later comments by Monroe and Henderson offer specific comments about what they found to be elements of "regional" poetry and explicitly decry "provincialism" in eastern critics accustomed to a Eurocentric view.[7] Ellen Williams's assumption that either woman would have fostered a limited "regional bazaar" in *Poetry* does not fairly hold up. While *Poetry* did encourage American writing, it did not limit its solicitation only to a few styles, and some of its greatest contributions, seen in retrospect, occurred through its introduction of minority writers and diverse ethnic traditions.

Ellen Williams also suggests that Monroe's greatest usefulness to modern poetry lay in promoting and publishing Pound; however, she accedes that Pound's poetic "revolution" was demonstrated through the same set of poems, presented repeatedly, which represented his own interests, and that Pound himself was not always attuned to the best new work (286, 288). This conclusion neglects the fact that Monroe and Henderson also promoted and published dozens of important figures other than Pound, and that if he were "crucial" to the magazine, the editors were more so.

As Ellen Williams notes, it is not easy to disentangle collaborative procedures. Fortunately, considerable pertinent information can be found in unpublished correspondence and in the magazine itself.[8] These materials demonstrate that Henderson's activities on behalf of *Poetry* had significant impact in terms of the issues raised by the magazine, the relations between *Poetry* and its contributors, and the continuing work of publication itself, notably in the anthologies (*The New Poetry*, 1917 and 1923) on which Monroe and Henderson collaborated.

On Monroe's part, evidence shows that she often sought others' opinions, not (as some critics assert) because she felt unsure of her own but for two better reasons: first, that Monroe wanted to share and test the works that passed through her hands, and second, that the sheer work of preparing a monthly magazine—reading hundreds of submissions, keeping up correspondence, arranging for printing, and so on—required help at least for the initial manuscript readings, which as Henderson pointed out were particularly important.[9] Additionally, Monroe's editorials reveal that she was neither prudish nor timid, as she has been accused of being, but a persistent spokesperson for innovation and expertise in modern poetic art, as well as a defender of those whose work was a bit too "modern" for her readers' tastes. The discretion she showed in not printing some materials is tied to her standards of integrity and good writing. She was not afraid to criticize magazines and organizations that she thought were not serving the art well, and she fought for respect for *Poetry*'s accomplishments and existence.

Henderson, too, was a vocal advocate for *Poetry*. She acted as Monroe's assistant, critical foil, confidante, and "sounding board" for ideas about the magazine. The two women's work in the pages both of *Poetry* and *The New Poetry* anthologies, and in private correspondence, demonstrates the extent of their dedication to modern poetry and poetics and shows the tenor of their editorial debates over some of the important issues their publications addressed. Henderson's greatest importance to *Poetry* lies in the mutuality that informed those first crucial years of publication, and in debating the merits of the various poems being printed, even though Monroe remains the central figure of the magazine. *Poetry* functioned as a locus of individually and mutually satisfying work for its editors, and as an instance of cooperative work between women in a literary world dominated by men.

Henderson was a spirited and knowledgeable critic as well as a poet. By the time *Poetry* was founded, she was familiar with the literary and artistic communities in Illinois, and had had experience as a book reviewer for newspapers in New Orleans and Chicago.[10] In August 1912 Monroe asked her for advice about making selections for the initial issue of *Poetry* and soon invited her to share the editorial work at the office on Cass Street.

Early letters from Henderson to Monroe indicate the hopes for *Poetry*—and the mundane details of production—that the two shared. A letter of August 1912 shows that Henderson was deeply involved in the magazine from the beginning, for she writes that she has forwarded "two letters from Mr. [Arthur Davison] Ficke, one enclosing a poem. . . . Mr. Seymour promises that I may have subscription blanks, separate, in a few days, to enclose with the circulars to poets. . . . If I can't find the white envelopes, or get them until your return, perhaps I had best send the poets' circulars in the blue envelopes? I am making good headway on the mailing list."[11] Ficke was, in fact, the poet who appeared on the first page of the first issue of *Poetry*. By the time the first volume had been completed, Henderson, like Monroe, was well versed in the operations of the magazine and outspoken in her editorial preferences. Not only did Henderson read submissions but also she was essential in seeing the magazine through publication and distribution. Her interest in promoting (and defending) *Poetry* informed many of her editorial contributions over the years.

The decision-making at the office seems to have been congenial if sometimes contentious; the spirit of their exchanges is suggested in Monroe's autobiography *A Poet's Life*, in which she notes that Henderson was "a well-nigh indispensible member of *Poetry*'s staff" (319) and wryly mentions that the two editors' disagreements never came to "bloodshed." Monroe also calls Henderson a "fine poet and intelligent critic . . . keen as a whip . . . [who] seemed the one fit person available to assist my project," and whom Monroe trusted as the first reader of manuscripts to detect and discuss any promising submissions (284). Monroe appreciated both Henderson's discrimination and her decisive nature. When Henderson left, Monroe wrote to her, "I want a young radical in the place."[12] Ellen Williams comments that "none of [*Poetry*'s later associate editors] had [Henderson's] critical trenchancy, and none of them could challenge and debate Harriet Monroe as a peer. . . . [Henderson's was] the mind which had shared *Poetry* with [Monroe] since the beginning . . . with which [Monroe] could enter into an unconstrained dialogue" (265).[13]

Given Henderson's level of importance, especially during the formative years of the magazine, it is intriguing that Monroe refers to Henderson very little in *A Poet's Life*. Monroe quotes from just two of Henderson's articles and none of her letters, refers only vaguely to differences of opinion that arose in the office, and does not mention their collaboration on the anthologies. Such omissions are the more intriguing because Monroe is very generous in her treatment of Pound. One might expect Monroe to have been annoyed with Pound as a result of his comments about *Poetry* when he abandoned it for the *Little Review*, but she quotes at length from Pound's correspondence and stresses the interesting aspects he brought to the magazine. There are several possible explanations for Monroe's emphasis, which has certainly affected critics' opinions about what mattered at *Poetry*. One important reason involves Monroe's disagreements with

Henderson over royalties for *The New Poetry*, as discussed below. But Monroe's virtual obliteration of Henderson from her memoir—which was not quite complete at the time of Monroe's death in 1936—necessitates that readers look elsewhere for evidence of early editorial debates at *Poetry*.

A letter of June 1915 indicates the frank tenor of Henderson and Monroe's editorial exchanges. Henderson writes:

> I enclose proof with two corrections in Our Contemporaries. Your sentence added to the Rupert Brooke item takes all the point out of the pointed brevity. . . . And oh, Harriet, whatever you do—*don't* speak of "*boosting the art.*" It is dreadful. . . . I don't mind your *cutting*, but I don't think you should add things that change the feeling. . . . And can't you get something better than *Massive* above the *Robert Frost* item. I don't think *massive* is right at all—Head it *Robert Frost's Quality*—or *Robert Frost's Poems.* . . . Your list for September looks encouraging!—Bravo![14]

It is precisely this sort of response that Monroe appreciated from Henderson; the latter's occasional combativeness and demanding tastes worked as a useful complement to the former's discretion and compromise. Even though Monroe sometimes responded in print to criticisms of *Poetry*, she usually decided not to expend energy on something she considered foolish, whereas Henderson preferred to engage and defend.[15]

Others of the women's letters indicate that they were in the habit of having animated discussions about many writers' works. In one of her first letters from New Mexico, for instance, Henderson wrote to Monroe commenting about the issue of June 1916: "Lindsay and the *Lament* two best in June of course. I like fairly well all but the last of Rosalind Mason's. . . . Shanafeldt half good and half affectedness (Imagism *does* tend toward *conceits*). Untermeyer's 'Magic' sheer bunk. . . . one sees so much stuff passing itself off as poetry that is nothing of the sort. . . . [Bynner's] little lyrics are so often hind-part-before. And he's such a bog of sentiment."[16]

Henderson's contributions to *Poetry*, both critical and editorial, rest in large part on her ability—and willingness—to criticize contemporary writing. She did not hesitate to make sharp comments about Monroe's choices for the magazine if she thought *Poetry* was not serving the art well, writing for example in August 1916:

The August number came yesterday—and it is pretty sad, honestly. . . . if I were you, I would *concentrate* in the first place, on *getting* and *keeping* and publishing all the *first rate poets*. . . . There is *absolutely* no use in encouraging the poet who has *one* passable poem in a lot of bad ones. . . . Encourage him to *keep on trying all* you want to. But let him try outside the magazine. Now *concentrate* on Masters, Lindsay, Sandburg, Ficke, Fletcher, Frost, Pound, the English ones—W.B.Y— Hueffer, Manning—etc. . . . Also of course *Wallace Stevens*[, Arensberg, Williams]. . . . And be very careful that the reviews do not degenerate too much into personal impressions and pre-ambling prefaces in regard to the book in hand without enough definite objective criticism.[17]

Henderson's opinions show her intention to discuss precisely what constituted "the best" in the new poetry. Her and Monroe's decisions and preferences had much more to do with determining which individual poems were suitable for publication, and what were the enduring qualities in contemporary writing, than with poets' personalities or one particular style of poetry. These aspects of their styles offer insight into their later disagreements over the aims and parameters of modern poetry as epitomized in their choices for the anthologies, and demonstrates that their editorial exchanges were quite different in intent from Pound's letters, in which he often baldly told them what to do. Both women expected the poetic community to engage in useful debate that would enliven the field, which is quite different from didactic pronouncement.

One instance of such pronouncement, at least as the two editors saw it, occurred in William Stanley Braithwaite's annual anthologies of poems he selected as "the best" for a given year. In these publications *Poetry* was often left out or given short shrift, and Henderson took up the issue. In the "Our Contemporaries" section of February 1914, she complained about Braithwaite's annual "pronunciamento upon current poetry in American magazines" and criticized his selection of "the seven leading magazines" by characterizing them as "mostly . . . solemn standpatters which print a little verse as a decorative incident," and by citing his listing of total poems printed in *Century* (58), *Harper's* (57), *Scribner's* (45), the *Smart Set* (169), and others, to suggest that Braithwaite had chosen from forums far less able than *Poetry* to represent a spectrum of current work.[18] She went on to state that, of the two hundred and eleven poems Braithwaite claimed to be "distinctive," only two are "by poets of some distinction, Mr. Robinson and Miss Cather, though 'The Field of Glory' and 'A Likeness' by no means represent them at their best" ("Our Contemporaries" 188). Henderson finished by quoting the first two lines of a poem by Mahlon Leonard Fisher that Braithwaite had praised, asking, "If this kind of opinionating passes for criticism in Boston, what can be expected of the shadowy region beyond the Alleghenies?" ("Our Contemporaries" 188). The region to which Henderson referred was deliberately vague but might be thought to intimate criticism of European as well as eastern critics; equally, it might suggest that *Poetry*, in the Midwest, was better able to evaluate the range of contemporary work than was the *Boston Transcript*. Both readings of Henderson's comment reveal her confidence in *Poetry*'s purpose and her ire at having been ignored in this supposedly comprehensive look at the poetic accomplishments of 1914.

In the anthology for 1916, however, Braithwaite not only virtually dismissed *Poetry*'s contribution but also suggested that Carl Sandburg, whom Henderson had discovered for *Poetry*, was a poetic "failure." Henderson and Monroe expressed their dismay to each other in a series of letters shortly after Henderson's move; Henderson, in fact, brought up the question of whether Braithwaite had asked permission to reprint the poems he had used from *Poetry* and suggested that Monroe's lawyer might try to collect some fees.[19] Henderson's inquiries about whether Braithwaite's deeds were "actionable" foreshadowed her later insistence on a formal agreement with Monroe about *New Poetry* royalties. Monroe's own response—that Braithwaite was not worth the expense of mental or legal energy—also foreshadowed her later reluctance to give Henderson a royalty agreement in writing. In this case, however, as when Pound tried to tell them what to do, the two women affirmed each other's vision of what their magazine was doing and could accomplish.

Henderson's ideas about poetic tradition in America and the possibilities of modern work comprise three major critical features: her beliefs about what a truly American poetic sensibility would involve; her analyses of specific examples of what was or was not successful in current poetry; and her insistence upon the need for criticism informed by contemporary experiments in writing. She also vigorously defended *Poetry* against others' criticism, misunderstanding, or neglect, and in so doing helped to create a climate of critical exchange about important current issues. Her strongest contributions to modernism arose from her defense of vers libre and her attempts to define the spirit of American poetry, although her disputes with Monroe over matters of critical taste were also valuable in that they explicitly affected the contents of *Poetry* and *The New Poetry*, and, by implication, the landscape of twentieth-century poetry.

One of Henderson's central concerns was defining a specifically American poetry that would express the racial and ethnic variety of the United States. Her discussion of what constituted American work also included her views about nationalism in poetry, for instance in "A Perfect Return" (December 1912) and "Too Far from Paris" (June 1914). These early articles stressed the importance of Edgar Allan Poe and Walt Whitman in the American literary heritage, but Henderson's point was that these writers were not truly appreciated in America until their work had been assimilated by Europeans. Repeatedly Henderson insisted that American poets ought not look to European models but rather create their work out of their particular experience in the United States. This insistence reflects Henderson's view that poets are thought especially valuable by their countries during wartime; the "personal emotion" of patriotism is well served by poetry if it reflects the life of the nation. Henderson's view of American art had two distinct aspects: appreciation for the particular character of the nation and for America's nineteenth-century poetic experimentation, and criticism for the lack of self-knowledge and self-confidence Henderson perceived in American poets.

Henderson's first editorial ("A Perfect Return") specifically labeled the reason for American poets' neglect of Whitman and Poe: American poets and critics lacked the mental rigor necessary to learn the true nature of Whitman's genius. In the article she explains, "It is not that America holds as commonplaces the fundamentals expressed in Whitman that there have been more followers of the Whitman method in Europe than in America, but that American poets, approaching poetry usually through terms of feeling, and apparently loath to apply an intellectual whip to themselves or others, have made no definite analysis of the rhythmic units of Whitman. . . . The hide-bound, antiquated conception of English prosody is

responsible for a great deal of dead timber."[20] Henderson's distinction between emulating the "feeling" of Whitman's expansive originality rather
than learning the lesson of his "new flexible chanting rhythms" lies at the
heart of her charge that American poets have borrowed a tradition—the
very problem Whitman's art was able to transcend. Therefore Henderson
called for "a new sense of responsibility" in poets and critics alike "to turn
the international eye, in private, upon ourselves." Such perspective could
avoid "parochial" limitations and help frame the broader values of American art without requiring "the approval of English or French critics" ("A
Perfect Return" 88, 91).

This article reflects in a number of ways upon *Poetry* as well as upon
poetry. In one sense, Henderson was qualifying Monroe's "open door"
policy by urging the need for higher standards in general, along with the
need for rigorous mutual criticism based on appreciation of the truly original elements in native poetic genius. Henderson's comments also made
much the same point as Pound's "To Whistler, American" and "A Pact"
but didn't simply dismiss American readers as "that mass of dolts"; rather,
she prepared the ground for her subsequent discussions of the invigorat-
ing qualities of American art, including its unique diversity.

Despite her criticisms, Henderson also declared that truly American
writing could be found and developed. She identified intrinsically American aspects, for instance, in the diction of Sandburg's free verse and the
"primitive" exuberance of Lindsay's rhythms. This interest in "other voices"
deepened after her move to New Mexico, when she became more involved
with regional ethnic literatures such as Hispanic-American and Native
American oral traditions and "cowboy songs" such as those of Charles
Knibbs. Henderson's support for indigenous writing and experimentation reflects *Poetry*'s position as a forum for such work. She helped to
establish the magazine as a champion of specifically American poetry, as a
place for discussion of what constituted the "American" aspects of current work, and as a venue demonstrating the democratic diversity of the
United States. Henderson's comments also served as a foil to Pound's
denigration both of American poets and the American audience.

Henderson's articles connected the issue of the poet's relationship with
an audience to the question of American poetic sensibility. Her article
"Too Far from Paris" noted that the times during which a nation faces

adversity are the times it will appreciate most the contributions of its poets. Mindful of the threat of war in Europe and of the currently renewed
feelings of patriotism that attach importance to the poet's role in forming
any "national make-up," Henderson pointed out that Americans ought
to reassess their own particular heritage, which arose from modification
of the traditional folk materials brought in by its various citizens and given
new impetus by nationhood: "in the United States we have naturally that
direct break with the past which is an artificial feature of . . . certain revolutionary European artists and poets. . . . All that we owe to the native
soil itself is Indian or negro, and the latter,—we can not say certainly
how much—is of African origin. These . . . are exotic [to us]. . . . Therefore, whatever contribution this country makes to the great international
body of literature or art must be largely individual. . . . The nation has
been expressed through the individual."[21] By obliquely invoking the Revolutionary War, as well as calling up the historical view of America as the
"new world," she stressed the unique background of this land and its political role in having shaken off imperial rule, thus becoming a model for
other countries—notably France, whose literary influence on the United
States informed Henderson's initial polemic ("A Perfect Return") in 1912.
As well, Henderson respected the integrity of the non-European traditions that have been absorbed into American life; her own budding interest in the "exotic" literary strains of Native Americans would later blossom into perennial involvement with both Indian and Hispanic folklore.
Thus, anent a nation still "finding itself" in an artistic sense, Henderson
declared it would be misleading to believe that America was "too far from
Paris" for its literary achievements to be taken seriously, especially since
"the creative source of much of the modern European movement is American in spirit," springing from a blend of multinational influences, "of
which the United States has certainly furnished heroic growths" ("Too
Far from Paris" 107-8).

Henderson's article located the importance of poetry in "the individual," both as artist and as audience. The crux of American mythology—unity in multiplicity—was neatly turned into a political and aesthetic statement, one which also reflected the modernist aim of drawing
unified artistic work from the fragments of earlier cultures.

Henderson's insistence upon exact technical analysis formed the basis for her contributions to the debate about vers libre, in which she along with Monroe helped to establish the legitimacy of free verse in English-language poetry. The articles in which Henderson most strongly present-ed her ideas on vers libre appeared in *Poetry* in the issues for May 1913 and December 1916. In Henderson's 1913 piece, she, like Monroe, found that the difference between "Poetic Prose and Vers Libre" rests "in the quality of the rhythmic phrase" in the latter.[22] Again emphasizing the need for precision in metrical analysis as she did in 1912, Henderson argued that free verse has more specific patterns of stresses and variations than does prose—that, in fact, one can discern "scientific divisions of wave lengths" in proper vers libre. Yet along with these internal structures, po-etry in free verse must also demonstrate the spontaneity and intellectual "action" required of all good creative work ("Poetic Prose" 100, 102). These guidelines reflect the sensitivity to rhythmic and stylistic originality that accounts for Henderson's enthusiasm over Sandburg's poetry, which she discovered for *Poetry*. Sandburg's "Chicago Poems" opened the issue of March 1914 and caused a sensation that well characterizes *Poetry*'s most dynamic years.

Three years later, however, Henderson's careful exposition gave way to impatience. In "Lazy Criticism," responding to what was then the much belabored question of whether such verse is indeed poetry or merely an assemblage of "ragged lines" (as the *Dial* had called Sandburg's work), Henderson had apparently decided that the patient analyses of vers libre by herself, Monroe, Pound, Amy Lowell, and John Gould Fletcher had gone on long enough. Henderson's recurrent insistence that all poets should "grow" clearly applied also to the critics repeatedly recrossing this ground. Henderson took issue with recent comments critical of free verse put forth by Max Eastman in the *New Republic*. "It is high time that a critic ob-jected to *vers libre*," Henderson began sarcastically,

not on the score of rhythm—a phase of the subject endlessly debatable, but on the score of style, and for a few moments it looked as if Mr. Eastman were about to prove the one exception who would establish the intelligence of the tribe. But alas, no. . . . No, instead of indicating that what keeps journalism from being literature is exactly what keeps much *vers libre* from being poetry—and also what keeps much metrical verse from being poetry—and literature, Mr. Eastman falls into the very pitfalls that all the other critics have dug, and he even falls deeper in—buries himself like an exploding shell.[23]

What was really needed, Henderson explained, was a rejection of the critics' usual "courage of generalities" in favor of the "courage to discriminate among . . . contemporaries," to discover precisely how the poem's "emotional image" gains power through the poet's metrical sophistication. The disagreements over vers libre, Henderson made clear, merely masked a deeper inadequacy on critics' parts to remain open-minded and well-trained—a problem that, it seems, no further amount of explanation could correct. "The poet knows that it is just as hard to write good free verse as it is to write good metrical verse," Henderson declared at last. "When either achieves the level of poetry, the distinction between the two is unimportant" ("Lazy Criticism" 148). Henderson's use of the "emotional image" of the bomb epitomized her own frustration over the futility of the free verse debate, which by 1916 she thought of as "back history."[24]

Although her interest in American poetry based on oral literature and rhythms of speech would seem to cast little emphasis upon precision in writing, Henderson also demanded technical expertise, as seen in her insistence that poets should make detailed analyses of Whitman's verse patterns and in her careful outlines of the metrical subtleties in free verse. She also defended the contemporary mode of Imagism even as she acknowledged its classical antecedents, thereby deflecting as irrelevant the charge that Imagism did not deal with the modern world.

At the same time that she supported free verse, Henderson was quite capable of satirizing the excesses and foolishness perpetrated under its guise. Henderson's more playful treatment of what she perceived to be a wearisome trend in contemporary verse once again embroiled *Poetry* in heated exchange. In one 1916 section of "Our Contemporaries," which Henderson often wrote, she presented her topic—in this case the writers in the *Others* anthology—with characteristic vinegar: "Replacing the outworn conventions of the I-am-bic school, we have now the I-am-it school of poetry[,] . . . not to be confused with *Les I'm-a-gists*, who are already out-classed and *démodé*."[25] This introduction was followed by excerpts from the *Others* anthology, in which the poets' use of the first person accumulates as an irritating affectation: "I am Aladdin. / Wanting a thing I have but to snap my fingers. . . . I dislike men loving too many women. / They are wrong. . . . / I am right. . . . I am the possessor and the possessed. / I am of the unborn. . . . Behold me! / The perfect one! / Epitome of the universe! . . . I laugh. . . . / I laugh. . . . / And I laugh. . . ." Henderson broke off abruptly at the bottom of the third page, stating, "We regret to say the printer announces that there are no more I's in the font" ("Our Contemporaries [A New School of Poetry]" 105). Henderson's point, of course, was that certain aspects of contemporary poetry had become self-indulgent or arrogant, a view with which subsequent readers may be sympathetic.

Even after expressions of outrage from Maxwell Bodenheim and William Carlos Williams (on behalf of *Others* editor Alfred Kreymborg), who didn't find the piece amusing, Henderson showed no inclination to recant, writing to Monroe in June that she still thought that "ninety-nine per cent [of the anthology] is sheer bosh. . . . I am personally sensitive to altercation etc. but a magazine has got to have a fighting edge to it."[26] Henderson was always willing, as Pound was, to provide that "fighting edge," whereas Monroe preferred a less confrontational style.

In this piece, Henderson lampooned a tiresome poetic trend while demonstrating her awareness of current writing. In her other comments, she also insisted that critics be informed of contemporary experiments in writing. She deplored careless criticism that did not carefully weigh such developments as vers libre, Imagism, and individual American voices such as Lindsay's and Masters's. Her particular editorial style included spirited criticism of poets, publications, and critics that did not seem to her to be doing their jobs, as for instance with Braithwaite's failure to credit *Poetry* in his annual ratings of verse in American magazines. This readiness to take issue served the magazine well in Henderson's spirited defense of Sandburg and her criticism of some of the weaker elements in current writing, which she perceived in the *Others* anthology as well as in numerous books and articles she reviewed. Her ideas, especially those expressed during the four years she was most closely tied to *Poetry*, helped to create a coherent critical approach to modernist writing, much as Pound's did, although Henderson was far more willing to discern good work in America.

While late twentieth-century readers may find Henderson's interest in American racial and ethnic groups laudable, it was nevertheless problematic, revealing a confusion characteristic of the times. In these years *Poetry* was publishing poems by Vachel Lindsay, Margaret Widdemer, Sherwood Anderson, and Henderson herself (as Alice Corbin) that were purportedly based on African-American or Native American oral traditions. The presentation of these spurious works may have been an outgrowth of the interest in primitive art that entered modernism most notably through Cubist painting, but which of course involved distortions of the original material. Related developments include such amalgamations as Pound's *Cathay* poems and "Propertius" and Amy Lowell and Florence Ayscough's Chinese poems. It is worthwhile to consider the possible connections between modern interest in exotic literatures, "translations" and rewritings of various kinds, and co-optation of "minority" literatures that was clearly going on during this time. Henderson's own interest in literatures and cultures of the Southwest led her in later life to promote and conserve such literatures. She was also quite capable, however, of insulting and dismissing Braithwaite—as did both Pound and Monroe—because he was a mulatto. The problems inherent to discussing what constituted an "American" literature in the early decades of modernism, then, are in need of considerable analysis. While *Poetry* went further than most such magazines in creating a forum in which different voices might be heard, it is clear that a "gatekeeping" ideology was still in effect. Monroe and Henderson, of course, did not anticipate the late twentieth-century climate of awareness about one's own critical "positionality"; they were concerned with keeping *Poetry* alive as a vital and varied platform for a much broader spectrum of new writing than had previously been available.

Henderson's and Monroe's articles cumulatively demonstrated *Poetry*'s editorial identity and enlivened its tone of artistic exchange. What they accomplished was not the sort of vigorous "conversation" that was Margaret Anderson's aim for the *Little Review* but rather a more particularized discussion of the nature of current poetry and an appreciation of certain trends and figures from the past, which Monroe and Henderson considered important for their continuing influence and their expression of humane values. When, for example, Monroe praised the "spirit of the west" shown in one poet's work and later rhetorically called for "all the prairie muses" to assist Vachel Lindsay's poetic message, she showed general support for things "midwestern" and "western" later echoed in Henderson's support for Masters's *Spoon River Anthology*, the "cowboy poets," and ethnic American writings.[27] They also reiterated each other's exhortations for poets to reject outmoded language and styles and to experiment in newer forms: Monroe's articles "The Open Door" and "The New Beauty" offer examples, and she added her support for the Imagists in "Its Inner Meaning" (1915).[28] Henderson gave her opinion in articles and reviews such as "Poetic Prose and Vers Libre," "Poetic Drama" (1915), her reviews of Imagist anthologies (1914, 1918), and "Our Contemporaries [A New School of Poetry]" (1916).[29] Other matters upon which both women wrote include antiwar feeling in America, the international spirit of modern writing, the need for support of newer poets, the difficulties of editorial duties, and the importance of a sympathetic—or at least an informed—public.

Monroe's own early editorial comments set out her artistic philosophy behind *Poetry*. First, she made it clear that she was willing to include any poem showing what she considered to be the true spirit of poetry, whether or not the poem itself was perfect in formal execution. Second, she stressed the importance of newly envisioned work written in a modern idiom. Both aspects of Monroe's thought have been misunderstood, and one reason lies at Monroe's own door; her writing on occasion shows a taste for the sort of "poetic" language that modernism was beginning to sweep away. Consequently her idealistic call for traditional human values in poetry has sometimes been read as an inability to appreciate contemporary language or as an intention to cling to outworn literary forms, at the expense of "the best" new work.

Monroe's first piece, for example, in volume 1, number 1, was a fable about a prince who had the power of beautiful speech; Monroe's own language used such archaic phrases as "fit thy speech to music, that men may hold in their hearts thy rounded words."[30] Although the outmoded nature of this language suggests that Monroe preferred traditional tropes, Monroe was using this language deliberately to convey her sense of true poetic spirit, expressive of human nobility and accomplishment and enduring throughout human existence, whatever form it happened to take. Still, Monroe apparently did not mean this archaic language to be ironic, for her insistence on the enduring, even ancient, value of the "poet as prophet" reappears elsewhere in *Poetry*.

Monroe's occasional use of old-fashioned language obscures the more important element of her philosophy, namely her call for lucid poetic structures and unembellished language. She wrote at one point that she preferred "straight modern talk which rises into song without the aid of worn-out phrases."[31] Yet the philosophy that guided Monroe's taste did not yield a clear statement of standards; thus both she and Henderson (and later Pound) could agree in principle about *Poetry*'s goals while disagreeing over specific details. For example, in an early review Monroe wrote that poetry sometimes "is an aspiration rather than an achievement; but in spite of crude materials and imperfect artistry one may feel the beat of wings and hear the song."[32] This is a telling comment, for in it one sees Monroe's editorial predilections: she was willing to credit the spirit of the attempt rather than insist upon a superlative product—a position quite different from Henderson's (or Pound's). In a sense her editorial tastes are broadly democratic and intuitive but not stuck on the idea that "anything goes." Rather, in this editorial she encouraged poets to write new works that tested poetry's methods and scope, even at the expense of refined artistry.

Although she said all forms of the art were welcomed into *Poetry*, Monroe was far from believing that all such forms were equally valid for modern writing, or that all contemporary poets were producing usable material. This point too has been misconstrued in the body of criticism on *Poetry*, although Monroe strove to make her point clear from the beginning. In her editorial "The Open Door," which appeared in the second number of *Poetry*, Monroe responded to her critics' "fear" that *Poetry* may become a refuge for "minor poets."[33] She retorted that minor architects and artists are not so maligned as are minor poets, and that minor works are a necessary concomitant of major achievements (63-64). The subtext, of course, was Monroe's defense of her own democratic editorial preferences, which admitted dross along with the gold, but in the absence of which, she believed, no gold could be mined at all. Monroe indicated that history might perhaps vindicate her, if her contemporaries would not.

Monroe was quite well aware of the limitations of her "open door" policy and defended them as a necessary result of keeping the door open. Not that the open door was an unmitigated pleasure: in the first issue of volume 2, Monroe's "The New Beauty" complained of the past half-year's submissions to *Poetry* as "pathetically ingenuous in their intellectual attitude," having apparently been written by poets not of the twentieth century but of "an Elizabethan manor-house or a vine-clad Victorian cottage. . . . This is true even of certain ones who assert their modernism by rhyming of slums and strikes, or by moralizing in choppy odes, or in choppier prose mistaken for *vers libre*, upon some social or political problem of the day."[34] As this passage shows, Monroe could be a harsh critic when rejecting plain "moralizing" and sloppy vers libre that did not meet her standards for modern poetic form and content.

Monroe made her own defense of vers libre early in *Poetry*'s second year, not in the terms of general descriptive pronouncement that Pound had used in March 1913 but in the context of a careful explanation of the musical basis of poetry throughout the history of English verse, in which she asserted, "*Vers libre*, whose rhythmic subtleties may be only at the beginning of their development, is a demand for greater freedom of movement within the [musical] bar and the [poetic] line."[35] Monroe praised vers libre as one means of radical change in poetry, writing: "My own feeling is that the familiar terms, iambic, anapestic, etc., might better be thrown away, and a system of musical notation observed more in accordance with musical laws. But though the practice of centuries cannot be changed at once, it may be subjected to question. Poetic technique is still a mediaeval province unillumined by modern scientific research" (110). Monroe's approach to vers libre rested on her analysis of earlier traditions in English poetry, presented via musical notation accompanying passages from Shakespeare, Wordsworth, Coleridge, Meredith, Tennyson, Shelley, Poe, and Swinburne. Monroe was fond of this approach to thinking about free verse, and promoted it in *Poetry* and elsewhere. The discussions about vers libre in *Poetry* provided a spectrum of opinions that helped to establish the twentieth-century versions of this technique.

Given the innovative nature of the magazine as she had conceived it, Monroe found herself repeatedly stating her position on the relative usefulness of literary traditions. In an editorial entitled "Tradition," Monroe noted that her article "The New Beauty" in the previous number (April 1913) had antagonized some critics who supported "the grand old English tradition" in verse.[36] Defense of tradition, she wrote, is for those who "need protection," and the makers of English verse traditions certainly didn't think of their work as "sacro-sanct." Tradition, Monroe carefully noted, is useless if it inhibits an artist—a point with which Pound agreed a few months later.[37]

Monroe has herself been accused of "inhibiting" poets through alteration of or objection to portions of their works. This situation has been treated in some depth by Ellen Williams, who discusses Monroe's actions and choices in this regard. It is true that Monroe's own tastes, and her deference to guarantors (later the Modern Poetry Association), led her to much-cited editing such as eliminating the line "He laughed like an irresponsible foetus" from T. S. Eliot's "Mr. Apollinax" and deleting the word "bloody" from Pound's "Phyllidula and the Spoils of Gouvernet" in 1916 (Williams 62-65, 190-192). Pound, of course, also altered others' poems (most notably those of Yeats and Eliot). Monroe, however, has been sharply criticized for her motives. Yet the survival of *Poetry* as a forum was an issue; since its supporters were publicly acknowledged, the magazine was vulnerable to popular opinion despite the editors' efforts to educate their audience. The alterations were ones Monroe thought necessary to avoid alienating her financial backers.

These actions do not obliterate the extent of Monroe's accomplishments, nor are they sufficient cause to dismiss her as a prude, as many critics have done following Pound's lead. Monroe made many forays against artistic inhibition. She protected her contributors, sometimes against her own taste, in her determination to keep the door open to new ideas. Pound, in fact, was the earliest to benefit from Monroe's defense when *Poetry*'s readers railed against his characterization of them as "that mass of dolts" in the poem "To Whistler, American," in the very first issue.[38] Monroe met the criticism in the "Notes" section of the fifth issue, defending Pound for giving the public "bitter medicine which possibly we need" and accounting for his exile by stressing America's neglect of poets—a factor that for her had been the strongest motivation for creating *Poetry*. Thus Monroe's defense of Pound's boldness, in a way, spoke for herself as well; one sees again her will to effect change in the modern literary landscape in her assertion that critical "blows" are easier to bear than indifference. This attitude clarifies Monroe's responses to the criticism of her readers about what *Poetry* published. Guided by her artistic philosophy although unable to implement it in her own poetry, determined to provide a wide open forum for new poetry despite the variable quality of submissions she knew she would receive, Monroe showed immense persistence and willingness to serve on the front line of modern poetry, allowing the accomplishments of the magazine to speak for her vision.

With Pound, Monroe and Henderson shared a relationship that gave off sparks that helped ignite the "poetry renaissance" but that also has led to tendentious interpretations of the editorial activities at *Poetry*. Pound's criticisms of the magazine are clear from a glance at his *Letters, 1907-1941* and have carried much weight in literary history. Monroe's own generosity toward Pound in *A Poet's Life*, as in *Poetry* generally, stemmed from appreciation for his work and his frankness about her magazine and her own poems; she seems to have viewed Pound as another participant in the lively debate she shared with Henderson. Pound's own assessment of Monroe in his obituary for her in 1936 placed much more emphasis on her qualities of tenacity, insight, and dedication than did "Small Magazines" in 1930 or his letters. Ann Massa notes that despite his criticisms Pound saw Monroe as a kindred spirit, dedicated to poets and poetry (39). Nevertheless, most critics have chosen to focus on Pound's disagreements with Monroe rather than on their mutual accomplishments.

On the other hand, Henderson and Pound sent each other manuscripts and books, traded gossip and news, and sometimes commiserated over *Poetry*, which Monroe knew about but accepted as another aspect of editorial debate.[39] Henderson's strong loyalty to *Poetry*, however, led her to stop communicating with Pound after his remarks about the magazine in the *Little Review* in 1916; her willingness to engage in critical exchange did not encompass what she viewed as defection and slander.[40] The coop-

erative spirit seen in both women's relationships with Pound, that difficult and valuable contributor, emphasizes the openness to experiment,
investigation, and variety—but not didacticism or self-seeking attitudes—
which characterized the magazine.

Poetry, operating as the sort of broadly based poetic forum that Monroe had envisioned, was able both to absorb and reflect the differences of
critical opinion between Henderson and Monroe, as well as the extremely
varied experimentation of its era. If it was not always able to attract "the
best new writing," that fact resulted in part from *Poetry*'s own success in
clearing the way for the many other publications created to print the new
work to which *Poetry* had given such a strong impetus—a surge of small
magazines that continues to this day. It is likely that much fine work in
less noticed regions of the country may ultimately trace its vitality to
Poetry's "open-door policy," which refused to neglect Midwestern and other
"regional" poets. As well, the variety and depth of modernism itself is
characterized by the contents of *Poetry*'s pages, which depict the currents
of subjects and modes of the era, which recall the past and help create the
future, and which present the success and failure of various contemporary idioms. In no small way, literary modernism was introduced into
America as a result of Monroe and Henderson's cooperative work in blending their critical skills with the raw materials of modern poetry.

Another collaboration between Henderson and Monroe, outside the
pages of the magazine, resulted in the series of anthologies entitled *The
New Poetry*. The women worked together on the first and second editions, published in 1917 and 1923; a third edition, in 1932, seems to have
been prepared by Monroe alone (Abbott, "Publishing the New Poetry"
106). Studying the assembly of these volumes sheds additional light on
the women's editorial exchanges and provides evidence of each one's opinion about the nature of good modern poetry. As well, the work of com-
piling these anthologies led to events that resulted in Henderson being
virtually written out of Monroe's autobiography—a factor that accounts
for the subsequent neglect both of Henderson's influence in modernist
literary history and of the dynamics of her editorial collaborations with
Monroe.

The editors' professional stakes in *The New Poetry* were somewhat different than for the magazine because, as Monroe put it, the anthologies were the only chance to make a little money.[41] In addition, Monroe's intuition that the prestige of *Poetry*'s name would assist the anthologies proved correct, and the first edition sold fairly well. Thus both profit and prestige were connected to the anthology for both editors.

Monroe proposed the volume to Macmillan early in 1915. Craig Abbott notes that Monroe had wanted the first edition of *The New Poetry* to represent poetry that was "new in kind" rather than simply the most recent work, as Edward C. Marsh of Macmillan urged ("Publishing the New Poetry" 92). Monroe had probably been having similar conversations with Henderson about this very topic. While there is little archival evidence of the exchanges between Monroe and Henderson during the compilation of the first volume, subsequent letters suggest that the women had discussed the focus and purpose of the anthology just as they had carried on friendly disagreements about editorial policies for *Poetry*. The women worked together selecting poems, making the paste-up, and conferring about what should appear in the book's introduction and bibliography. Much of the first version of the book that Monroe sent Marsh was in fact drawn from *Poetry*'s pages, which led Marsh to suggest greater inclusiveness and a smaller number of poems by each poet; a second paste-up, also criticized by Macmillan, was defended by Monroe on the grounds that the greater space given to some figures was necessary because of their influence and by Henderson on the grounds that more "orthodox and classical" poets balanced out the newer ones (Abbott, "Publishing the New Poetry" 93). After a few more substitutions and alterations, some by the poets to whom Monroe had written for permission to use their work, the final version was a volume that reflected *Poetry*'s "open-door policy" by including a broad range of minor poets while still emphasizing such major figures as Pound, Lindsay, Masters, Sandburg, Robert Frost, H.D., and Edwin Arlington Robinson.

The New Poetry became Macmillan's "best seller in the poetry field," as Monroe wrote to Henderson in August 1921.[42] Problems had arisen, however, during the preparation of the volume that were more serious than the disagreements over the contents. Although both women had combed back issues of *Poetry* and individual authors' volumes in search of selections for the anthology, Henderson's tuberculosis and subsequent removal to New Mexico in 1916 interrupted her work. Monroe finished the volume herself after considerable effort, as her letters to Henderson make clear; the sheer volume of work necessary to create such a book had caused her to vow, at one point, "No more anthologies for me!"[43] Henderson's departure complicated the question of how much work each woman had done for the anthology; as a result, the women argued over the amount of royalties each should receive. Thus, when Macmillan raised the possibility of a new edition in 1920, the way was already paved with difficulties.

Monroe felt that she had done the lion's share of necessary clerical and mechanical work in 1915 and 1916. The earlier contract with Macmillan had not specified any division of royalties between the two editors—Monroe alone had signed the contract, despite Henderson's request to be included, because Henderson was out of town at the time.[44] After some argument with Henderson, Monroe had reluctantly granted Henderson a one-third share of royalties, later stating that she had done so only due to exhaustion and distraction at the loss of Henderson during a stressful time. After the second edition was proposed, Monroe stated that she thought Henderson's proportion of the royalties should be reduced. Henderson, on her part, contended that the contents of anthologies were what sold the book and that her effort in selecting those contents for *The New Poetry* had been as important as securing details of permissions and production; therefore, her royalties should not be reduced. This disagreement carried on throughout the preparations for the second edition, and, as a result, the editorial discussions about the second edition encompassed far more than questions of poems' artistic value.

It is apparent that the very success of *The New Poetry* led to the destruction of Monroe and Henderson's editorial collaboration. Part of the blame may be laid at Monroe's door, as a result of her solicitude during Henderson's illness in 1916. At that time, although both had been deep in preparation for the book, Monroe's letters to Henderson urged her to regain her health and not to worry about the anthology. On her part, Henderson felt bad that Monroe had had to shoulder so much of the clerical work for the first edition. Shortly after her depature, she wrote to

Monroe, "I am *terribly sorry* that the anthology turned out to be such a burden!—I can't help feeling indirectly grateful to it, for if I had not stayed up so many nights reading for the thing, I might not have discovered my condition in time!! As it is—it is a long, *slow job*, as Sandburg would say."[45] Early in 1917, she reiterated her regret over leaving her editorial work but indicated her continuing interest in promoting the anthology.[46] Henderson's comments about the contents of *The New Poetry*, in this case, also indicate some of the grounds on which Henderson had disagreed with Monroe over the years, which in turn suggest Henderson's influence on the editorial direction taken by *Poetry*. Late in February, for instance, Henderson noted,

I like your introduction to the anthology. I'm not sure I agree with you on all points, but that doesn't matter. . . . As for the anthology itself, I don't believe you'll regret the hard work. It's a pretty good *monument*. It is probably too inclusive, but as long as it doesn't run to the extremes of Stedman's, not a bad fault. Of course there is too much in it—for the title; some stuff that has no business there at all, I think. (Including some of mine) Aiken is a sore trial. . . . I think the anthology is a monument, just the same, of your five years' endeavor. You must, as Lindsay said, advertise it to the full hilt, in Poetry, and without modesty elsewhere.[47]

The "five years' endeavor" for which she gave Monroe credit was not the anthology but the magazine itself. Calling the anthology a "monument" to *Poetry*'s role in encouraging "the modern movement" in poetry, Henderson expressed once again her interest in the relationship between important nineteenth-century influences and their twentieth-century respondents. This viewpoint formed the basis of many of her disagreements with Monroe, including those about the contents of the second *New Poetry*. As a related matter, Henderson's belief in the extent of her own contributions to this "modern movement" through her work for the anthologies and the magazine supported her position that she deserved no reduction in royalties.

Monroe probably contributed to the argument unwittingly by taking the same stance toward Henderson's involvement—and another bout of illness—in 1921 as in 1916. In letters to Henderson discussing plans for the new edition, Monroe's tone was as solicitous as before. Even though she requested Henderson's suggestions for the new book, Monroe also urged Henderson to guard her health and not worry about the anthology: "I fear I have not realized how far from well you are just now," she wrote in June 1921. "I dont [sic] want you to bother about reviews, or the New Poetry, or anything else. . . . Thank you for your suggestions, with most of which I agree. But please don't bother—just be quiet and get well."[48] Such mixed messages about Henderson's participation set the stage for the women's bitter dispute over Henderson's share of the royalties. The women's earlier tendencies toward compromise (Monroe) and confrontation (Henderson) in editorial matters resulted in this case in figurative "bloodshed," which caused a permanent schism between them, demonstrated most obviously in Monroe's virtual erasure of Henderson from the discussions of Poetry in A Poet's Life.

The women's exchanges about the actual contents of the second New Poetry add considerable depth to any reading of their editorial views. From an examination of the two editors' discussions about selecting the contents for the second edition, one finds that Monroe was not as conservative as she has been painted, since she would have preferred to assemble an all new volume of contemporary work, although her preference for being broadly inclusive still obtained. Henderson was more interested in demonstrating the whole stream of influences that fed into modern poetry, adding work by such poets as Yeats, Robert Bridges, Gerard Manley Hopkins, and Emily Dickinson, while excluding some of the poets who had not shown any growth since the first edition, so the anthology would demonstrate in depth the historical changes that had led to "the new poetry."

Early in 1921, Monroe wrote to Henderson asking for her input about omissions from the first volume but qualified her request by noting that she found few poems she would take out. She was also quite clear about her desire to make the second edition current, asking Henderson's advice about inclusions from more recent issues of Poetry.[49] Monroe had already made a virtue of necessity by explaining in the first edition why Yeats's poems (which he had refused to give at a price Poetry could pay) were not appropriate to the aims of the book; she saw no reason to go back in time to find more of that sort of poetry when so much new work could be anthologized.[50]

Henderson, however, proposed in June that the revision be made "a competent and authoritative text-book" by including work from important earlier writers who showed the modern spirit as well as keeping good writers previously represented.[51] She suggested cutting or omitting Conrad Aiken, Mary Aldis, Alfred Kreymborg, Amy Lowell, and Louis Untermeyer, while including Yeats, J. M. Synge, Padraic Pearse, James Joyce, Edward Thomas, Wilfred Owen, Siegfried Sassoon, Sherwood Anderson, Arthur Waley, and Elinor Wylie, as well as newer poems from certain poets such as Edna St. Vincent Millay, Edgar Lee Masters, and Wallace Stevens. Henderson's suggestions look both forward and backward, culling from earlier years as well as from interesting contemporary writing and including some of the best World War I poets, the influential translations by Waley, and members of the Irish Renaissance. She saw no reason to stick to an arbitrary time line, because the "spirit" that infused modern poetry had begun earlier; in fact, she noted, Dickinson had never appeared in a proper edition although her influence had been strong because her work was so "modern" in tone.

In response, Monroe reiterated her preference for more contemporary work: "I am dead against your suggestion to go back to Synge, Bridges, Moody, Moore, Kipling, even Yeats. I shall stick to a 1900 line, and if a vol. II, to a 1916 line. I am not going to rake up the 90's. . . . in my opinion that would be a tremendous mistake, would contradict the whole intention of the anthology."[52] Thus the lines of disagreement were drawn, with Monroe on the one hand urging a broad contemporaneity, while Henderson preferred more depth and a more exclusive focus covering a longer period of time.

What eventually occurred was a compromise, first between Monroe and Macmillan, then between Monroe and Henderson, leading to an expanded edition of the book from which a few minor poets had been excised, a number of both major and minor poets added, and a large number of additional newer poems from poets already represented included as well. Monroe had tried to arrange a more substantial change via a new volume; she had written Macmillan several times, at one point quoting

Witter Bynner (then president of the Poetry Society of America as well as a businessman), who urged her to do not a revision but rather a supplemental volume.[53] Monroe feared that a mere revision would confuse the book's audience and would "fail to continue the present vogue" (*The New Poetry* had become a reference work). George Brett of Macmillan had suggested that a new edition simply include supplementary pages, which would be easier and cheaper to publish.[54] Monroe proposed instead "a strong new volume, which would have a personality of its own and would not interfere with the first one," and if need be, printing a "thin-paper edition" of both together for the schools. She also preferred that the second volume be "somewhat smaller than the first." For a few months in 1921 the two women discussed this idea. None of these suggestions prevailed, however; Macmillan insisted upon a one-volume work that would remain competitive in the college market, and Monroe reluctantly acquiesced, agreeing to add to the previous contents about fifty percent more new work (her actual estimate of new work, once she had sent in the second edition, was almost seventy percent).[55] When hopes for a supplementary volume were dashed late in 1921, Monroe proceeded to plan for the revision.[56] Abbott notes that the 1917 edition contained 431 poems by 101 poets, whereas the 1923 edition contained 783 poems by 140 poets ("Publishing the New Poetry" 95, 103). Monroe's wonted persistence did pay off, for she persuaded Macmillan to pay for the permissions because the magazine could not support that expense.[57] This format is not what either woman thought best, yet its breadth seems more to reflect the "text-book" Henderson wanted than the post-1916 update that Monroe would have preferred.

It is interesting to compare the two women's suggestions about which poets to omit, include, and expand in *The New Poetry*'s revised edition. In only two cases—Witter Bynner and Conrad Aiken—were substitutions or rearrangements made, and these occurred at the suggestion of the poets. Only four authors were deleted entirely (Skipwith Cannéll, Scharmel Iris, Seumas O'Sullivan, and Hervey White).[58] Despite Henderson's strong dissent, none of the remaining authors' selections were cut, not even Amy Lowell's "Patterns," which Monroe at one point said Lowell had agreed to delete. Henderson's urging to include Yeats prevailed over Monroe's reluctance to approach him again for poems, and Monroe then complied by making good suggestions for his section. Ultimately the volume was strengthened through the inclusion of several of Yeats's important poems.[59]

The specter of royalties had, as might be expected, interrupted and slowed this work. When Monroe had suggested a reduction from one-third to one-fourth of royalty payments to Henderson, the latter replied with characteristic vigor:

Of course I shall want to make suggestions and do my full share in the revision. . . . I was much hurt and shocked by your letter of August 5th, in which you questioned my 1/3 interest in the proposed second volume. If, during the three or four years when I have been urging you to get out a new volume or a revision, I had made a new volume myself—instead of remaining loyal to a supposed partnership—you would doubtless have thought me a better business woman than a friend! . . . you must realize that I had something to do with the success of the anthology; and that I am naturally jealous of its standing, and of course I should be unwilling to have it revised without my full co-operation and responsibility. . . . I have been ready all summer. I sent you my outline for the revised volume last June. . . . Please let me have this again, or make a copy of it for me, as I want to check up on it the work that I have done since.[60]

Henderson's perception of her editorial contributions to *The New Poetry* was clearly premised upon reading and making suggestions for the overall thrust and contents of the volume. Her acceptance of a one-third share of royalties in 1917, she thought, acknowledged the fact that Monroe had singlehandedly completed the clerical details only because of Henderson's departure, not because Henderson's editorial work had been of lesser importance. Henderson's expectations about her own contributions in 1921 obviously followed the same lines. A few weeks later, she wrote,

As you remember, the original agreement between us on the anthology was for a 50-50 division of the royalties. . . . You may remember, too, that it was I who urged and urged the idea of the anthology upon you, and prepared the first lists of poets and drafts of letters to Macmillan. . . . I had made not only the dummy from "Poetry," but the general selection as well (modified a little in the final printing), had done some work on the bibliography, and had made, at your request, suggestions for the Introduction, when I was taken sick. . . . The burden of the clerical work was thus left to you, and on that account, when the book came out, you suggested 1/3 instead of 1/2 as my interest in the book and I accepted it.[61]

For her part, Monroe maintained in a letter of December 1921 that Henderson had no legal ownership in the first *New Poetry*, since Henderson was not mentioned in the original contract with Macmillan; however, Monroe wrote that she was yielding to Henderson's wishes not because she thought Henderson rightfully entitled to one-third of the royalties, but "because I am disgusted with the whole business, and besides I have a human desire that you should, if possible, be satisfied."[62]

The work proceeded rapidly after that point, with Henderson and Monroe exchanging lists of suggestions and Henderson at times requesting copies of books and poems. Monroe sometimes lost patience with Henderson, since the *Poetry* offices were being moved to a new address in April 1922 and she could not arrange to send copies of books and back issues for Henderson's perusal. With her characteristic good nature, Monroe tried to incorporate Henderson's ideas, although it seems that Henderson, in trying to resolve the royalty situation to her own satisfaction, had waited so long to make her suggestions that Monroe was only able to use some of those ideas as a result.[63] A letter of February 1922 indicates that Henderson's earlier suggestions had had only moderate bearing on the new edition as Monroe assembled it. Monroe wrote that she had misplaced Henderson's earlier list of ideas, but said that those "few casual and very indefinite suggestions" didn't constitute an outline anyway. "You have sent me nothing since summer, though you knew the work had to go on," Monroe complained, noting that it was getting almost too late to consider "inclusions and omissions."[64]

Henderson, however, believed that she had made good-faith efforts to indicate her preferences and wrote on April 15:

Your letter of April 6th, indicating that you were sending letters to the poets asking permission to use certain poems, without waiting for my agreement or objections to your selection—without in fact giving me time to make any suggestions whatever—surprised me considerably. If you have sent many such letters to the poets, I fear that it will muddle things up very much. . . . The anthology of course purports to represent our joint judgment, and must do so, even if publication is thereby delayed.

I have been going over your list very carefully and conscientiously. I sent you my list on February 23rd, and you had at least five weeks to consider it. I got yours Sunday night, April 2nd, and judging from your letter of April 6th, you evidently expected me to spend only three days on it. . . . I feel sure that we can come to an agreement about most of the poets; but it seems to me that you should not ask any permissions until we come to a complete understanding about the contents.[65]

Henderson may have felt compelled to make a strong case for her disagreements in this instance since she had missed the editorial give-and-take, to which the two women were accustomed in the *Poetry* office, which would have accompanied their preparations for the 1917 edition.

Monroe, on the other hand, continued with the clerical duties as she had done for the previous volume. By April 1922, she had completed most of the dummy, which she used to estimate page count. She made a few compromises based on Henderson's latest comments, which were fairly extensive, encompassing "no less than 48 of the poets represented."[66] Even in the final stages of preparation Monroe made efforts to respond to and incorporate some of Henderson's suggestions. In August, for example, Monroe related her last-minute negotiations with Conrad Aiken, Witter Bynner, and Harold Monro, and said that she wanted to add some work by Francis Shaw and Oscar Williams and delete Charles Knibbs (a poet Henderson supported). She also asserted that she wanted to include Genevieve Taggard—a longstanding patron and assitant to *Poetry*—despite Henderson's objections, although Monroe's tendency to compromise is evident in her suggestion that Taggard's long poem "Ice Age" be used if the poet agreed to shorten it; it did not appear.[67] Monroe's interest in "Ice Age" expresses her willingness—stated in the earliest issues of *Poetry*—to accept poems in unconventional or inconvenient forms.[68] Her wish that she could have done so in the anthology appears in her words to Henderson, written as preparations neared completion: "We are in danger of including in the *N.P.* a crowd of perfect *little* poems, and excluding things of size."[69] Her encompassing position could hardly be more clearly expressed—yet it is also true that the "things of size" (and substance) appearing both in *Poetry* and in *The New Poetry* cannot be judged only according to line count or format.

Even after Monroe's letter of December 1921 informally agreeing to a two-thirds to one-third split in royalties, Henderson insisted on having Monroe sign an agreement that had been drawn up by a lawyer and that verified her one-third share of the royalties for the 1923 and any subsequent edition of *The New Poetry*. Henderson had also been in contact with Macmillan through her lawyer, not only to see whether Macmillan would honor Henderson's request to be part of the second contract but also to warn them that, since her name was on the book, she would need to approve of its contents—which, for the preliminary copy Monroe had sent the publisher in April 1922, she did not. Although Macmillan had indicated earlier it would "lose interest" in publishing a volume that might elicit litigation, the company tried to steer clear of the matter. It was Henderson's lawyer who finally persuaded her that she might damage her own reputation if she pursued the matter, but who also arranged for the two women to sign the agreement, which was finalized in June 1922.

Although the two women continued to correspond after the appearance of the second *New Poetry*, it is clear that the rift between them seriously disturbed their longstanding friendship. Henderson's willingness to take legal action, foreshadowed in her earlier complaints about Braithwaite's use of poems from *Poetry*, ran up against Monroe's sense of investment in both the magazine and the anthology. Monroe's own sense of honor led her to believe that she had done all that was necessary by agreeing in her December 1921 letter to give one-third of the royalties to Henderson. The strong sense of self-assertion in each woman—an assertiveness that had proven crucial to *Poetry*'s success—combined with each one's belief that she had put in substantial amounts of work for *The New Poetry* and created a situation in which the women's customary pointed bantering lost its humor. The aesthetic disagreement between the two women significantly affected the first two volumes of *The New Poetry*, as it had enlivened the magazine. Critics should be grateful for the blending of intellects with which Henderson and Monroe helped the poetic "renaissance" to its feet. Their personal argument over royalties for the books, however, marks an unfortunate chapter in their relationship, one that seems effectively to have silenced Henderson's voice, despite her many contributions, within the pages of literary history.

Monroe's virtual excision of Henderson from *A Poet's Life* not only has diverted attention from Henderson's contributions but also has changed the emphasis given Monroe's editorship and *Poetry*'s impact on modern literature. Both women were involved in *Poetry*'s most significant contributions: introducing Imagism to America, encouraging the experiments of scores of modern poets, broadening avenues of public access to poetry, and helping to encourage an international sensibility as well as reconsidering America's role in the critical debates about new work. *Poetry* argued for the existence of a distinctly American poetry and tried to display the range that such poetry could take by supporting minor as well as major poets, regional work and poetry societies, other little magazines, small-format publications, readings, prizes, and many other aspects of literary activity that are now taken for granted. *Poetry* was also a leader in the controversy over vers libre, analyzing and defending the technique during the years that important innovations were taking place. Had *Poetry* not printed and supported Sandburg, for instance, the pronouncements by the *Dial* dismissing his free verse as "ragged prose" might have prevailed—if and when Sandburg had been able to publish at all. Monroe's and Henderson's reviews of the several Imagist anthologies, as well as the space *Poetry* gave to Amy Lowell during the years of her promotion of *Some Imagist Poets* (1915-17), added impetus to the introduction and critical discussion of these developments. The magazine also served as an example challenging the whole concept of what a "poetry publication" could be: its editors were unafraid to touch upon, directly or obliquely, political topics of the day, including women's rights, wartime sentiment, racism, poverty, and jingoism.

Monroe and Henderson's support for many different kinds of experimental poetry—the "lesser growth" that Monroe saw as necessary to give rise to masterpieces—provided an important sense of context or audience for modern writing. Their editorial agenda differed from the elitist position of some modernist writers; *Poetry* provided a democratic space that encouraged inclusiveness and extensive scope in modernism at a crucial time. Far from being timid, frail, and provincial, Monroe showed a courage and equanimity that continually tried to preserve idealism and cooperation, even in the face of a world at war, and engaged a spectrum of topics in her editorials. While her taste and moral scruples have been faulted because they affected what appeared in *Poetry*, Monroe's editorial choices were in part based on a hard-won knowledge of the difficulty poets had in being recognized for their work and on her strong determination to keep *Poetry* going as a paying venue, even if that meant occasional compromise to please her guarantors. Her sense of loyalty was strong and permitted her to be gracious toward most of those who disagreed with—and even openly insulted—her. Her dismissive treatment of Henderson in her autobiography stands as a notable exception, and even then, a close examination of their correspondence during their work on *The New Poetry* demonstrates a certain level of courtesy that was never breached, despite both women's obvious ire.

The collaboration between Monroe and Henderson clearly energized *Poetry*, bringing much good work to its pages and providing an editorial milieu that served the magazine well in its important early years. Not all of the editors' decisions were good ones; most of the published work was not of enduring quality; but the most important task, of providing a paying place for poets where their work could receive critical response, was indeed met. Monroe's insistence upon giving place to many kinds of new work helped provide the basis for the range of experimentation and accomplishment that characterizes early twentieth-century poetry. Henderson's strong sense of the nineteenth-century roots of modern work helped her defend free verse and discern what was important in the new poetry. Together, these women collaborated to produce the magazine that served as the catalyst for modern poetry in America.

3 READER CRITICS

Margaret Anderson, Jane Heap, and the *Little Review*

Among the little magazines identified by Frederick J. Hoffman, Charles Allen, and Carolyn Ulrich as vital to the development of twentieth-century literature, the *Little Review* serves as the paradigm. Its irreverent tone, its eclectic selections, and the idiosyncratic opinions of editors Margaret Anderson and Jane Heap characterized the magazine throughout its run of fifteen years, from 1914 to 1929, during which time it became the premier forum for avant garde literary and artistic activity. Even for the explosively creative age in which the magazine arose, the accomplishments of the *Little Review* are impressive, including serializations of works by Ford Madox Ford, James Joyce, Wyndham Lewis, Ezra Pound, Dorothy Richardson, and May Sinclair, and shorter pieces and reproductions of artwork by such figures as Sherwood Anderson, Jean Cocteau, H.D., T. S. Eliot, Juan Gris, Marianne Moore, Francis Picabia, Gertrude Stein, Joseph Stella, William Carlos Williams, and W. B. Yeats. Although the register of contributors attests to the magazine's importance in the development of twentieth-century arts, this roster of names alone cannot account for its success, for the *Little Review* created its greatest legacy through inviting and enacting opinionated debate about the nature and value of art, between the two editors as well as between the magazine and its readers and contributors—a form of critical exchange reflecting the multifaceted nature of modernism itself. This insistence on response and interaction demonstrates Anderson's expressed reason for developing the magazine in the first place: her boredom with a life that did not include "inspired conversation" every minute, and her belief that publishing a review would place her in contact with persons with whom she could always have an interesting exchange of ideas.[1] The "conversation" embodied in the *Little Review* became one of the forces that moved modernism.

Studies of the magazine, however, have tended to treat Anderson as a foil for Ezra Pound—who was highly visible as "foreign editor" during 1917-19—or to focus on Anderson's personality, discussing the *Little Review* according to stereotyped expectations surrounding women's appearance and demeanor rather than according to the editors' actual accomplishments. As well, discussions of the editorship of the *Little Review* have often failed to distinguish Anderson from Heap or to note the two women's interactions in print, which helped to account for the review's spirit of lively exchange. In fact, little attention has been paid to the particular contributions of Heap, who joined the magazine in 1916 in collaboration with Anderson and who later took over editorial duties, significantly changing the nature of the magazine. When one reconsiders *Little Review* editorial policies and achievements in light of the fact that its editors were lesbian lovers, resisting the dictates of a patriarchal world, their dedication to the unconventional in modern art and literature can be seen to carry strong personal as well as aesthetic import.

The critical interactions in the pages of the *Little Review* show a level of editorial confidence that defies traditional assumptions about women's roles in the arts—that is, expectations that women would be "midwives to the arts," or would act as muse or nurturer for men who were "really" making literary history. Of equal importance is the fact that Heap and Anderson radically altered the parameters of the role of magazine editor. They refused to use editing as a passive facilitation of others' works and were instead visibly confrontational, juxtaposing editorials, reviews, and articles in order to highlight critical controversies, and including their own parenthetical responses to articles and to letters in the "Reader Critic" and "Comment" sections. Yet rather than merely showing off as a rebellious arbiter of "the new," presenting experimental writing and ideas simply for shock value, Anderson and Heap's magazine provided them an arena for discussion with some of the finest modern artists during a time when traditional forms and conventions were changing dramatically. The *Little*

THE LITTLE REVIEW

THE MAGAZINE THAT IS READ BY THOSE WHO WRITE THE OTHERS

MARCH, 1918

MARGARET ANDERSON, *Editor*
EZRA POUND, *Foreign Editor*

24 *West Sixteenth Street, New York*
Foreign office:
5 *Holland Place Chambers, London W. 8.*

25 cents a copy $2.50 a year

Entered as second-class matter at P. O., New York, N. Y.
Published monthly by Margaret Anderson

Table of Contents for the *Little Review*, vol. IV, no. 11, March 1918

Review was a vehicle of critical exchange that mirrored the "cubist" interest in multiplicity of viewpoint and in breaking down objective authority.

At the same time, at a level less obvious to the public, the two editors expressed their relationship by encoding private meanings within their published writings. The *Little Review*'s editors not only displayed their intellectual views but also made jokes between themselves and explored ideas that amused them and about which they disagreed. These exchanges occurred in conjunction with the major discussions carried on in the magazine about aesthetic principles, censorship, and the roles of artist and critic; in each case, the question of form was central. The *Little Review* can be viewed as a forum for interrogating the problem of form, even as its editors' lives were as unconventional as their magazine, not acceding to traditional assumptions about what magazine editors (or women generally) "ought to do." Concomitantly, critical response to the editors and to the *Little Review* has frequently used gender-inflected language, which suggests public discomfort with this type of female nonconformity.

It is important to keep such discomfort in mind when one approaches critical assessments of the *Little Review*, for much published material discusses the magazine in the context of the personal attributes of its editors. Many commentators have mentioned Anderson's physical attractions—hair, face, and dramatic gait—and her talents as a pianist, in comments that reflect traditional expectations about women's appearance and "accomplishments."[2] Such remarks would merely bemuse a reader were it not for the value judgments placed on such attributes and their implications about Anderson's professional work. For instance, in the first extended examination of the magazine, in 1965, Jackson Bryer wrote, "[Not] to be dismissed lightly, is the important role in her success as an editor which Margaret Anderson's physical beauty and personal magnetism played. . . . [As one man remarked,] 'If Margaret Anderson had had a different face and a dowdy figure, her story would have been quite something else.'"[3] Some authors mention the ways in which Anderson solicited money for the review through reliance on charm and impassioned pleading; Ben Hecht gives the impression that Anderson shamelessly used her personal attributes to charm her creditors into forgetting their bills.[4] Such charm was also assumed to operate in Anderson's ability consistently to persuade Mason and Hamlin, the piano manufacturers, to "lend" her a piano for several of her residences—a habit of hers that contributed to the impression that she was a frivolous person who had conceived of her magazine in a passion and kept it going for years on little else, rather than being read as evidence of a resourceful person who had to figure out ways to circumvent a lack of funds while accomplishing her ambitious goals.

On the other hand, Jane Heap, Anderson's coeditor and an artist in her own right, has been described in language associated with traditional (male) ideals of success; she is called handsome, redoubtable, intellectually powerful, and the wielder of a "peculiar intimidating wit," which helped set the aesthetic tenor of the magazine.[5] Her physical appearance, which was tailored and deliberately "masculine" (she had cross-dressed for years),[6] has drawn fewer personal comments than has Anderson's, a fact that may be linked not only to her apparent alignment with "male" imagery but also to her relative obscurity compared with the flamboyant persona that accrued around Anderson. Thus one finds that the language used to discuss these two editors, whatever its basis in aspects of the women's real lives, has often been founded on assumptions about gender roles either according to "feminine" traits suggestive of a prima donna or according to "masculine" traits traditionally associated with success: wit, intellectual power, "one-upmanship."

It is therefore especially interesting that the editors themselves encouraged, even initiated, the use of such stereotypes. Both Anderson and Heap to some degree courted stereotyping in their editorial comments, and both wrote short dramatic sketches characterizing the editorial interactions at the *Little Review* in terms of the stereotypes they inhabited. The editors' reasons for using stereotypes to describe themselves were deeply radical, part of a strategy of public expression in which meanings occur on several levels, not all of which may be available to the casual reader who lacks awareness of the ways the editors presented or thought of themselves as "other."

Anderson began the magazine by creating an image of herself as youthful, passionate, and extravagant, although she also insisted on the validity of her critical comments; one of the points she made by this strategy was that readers ought not simply to assume that a certain type of woman

Drawings by Jane Heap from the so-called "blank" issue of the Little Review, showing Margaret Anderson at work and play.

would have nothing intellectual to say. Heap was more restrained in portraying herself in the *Little Review*, relying on incisive criticism and dry wit in her signed pieces, and usually printing her imaginative writing—which often explored lesbian themes—anonymously.[7] Anonymity helped to preserve Heap's image as austere and demanding while allowing her to play with words in a way not traditionally permitted to critics. Her first "appearance," in the number of August 1916, was as a figure in her own sketches, which prefigured the humorous and ironic work she would later produce. Close readings of the *Little Review* detect hidden resonances that suggest several ways in which the editors viewed their work, the magazine itself, and their public.

It is pertinent to consider Anderson's persona in the context of the "New Woman" figure of the time. This figure, an imaginary composite based on public perceptions of women who supported such issues as suffrage and sexual freedom, was the focus of considerable social anxiety. In part, this anxiety resulted from movements for social reform demonstrated in the activities of such women as Carrie Chapman Catt, Alice Paul, Emma Goldman, Margaret Sanger, Susan Glaspell, and "Mother" Mary Jones.[8] In part, also, investigations by such researchers as Havelock Ellis into the nature of sexuality, particularly "inversion" or homosexuality, fed perceptions of linkages between lesbianism and feminism. When Anderson began her magazine with a flourish, declaring her allegiances to feminist and other radical ideas, she deliberately tapped into the social discomfort about, as well as the social movement represented by, "New Women" of the time. She had a number of reasons for doing so, most of which have been overlooked by literary critics or conflated under the misleading claim that the *Little Review* was a vanity magazine.

Anderson's early editorials may be read for clues about how she viewed her role as editor, her responses to being a woman in her particular social milieu, and her thoughts about how art can elevate humanity above the limitations of that milieu. Particularly, her ideas about art encode her frustration with society and her preference for a world of ideas in which minds may meet on equal terms, unrestricted by conventions. In this way, Anderson's early pieces foretell the boldness with which she met the censorship that truncated the *Little Review*'s publication of *Ulysses*, as well as suggest some of the ways she nurtured her individuality in a world that had little place for intelligent, self-reliant women.

In the first issue, for instance, Anderson flouted traditional expectations of what an editor should be when she proposed to run a magazine based not so much on the purportedly objective criteria of aesthetics but on things that interested *her*, a proposal that has led some critics to call the *Little Review* a vanity publication, or, less pejoratively but still with implications of frivolity, a "personal" magazine.[9] Such a reduction of Anderson's intentions, however, obscures their deeper implications, and does not do justice to her importance as an editor and her fortitude in persevering when the editors of many other magazines could not. Such an interpretation also discounts Anderson's antiauthoritarian sentiments, which she reiterated throughout her writings.[10] Thus, if one is alert to Anderson's irony and social criticisms, one finds in her editorials and reviews far more than just the apparent musings of a young, flippant intellectual.

It is telling that, apropos of Anderson's interest in critical exchange, she began her magazine with an editorial discussing the necessary correlation between art and audience appreciation. In effect, her editorial agenda was based on an audience functioning as a critical entity, with conversation serving as Anderson's paradigm: "Appreciation has its outlet in art; and art (to complete the circle and the figure) has its source in—owes its whole current—to appreciation. That is, the tides of art would cease to ebb and flow were it not for the sun and moon of appreciation. This function of the sun and moon is known as criticism. But criticism as an art has not flourished in this country."[11] Anderson asserts that "the quality of our appreciation is the important thing," so that one might apprehend the beauty of life through the vitality of an "eager, panting Art," which by implication may include the "art" of response—an unusual assertion for a little magazine. Anderson implies that critical writing could be as original and useful as art.

In the same editorial, Anderson ironically refers to her own undertaking as she imagines it will be received by a critical society, and casts the terms of social response in specifically gendered terms. She creates an imaginary conversation in which she refutes a hypothetical reply with an example based in women's experience. By using the plural pronoun "we," she not only draws on editorial convention but also slyly undercuts masculinist authority through appropriation, as is clear in this particular context:

We may as well acknowledge right here that we've never had a friend . . . who hasn't shaken his head at us paternally about this attitude toward art. "It's purely transitional," he says, tolerantly; "life's so much more interesting. . . . It really doesn't matter so much that Alice Meynell wrote 'Renouncement' as that Mrs. Jones next door has left her husband." Well, he's wrong. . . . It's not a question as to which is more important—"Renouncement" or Mrs. Jones. We're merely trying to say that we're intensely interested in Mrs. Jones, but that Mrs. Meynell has made our lives more wonderful—permanently. [1]

It is telling that Anderson sees the experience of art as the way to heighten and to improve, or even to draw attention away from, everyday life, characterized here by a situation in which women—both "Mrs. Jones" and the speaker in Meynell's poem—have freed themselves from masculine or romantic attachment. Anderson also has pointedly created a patronizing attitude on the part of the male "friend," who entirely misses the significance of linking the elevated nature of art with "leaving one's husband." Anderson disagrees with this avuncular voice through the figure of "Mrs. Jones," indicating her wish to be free of the patronizing aspect of society that is reluctant to see women's experiences as valid. Anderson's use of the editorial "we" also implies a consensus in her challenge to authoritarian male pronouncements, as if she expects her "audience" to include other women who understand and applaud her resistance.

Anderson's use of sex-linked imagery is not, however, transparent; it becomes problematic as the article proceeds. The *Little Review*'s "ambitious aim," she writes, "is to produce criticism of books, music, art, drama, and life that shall be fresh and constructive. . . . For the instinct of the artist to distrust criticism is as well founded as the mother's toward the sterile woman. More so, perhaps; for all women have some sort of instinct for motherhood, and all critics haven't an instinct for art. Criticism that is creative—that is our high goal. And criticism is never a merely interpretative function; it *is* creation: it gives birth!" ("Announcement" 2). This is, as Anderson admits, a "time-worn illustration." Why then would she—an editor who on the same page asserts that "the degree of [our feminism] is ardent!"—use it? The answer seems to be that Anderson knew exactly what she was doing: using traditional images ironically to indicate her dissatisfaction with the (explicitly) patriarchal voice of current aesthetic discussion, which would include such "time-worn illustrations" of what artists and critics were doing. Anderson's imagery suggests that women might make better critics—of society as well as of art. The "distrust" of sterility reflects a tradition of schism between artists' creativity and critics' lack of creativity, a perception Anderson specifically challenges.

Anderson also affirms the *Little Review*'s intention not to be "restrictive" but to present "the several judgments of our various enthusiastic contributors . . . in the same issue. The net effect we hope will be stimulating and what we like to call releasing" ("Announcement" 2). Since Anderson had already indicated her dissatisfaction with patriarchal voices telling her what to do, and since a plurality of voices implicitly questions the status quo, the "release" Anderson wants seems specifically linked, at least in part, to social restrictions on gender roles.

In her final paragraphs of "Announcement," Anderson's language anticipates (and probably provokes) the sort of gender-based stereotypes that later arose about her. In the context of Anderson's previous gendered imagery, her pride and self-confidence gives added meaning to her plans to invigorate current critical exchange:

Finally, since *The Little Review,* which is neither directly nor indirectly connected in any way with any organization, society, company, cult or movement, is the personal enterprise of the editor, it shall enjoy that untrammelled liberty which is the life of Art. And now that we've made our formal bow we may say confidentially that we take a certain joyous pride in confessing our youth, our perfectly inexpressible enthusiasm, and our courage in the face of a serious undertaking; for those qualities mean freshness, reverence, and victory! At least we have got to the age when we realize that all beautiful things make a place for themselves sooner or later in the world. And we *hope* to be very beautiful! [2]

It is easy to detect the brashness that became the hallmark of little magazines. It is also easy to see that Anderson, who was young, spirited, and good-looking, played on these traits in creating the image of herself as bold and new. Even as she participated in stereotyping herself according to her youth and her sex, however, the blatancy with which she did it indicates that she may have been baiting people who would think her intellectually limited because of these traits. She also teased such people by including at the end of her "Announcement" quotations from Samuel Butler and Ralph Waldo Emerson that echoed her own ideas about the prevalence of art in life and the need to distrust "academicism." By using these quotations, Anderson showed that she knew the work of "the great writers," and that some of them (who were men) have shared her ideas. These quotations, not incidentally, have to do with trusting oneself to find beauty and poetry in the world. Thus Anderson's self-assertiveness indicates more than just the fact that she was starting a magazine to enact critical exchanges and express her own views; it also carries a subtext that Anderson was well aware of the gender-based criticism that would come her way, and part of her approach would be to maintain a tone that would carry deeply ironic meanings for those who (as she did) refuse to be limited by traditional expectations.

Characteristically, Anderson initiated the *Little Review*'s custom of including readers' comments in the very next issue, apparently enjoying the disagreements as well as the approval and confusion her debut had provoked. If one recalls Anderson's stated desire to achieve "inspired conversation every minute" and matches that sentiment with the segment from *My Thirty Years' War* in which she claims she decided on having "a victory a day" in order to keep going, one may deduce that what really inspired Anderson was the edgy liveliness of debate, the "resistance" that made talking "worthwhile."[12] This savor for confrontation clearly undergirded her championship of such reformist ideas as feminism, anarchy, and socialism that were being debated, often heatedly, at that time. In fact, her taste for confrontation brought these ideas into contact with each other in ways that would not have been possible in a magazine with a more controlled scope. The very eclecticism of Anderson's enthusiasms reflected, and doubtless encouraged, the artistic and philosophical explorations of her time.

Another of Anderson's editorials a few months later specifically linked the situations of artists and women as being equally constricted by traditional societal expectations.[13] This emphasis reflected the *Little Review*'s early discussions of sexual morality in literature often carried on in book reviews and articles.[14] In this case, Anderson suggests that social pressures force the distortion of women's humanity and that the artist's accomplishments are concomitantly limited so long as the free expression of one's personality and sexuality is restrained by a delusory "morality." Anderson opens by citing an anonymous female novelist's statement that American women are "oversexed" and that there should be "a reaction against" the current emphasis on sex in dress and popular culture. Having noted this, Anderson takes her conversational turn by disagreeing:

[The] pity of the whole thing is that the critics who keep lecturing us on our oversexedness don't realize that what they're really trying to get at is our poverty of spirit, our emotional incapacities, our vanities, our pettinesses. . . . "sex" continues to shoulder the blame for all kinds of shortcomings, and the real root of the trouble goes untreated—even undiagnosed. One thing is certain: until we become conscious that there's something very wrong with our attitude toward sex, we'll never get rid of the hard, tight, anaemic, metallic woman who flourishes in America as no where else in the world. ["Incense and Splendor" 1]

Here "sex" refers to the whole body of expectations and limitations placed on women, that stress appearance at the expense of a free range of human feelings and activities. The motif of appearance and clothing as a measure of human character, which Anderson examines in the article, links Anderson's concern with gender issues to her belief that art—the elevated experience of life that a higher sensibility can provide—should transcend petty "bickering" about morality, which to Anderson suggested arbitrary restrictions upon individual self-expression. Anderson's concern for "Art" is revealed here, in fact, to be a radical vision for social change based on the freedom from convention that Anderson links with the artist:

> Some day we're . . . going to realize that the only person who doesn't *err in relation to values* is the artist; and since the bigger part of the artist's equipment is simply the capacity to *feel*, we're going to begin training a race of men toward a new ideal. It shall be this: that nothing shall qualify as fundamentally "immoral" except denial—the failure of imagination, of understanding, of appreciation, of quickening to beauty in every form . . . the failure to put one's self in the other person's place; the great, ghastly failure of life which allows one to look but not to see, to listen but not to hear—to touch but not to feel. ["Incense and Splendor" 3]

Failure to feel leads to "denial," affecting one's own nature and ultimately the entire culture. Thus Anderson's reference to raising a new "race of men" pointedly suggests that men's opinions need to change; by implication, the position of women demonstrates the failure of society's vision. Although Anderson followed the linguistic conventions of her era by referring to "the artist" as "he" frequently throughout her writings, these ironic moments suggest the complexity of Anderson's manipulation of sex-role stereotypes.

This early passage fits with others of Anderson's editorials and reviews that promote greater sexual openness. Anderson even dared, as Holly Baggett points out, to include a clue to Anderson's own sexual orientation in her March 1915 article, "Mrs. Ellis's Failure." In this piece Anderson discusses a lecture given by Edith Ellis, who was Havelock Ellis's wife and a lesbian, criticizing her for apparently failing to provide the inspiring talk that would have promoted a greater understanding of homosexuality for which Anderson had hoped. In the article, Baggett notes, Anderson refers specifically to sexologists' current ideas about homosexuality and "intermediate sexual forms," demonstrating her familiarity with the debate and her support for greater sexual openness and tolerance toward "other" orientations (108). Anderson saw sexuality as a public as well as private aspect of life, thoroughly integrated with intellect and social interactions and in need of liberation from stultifying conventions, as Anderson's fervid support for Margaret Sanger makes plain. Even from its earliest years, the *Little Review* proved itself to be open to publishing pieces treating themes of homosexuality—for instance, Gertrude Stein's "Bundles for Them," Bryher's "Chance Encounter," Hemingway's "Mr. and Mrs. Elliot," and Jane Heap's "I Cannot Sleep"—which increased its importance to the avant garde but also increased its danger. As Baggett points out, even the trial over the publication of *Ulysses* had more to do with authoritarian distaste for the editors' lesbianism than with the book's "immorality" (243, 257), which hearkens back to Anderson's critique years before of the kinds of "denial" that betray a fundamental "failure of imagination" in American culture.

The complexity of Anderson's play with sex-role stereotypes certainly relates to her own ironic play with norms of female appearance and behavior. She believed that "moral offense" lies in one's state of mind, and that, under pressure to conform to socially prescribed roles, women as well as men participate in limiting human options. To establish the connection between artist and audience, Anderson used a broader definition of "sex": the capacity to feel intensely, which Anderson saw as the integral experience of life. Arbitrary limitations upon women, as well as upon artists, seemed wasteful to her. For Anderson the role of the artist in teaching others to feel implied a revision of the entire social mechanism. It is clear that she used her language in the *Little Review* "to make critical statements about the psychosexual and sociocultural construction of women," creating in her editorials the same sort of disruptive narrative strategy that Rachel Blau DuPlessis identifies in women poets and fiction writers (*Writing Beyond the Ending* 4).

Early in the history of the *Little Review*, Anderson's interest in social reform took a new turn—a rather theatrical one, as she described it later. After attending a lecture by Emma Goldman, Anderson noted in *My Thirty*

Years' War, she "had just time to turn anarchist before the presses closed" for the May 1914 issue of the magazine (54). To "turn anarchist" in this case meant Anderson wrote and printed an energetic promotion of Goldman's radicalism, "The Challenge of Emma Goldman," and a number of subsequent articles promoting anarchist ideas. The tone of Anderson's statement in her memoir no doubt has fed the criticisms of those who believe Anderson's interests—encompassing as they did feminism, anarchism, Imagism, Dadaism—were insincere. The arch quality of this statement may indeed seem inappropriate since it is so at odds with the fervor of Emma Goldman's message and the seriousness of the legal sanctions that Goldman suffered in the United States. Equally, though, one might interpret Anderson's statement as further evidence of her desire for immediate, ongoing discourse about ideas she thought valuable, and in her excitement to initiate conversation about the topic of anarchism she did not want to wait for another number of the *Little Review* to be produced. This interpretation fits better with the importance Anderson attached to Goldman's work, as is clear from the pages of the magazine and *My Thirty Years' War*.

Anderson's interest in anarchism led to a personal friendship with Goldman and a series of articles in the magazine promoting anarchist and pacifist ideas, fueled in part by the outbreak of World War I. Anderson saw the war as a terrific waste, linked to the dogmas of capitalism and social intolerance.[15] Baggett points out that another of Anderson's articles in the September 1914 issue of the magazine—protesting the death of labor organizer Joe Hill—drew the attention of the FBI (118), while the cumulative effect of her interests lost Anderson her initial financial backer and initiated the magazine's first real fiscal crisis, which led to Anderson's famous six-month sojourn in a tent on a Lake Michigan beach (*My Thirty Years' War* 86-92, 99-102). The several forms of discrimination to which Anderson was subjected as a result of her promotion of anarchism included withdrawals of magazine funds and landlords' refusal to rent to her, earlier versions of the contretemps that were to occur over the printing of so-called obscenities. Throughout these adversities, Anderson maintained her composure and her courage, continuing to speak out in favor of social causes as well as art that she thought important.

Another significant feature of the literary landscape in 1914 was Imagism, which had been launched in America by Harriet Monroe's *Poetry* and was picked up, with her usual enthusiasm, by Anderson. Anderson's interest in the movement was predicated on her enjoyment of its descriptive style, which she emulated in pieces of her own writing, although from such pieces it is clear that Anderson did not pay much attention to the kind of close rhythmic analysis that Monroe and Alice Corbin Henderson offered in *Poetry*. "I am convinced that the secret and beauty of the Imagists lies somehow *in the look of the words*, and that if you have only a feeling for the sounds of words you will never love Imagism," Anderson wrote in a short editorial of March 1916. This editorial, a response to a lecture by Mary Aldis, who was "unmoved" by Imagism, noted approvingly Henderson's claim that Imagism "isn't a matter of technique: it is a matter of vision."[16] Whether a result of vision or metrics, the effect of Imagism on Anderson led to her promotion of the movement in America during the years of *Some Imagist Poets* and provided crucial support for Amy Lowell's extensive series of lectures on the topic. Baggett finds that Anderson used the controversy over Imagism as a way of emphasizing her policy of "conversation" in the *Little Review*, encouraging Lowell to send submissions but also printing Eunice Tietjens's critical article "The Spiritual Dangers of Vers Libre" in November 1914 and a preface disagreeing with Huntley Carter's article "Poetry versus Imagism" in September 1916 (135–36, 144). Anderson's side of the conversation, however, was clearly supportive of this poetic innovation, since the *Little Review* included a considerable number of relevant poems, articles, and reviews of Imagists' books many times during 1915–16. Thus the *Little Review* became one of the foremost venues in the United States for materials concerning Imagism, which of itself has been extremely influential in twentieth-century literary history. Not incidentally, Anderson's strength of character as well as of opinion is obvious in her refusal of Lowell's offer to subsidize the *Little Review* in exchange for editorial leverage (*My Thirty Years' War* 60–62), even after Anderson's several removals and sojourn on the beach because she could not afford rent.

In these articles, and throughout the years of her close engagement with the *Little Review*, Anderson's writings and editorial style drew con-

nections between traditional expectations about gender roles and a vision of social reform articulated through the interactions of artist, critic,
and audience. Heap, who joined the magazine in 1916, surely debated
these issues with Anderson, as the latter suggests in *My Thirty Years' War*,
in which she characterizes Heap as "the most interesting thing that ever
happened" to the magazine because Heap was "the world's best talker"
about ideas (102-3). The two women met at the Fine Arts Building in
Chicago, which housed the *Little Review* offices and Maurice Browne's
Little Theatre company, with which Heap had become associated after
moving to the city to study and exhibit her art. It is clear that Anderson
had found someone who, despite their marked differences in moods—
Anderson was busy and optimistic whereas Heap was quiet and prone to
depression—struck sparks of "discussion" that energized a generation of
the avant garde. At the same time, as Anderson noted wryly, the two
"formed a consolidation that was to make us much loved and even more
loathed" (*My Thirty Years' War* 107). Their lesbian relationship made the
critical questions raised in the *Little Review* about "following forms," about
censorship, and about the integrity of experience deeply meaningful in a
private way as well.

Jane Heap's critical work in the *Little Review* first appeared in the
column, "And—," in September 1916, November 1916, and January 1917.
Heap's distinctive critical approach is at once evident in these collections
of short paragraphs commenting on literary and artistic matters. Although
she was unknown as a critic, she was willing to assert her ideas in a
language that exudes knowledge and self-confidence through its terse,
aphoristic style. If this was indeed her manner of speaking, as Anderson
suggests when she claims that she had to beg Heap to write for the magazine (*My Thirty Years' War* 110), one can see how Heap's conversation
would certainly have provided the "resistance" and freshness Anderson
craved. Heap's use of dramatic and provocative opening statements is characteristic; her pieces often began with such lines as "Here is another man
[Sherwood Anderson] who hasn't written the great American novel," or
"We are *Ulysses* mad."[17] One short example gives a general sense of Heap's
style: "Rabindranath Tagore is coming back to America to lecture. Go, if
you have never seen that slight presence with features drawn of air—with

eyes that seem never to have looked out—and let him put that white spell of peace upon your complex futility. You sometimes wonder why men like Dr. Coomaraswamy come telling us border-ruffians of Art about Ajanta frescoes and sculpture and the music of India. Perhaps they know our homesickness and know that alone we can't even find the road."[18] This complete comment, one of Heap's first for the *Little Review*, contains some important features. First, her writing, blended of elliptical comments, apt descriptions, and a sharp sense of irony, requires readers to use their imaginations to fill in the logical backgrounds for her statements. Without sacrificing clarity, Heap creates in her critical writing the same sort of interaction between artist and audience presumed by much modernist art. Second, Heap is interested in the ways in which the experience of art (in this case, hearing Tagore's lecture) could help people to forget the "complex futility" of their lives. This interest not only echoes Anderson's comments about the power of art but also foreshadows both editors' attachment to Gurdjieff's mystical community in France in later years, an attachment that reveals the integrative nature of their critical and artistic beliefs. Finally, Heap's directness and brevity reinforce her critical comments by refusing to "spell everything out," a tactic suggesting that anyone who cared to differ with Heap's conclusions must bear the burden of proof. Heap's opinions, standing on their own and requiring work on the reader's part, challenged traditional expectations about what a critic should do.

Anderson herself characterized Heap's style in *My Thirty Years' War* as follows:

She talks usually in monosyllables, with here and there an important word placed so personally as to give it a curious personal significance. It is impossible to quote her. You can hear that done, with appropriate disaster, by anyone who tries it. I will try.

Take a group of people discussing sophistication. . . . You hear every possible definition of sophistication—you already know them all. Then Jane says:

A really sophisticated person? I should say a person who is used to being a human being. . . .

A phrase of Jane's I have always remembered was one she found as a tribute to someone who (briefly) understood her: A hand on the exact octave that is me. [103-4, 106]

Despite Anderson's claim to failure, readers indeed get a sense of the boldness and interest of Heap's style. There is also a hint of their private relationship in Anderson's approving quotation of Heap's characterization of an understanding friend as a "hand on the exact octave that is me." To Anderson, who was a skilled pianist, this description must have carried profound personal as well as aesthetic appeal.

Heap's reputation as an austere critic does not accurately reflect the tone of all her writings for the magazine. There are instances in which Heap's imagery adds emotion as a component of her criticism, for instance in her first longer piece for the magazine, "Paderewski and Tagore."[19] This article weaves the story of Heap's and (presumably) Anderson's attendance at a concert by Paderewski with a meditation about the independent nature of cats and a description of seeing the Indian poet Rabindranath Tagore at the concert. Along the way, the article uses some gendered imagery that, as in Anderson's case, makes any easy assessment of Heap's critical language problematic but that also casts light on Heap's sense of the nature of art and of herself as a critic.

Heap begins meditatively: "This morning I lay in bed looking at the ceiling and thinking about cats. How *elegante* they are, and impenetrable, and with what narrow slant-eyed contempt they look out upon the world. . . . Anyway I thought of cats, and of violin strings made of catgut, and wondered about cats and music. Is it because violins are made of living things—wood and catgut and mother-of-pearl and hair,—that they make the most beautiful music in the world?" (7). The praise for cats' "impenetrable" nature, which allows them to view the world with "contempt," suggests Heap's own predilections as a critic, catlike, looking on the world of art and society with appreciation for the beauties and scorn for the follies. There is also a serious undertone in her connection of violin music with things once living. Any animal lover would not be pleased to be reminded of catgut, taken from animals that have been killed; Heap did not apologize for this reminder, but by using it hinted that music necessarily contains the violence as well as the beauty of life. Even this early piece has an edge to it, indicating the strength of Heap's opinions and her willingness to manipulate public discomfiture.

After this opening Heap describes going to the theater for Paderewski's recital, wondering whether Tagore, who was visiting San Francisco, would also attend. As she looks at the crowded house, thinking, "There [are] too many people," she notices Tagore and responds physically:

And then with tears hurting my eyes and an ache in my throat choking me I called out: "There—there's Tagore—in the third box!"—and made them look quickly so they wouldn't see me cry. There he sat in the first chair in a robe the color of grass-cloth and a pale violet cap upon his head. . . . I watched him until I was almost in a trance: the angle at which his head was put on, the cheek bones that were like an extra feature. . . . Everything that lies beyond the reach of thought and wonder seemed concentrated in that dark Stranger. I trembled, frightened by my imagination and a little melancholy. [7-8]

The ironic juxtaposition of Heap's comments—finding "too many people" but being glad that Tagore, too, was there—is obscured by her emotional reaction to seeing the man. Her description of Tagore makes explicit the connection between physical beauty and mystic understanding, a sense of transcendence both desirable and discomfiting. Thus Heap's confession that she cried, while it might be read as evidence of women's emotional nature, also ironically expresses her identification with Tagore's psychic intensity, as she had linked herself earlier to the cat.

These linkages—between Heap as critic, cats, the artist, and the mystic—are reinforced later in the article. Paderewski, the artist, is called "*elegante* and impenetrable," watching the audience's call for encores with contempt, "eyes narrowed . . . a great cat! . . . striking the keys with a sheathed paw," demonstrating the artist's critical purview of the world (9). In contrast, the quiet figure of Tagore, which might be thought to stand for spiritual elevation, is described as having "smiled and leaned forward" during "some brilliant harsh thing of Lizst's," as if he empathized with the combined brilliance and harshness of art. Heap emphasizes the relationship between the two men and herself when she calls seeing Paderewski and Tagore at one time "a bright heaven beside a still universe," a combination through which "I was so filled there was no room left in me for the music" (9). This expression of rapturous delight in art recalls Anderson's; also like Anderson, Heap suggests that the artist and audience must interact, that appreciation and informed critical response are necessary in order to create a whole and intuitively meaningful experience. Heap is somewhat more exclusive, suggesting that engagement is more important in the case of "the few" whose qualities of mind and personality set them apart from audiences in general.

In all, the article, written to appear episodic and impressionistic rather than calculatedly "critical," expressed Heap's pleasure in the private aspects that inform the artist's life and personality, not simply the performance. The entire structure of the piece was crafted around Heap's emotional experience, combined with Paderewski's and Tagore's experiences in performing and listening—an unexpected critical approach that layers Heap's knowledge of music with her appreciation for Tagore's philosophical and literary writings, which were enjoying a vogue at the time. Her use of elements that might be linked to female stereotypes (her appreciation for Mme. Paderewski's dolls, her tears) is subtly offset by the tone of competence and knowledge. It is also clear that Heap's portrait of herself as critic includes both emotion and knowledge in responding to the work of artists and philosophers, a position that anticipates Heap's later involvement with the spirituality of the mystic Gurdjieff.[20] Heap's belief in the symbiosis between artist and critic fit well with the intentions Anderson had already expressed for the *Little Review*. This article, in effect, may be read as one of Heap's responses to Anderson, the pages of the magazine being used to intimate their private conversations.

The very title ("And—") of Heap's first critical column suggests that editorial work served as an important link between the two women, for it gives the impression that Heap was a respondent (perhaps ultimately "the" respondent) in the conversation that Anderson imagined for her magazine. Certainly, Heap's comments affected the tone of exchange heretofore found in the magazine. Her critical pieces generally expressed strong opinions about the importance of avant garde ideas, both as means to energize art and as expressions of social dissent. Heap's aphoristic style and self-confidence may be the reasons she was considered intimidating— she expressed herself so well in few words that argument seemed foolish, as distinct from Anderson's tendency toward first-person elaboration. Between these two styles, it is easy to see why the women of the *Little Review* have been characterized in male-oriented literary histories as arrogant.

Another reason for the *Little Review*'s significance in modern letters is that it courted controversy not only through provocative interchanges about anarchy and feminism but also through its play with the magazine format itself. The excerpts Heap and Anderson used in the "Reader Critic" sections, for instance, were clearly chosen as humorous and often pointed demonstrations of the interaction between the *Little Review*'s readership and its editors. The comments about the so-called "blank" issue of September 1916 offer perhaps the most obvious case. This number sported sixteen empty pages, a number of drawings by the recently arrived Heap, and some commentary pronouncing on the nature of "Art" and criticizing the lack of high-quality submissions. This half-blank issue struck many as a superb example of avant garde insouciance; certainly Heap and Anderson reveled in the attention this issue drew, and they printed a number of responses in later issues of the magazine, including Ezra Pound's first contribution, "Das Schone [*sic*] Papier Vergeudet."[21] Even in the issue itself, the editors printed letters commenting on the "threat" of leaving pages blank, which Anderson had made in her August 1916 editorial.

"Congratulations!" one Reader Critic began. "You have the capacity for suddenly turning back . . . to say 'All or nothing.' And subconsciously realizing that you will get mostly nothing, you threaten your readers with blank pages. . . . [Who] are *you*, to expect a staff of ready geniuses to fill your pages? You should be grateful for one pearl you may find among hundreds of near-jewels."[22] Frank Lloyd Wright wrote praising the magazine, saying, "Your resolve is interesting—but it looks like the end. . . . I wish I had a million or a pen."[23] Other responses varied from "Don't you think you're asking a little too much?" to "Bravo!" to one reader's plaint that prefigured a good many future letters: "The *Little Review* sickens me. I don't understand why in the devil you talk imagism and color and beauty and fill your magazine full of that sputtering trash, that colorless-degenerate edgarleemasters junk."[24] After the rest of the letter, which continued in the same tone, Heap sliced it off with her own response: "You say *The Little Review* sickens you? With the above temperature and tongue? I should diagnose the case as autointoxication."[25] Sometimes the editors replied, sometimes they left the letter or excerpt to stand alone, but the cumulative effect was of spirited controversy in which the editors maintained the upper hand, although they were quite willing to print material critical of themselves.

The subsequent issue included responses to the editors' responses, complicating the conversation but obviously adding to the editors' savor for challenge. In one letter, for example, although the writer claimed that Heap "may wreck your ship," he went on to explain that her witty contributions would "save your soul and this issue she certainly has saved. . . . it's just the touch to put you in Abraham's bosom at the last," a compliment the editors no doubt read with amusement.[26] Other selections, including one from Alice Groff, a Philadelphia poet, were much less complimentary; Groff called the editor "a mad little self-made God, setting yourself on a pedestal as the *only* judge of Art. . . . All that an editor can ever be as to art is a medium between the artist and the world. . . . The editor who fails to do this is unworthy to be an editor."[27] The heading appended to this selection, "Officer, She's In Again!" implies Groff's letter was from a crank and suggests that the editors saw themselves as indeed having an active role in arbitrating the "art" they printed. Immediately following this missive, Anderson and Heap included two encouraging excerpts, again with humorous headings that, this time, "answered" the letter writers with agreement and implicitly refuted Groff's criticisms. In the first of these, the letter writer announced, "I have never enjoyed any number of *The Little Review* so much as the September. Those blank pages linked with the cosmos: space before creation. I await Prometheus," to which the editors added the heading "We Also Await."[28] In the second, reader Daphne Carr commented, "I bless your new enthusiasm and its effects. That half blank number was splendid—what there was of it, but I wanted to see as spirited things on the other pages too." Heap and Anderson gave this excerpt the heading "So Did We."[29]

Even in this detail—the use of titles that require one to read the selection in order to get the joke—the editors reinforced the sense of interaction fostered by the magazine. Editorial prerogative obviously delighted Heap and Anderson, whose use of such headings, postscripts, and excerpts created a subtle means of asserting control over their authors and correspondents, especially those who disagreed with and even insulted them.

Heap's and Anderson's responses to their readers as critics exemplified their collaborative work for the *Little Review* and demonstrated how they saw their work as interactive and mutually supportive. To both women the "Reader Critic" often responded in support and in disagreement. If a reader attacked an editor or contributor, the other editor came to the defense; sometimes, both editors responded to a letter they found particularly foolish or ill-informed. Heap pointed out in one response the confusion that caused (and continues to cause) some readers to conflate Anderson with every other contributor to the magazine, including her coeditor: "We have noted with much amusement that whenever there is an article in the body of the magazine or a comment in the Reader Critic, no matter by whom signed, which seems 'disgusting, ridiculous or immoral' to some struggling soul, in comes a letter addressed to Margaret Anderson, saying '*Your* article, *your* comment.' . . . The only hope the editor can have out of so much generous accredit- [*sic*] is that some one sometime will write in giving her credit for Yeats's poems."[30] This sense of solidarity does not mean, however, that the editors always agreed with each other. Rather, they supported and defended the expression of each other's opinions, particularly when their disagreements delved into issues they found important concerning art, aesthetics, and knowledge. Such an attitude not only preserved the sense of conversation in the magazine but also insisted that the *Little Review* serve as a forum for new and radical ideas engaging authors, critics, and audience in the kinds of debate necessary for vitality of the mind.

The women's experimentation with magazine format is significant in another sense also. By refusing to print items just for the sake of using precious page space, Heap and Anderson defied expectations about what literary magazines should do. While the blank section dramatized the dearth of first-rate contributions, it also could be seen as a form of silence demonstrating resistance to social expectations. In addition, the half-blank number's reliance in large part upon the editors' own work—Heap's sketches and critical comments by both women—shows a self-confidence that again seems deliberately to give the impression the magazine was a vanity publication, rather than a substantial critical magazine that had already published well-known writers dealing with a broad range of topics and issues. In another sense, part of the motivation behind making a partially blank issue may have had to do with Heap and Anderson's fairly new relationship, fostered in the summer of 1916 by their retreat to a cabin in California; the format of that issue could be read as an oblique statement that each found the quality of the other's company and private conversation more interesting than nearly everything else.

The printed "conversations" between Heap and Anderson took several forms. Sometimes the two took turns answering letters about certain topics in "The Reader Critic" and sometimes their reviews addressed similar aesthetic points in a cluster of short pieces or in sequential issues, so that one may read their critical statements operating interactively. As well, Anderson and Heap were able to encode private meanings within their professional writings, expressing themselves publicly in coded ways.

This habit of exchange informs even their early collaboration. In March 1916, for instance, one of Anderson's editorial comments links her belief in the nature of art to both spiritual and social (r)evolution by connecting Bill Haywood's labor organizing efforts with the visionary renewal Anderson perceived in John Cowper Powys's lectures. Anderson at first disagrees with Haywood that a revolution was underway socially: "I see evolution at work in labor—not revolution. But I see something more than evolution at work in the arts." It takes "one's own dream of beauty or of power" to create both art and revolution, she asserts—a neat linkage that demonstrates how Anderson's enthusiasm for anarchism stood alongside her love of art in the pages of the *Little Review*. "How horrible it is to realize that when a man is slaving for his very life he can not be selective in what he does, that he has no dream left to magnify," Anderson writes. "This is why I would go to hear John Cowper Powys. . . . Boycotts are important, but they will not help a revolution as a dream will. Mr. Powys will help you find both an exaltation and a dream."[31]

A few months later, Heap also defended Powys's lectures, but using her own distinctive style. "Powys should never write anything," she begins, in a manner sure to catch the reader's attention. Her support for Powys also rests on the spiritual inspiration of his vision, although her defense is not concerned with integrating art and revolution but rather with criticizing those who would deny the ineffable quality of Powys's words: "People like Q.K. in the *New Republic* come about as near to getting Powys as they would come to catching a comet. Powys is not for culture-snatchers, matinee girls, or glorifiers of the obvious. He is merely for those possessed enough of their imaginations to fall for a miracle when they see one."[32] Like Anderson, Heap displayed great self-confidence in her critical sense, demonstrating even in a short comment that she was quite able to refute an established critic. Heap also uses a gendered stereotype ("matinee girls," who could be considered "glorifiers of the obvious") to express scorn for popular taste, which suggests that she and Anderson had talked over the problems of gender roles (which Anderson had derided in similar language earlier in the *Little Review*) as well as the elusive nature of inspiration provoked by Powys's talks and inherent in the kind of art the editors wanted to print.

Sometimes the editors seem to have been engaged in dialogue with each other, using "Art" as their pretext but themselves as subtext. One example involves their numerous comments about Mary Garden, who was an actor, dancer, and singer and who served as a sort of cultural emblem for Heap's and Anderson's aesthetic concerns, particularly the role of the artist and the importance of deep feeling informing critical response. They often referred to Garden in passing as if the mere mention of her name served an obvious conversational function as a reminder of earlier discussions about the nature of art. Generally the editors, particularly Heap, defended Garden against the charge that her art was lacking or was "decadent" by pointing out the great energy and "life" with which Garden performed. "Mary Garden gives us grand opera; she gives what the closed hand holds," Heap wrote in 1917. "She gives as generously of her undraped body as a Rodin statue; and the audience gives her back their applause, grudgingly, not knowing the great art of her."[33] Here Heap's stereotype of the unclothed female muse serves as a symbol of inspiration for the critic, not the public. In another issue, Heap praises Garden in terms that again link a critical approach with the personal or spiritual sense: "The creative artist takes the character to himself [*sic*] and then creates from his imagination in his own image. . . . It breaks your heart in a strange way, because [Garden] makes you feel more precisely our brief longing, our frail tenderness and our deceiving hope."[34] Heap, although she uses conventional language that implies a male artist, admires Garden's sensitive evocation as muse for the spectator's private sensations. Anderson, however, although she also praised Garden in her writings, shows her side of the discussions she clearly had with Heap over the interaction of criticism and feeling to be slightly different. In a review of Isadora Duncan, which appeared in a later issue of the *Little Review*, Anderson criticizes Duncan's clumsy interpretation, writing ostensibly to her magazine audience: "If you were much moved by what Isadora suggested to you . . . why not realize that you can feel these emotions, if you feel like it, in the performance of the cheapest amateur. But that is no criterion of Art. . . . You are talking only of what Isadora made you feel, not what Isadora *made*."[35] It is as if Anderson is defending herself, or the stereotype of herself as overemotional, against the popular conception of Heap as the "aesthetic analyst." It is as if Anderson is reminding Heap that immersion in one's own intellect and feeling is not enough. In *The* Little Review *Anthology*, a collection she prepared for publication in 1953, Anderson positioned this review immediately after Heap's and included an editorial notice of disagreement, almost as if getting the final word in an encoded, disguised dialogue that had taken place over the years, both in and out of print. Anderson's running comments in the *Anthology*, in fact, operate as if she were getting the last word in a number of conversations.[36]

The mutuality between editors and readers also extended on several occasions to the *Little Review*'s contributors. One aspect of the debate fostered by the *Little Review* involves the editors' support for Pound. Over a period of several years during Pound's affiliation with the magazine, the *Little Review* defended Pound's writings, tastes, and actions on a number of fronts, on one occasion assembling under the general title "Ezra Pound's Critics" a selection of negative comments from readers interspersed with more positive comments by Heap and Jean de Bosschère asserting the value of Pound's work.[37] On another occasion, three articles by Anderson, Heap, and "Raoul Root" (Pound writing under one of his pseudonyms) discussed and defended Pound's work, an irony that was no doubt to their taste. In addition, the editors frequently expressed their belief in Pound's work when responding to negative letters in the "Reader Critic" section. It is noteworthy that Anderson and Heap published letters critical of Pound as well as pieces in his defense. The editors were well aware of the controversies surrounding him, and such publication simultaneously encouraged attention to the disputes while asserting the editors' interest in Pound's contributions. The defense of Pound clearly did not come because the editors were in favor of all his methods or pronouncements, but because Anderson and Heap found in Pound a fellow writer and critic doing valuable work at the front lines of literary innovation, including gathering interesting materials for their magazine. The editors' patience with Pound, despite his attempts to tell them what to do, demonstrates their resolve to preserve the freedom of diverse critical exchanges in the arts.

Anderson and Heap's interest in Pound finally flagged, although the rift was not obvious in the pages of the magazine until November 1918. The month before, Pound had arranged for the reprinting of "The Western School," an attack by English critic Edgar Jepson on *Poetry*, which had first appeared in the *English Review* of May 1918. In November the *Little Review* reprinted Harriet Monroe's response to Jepson as well as Heap's comment. The incident had soured Heap on Pound, leading her to declare that Pound as "foreign editor" was "foreign to taste, foreign to courtesy, foreign to our standards of Art."[38] Heap made it clear that the editors had taken what they wanted from Pound's suggestions and contributions over the years but that his "animadversions" and spleen had begun to "induce a sullen boredom and a greater inattention of the arts," not to mention (which Heap did) the offense given by such slurs to *Little Review* readers, who formed an integral part of the magazine's critical exchange despite its motto about "making no compromise with the public taste." Matters of personality, Heap noted, had nothing to do with editing a magazine; her point was clear, although her article ended by defending the materials Pound had sent: "[There] is not enough resistance in the whole country for one grown human being. As long as Mr. Pound sends us work by Yeats, Joyce, Eliot, de Bosschere,—work bearing the stamp of originality and permanence—we have no complaint of him as an editor. If we are slightly jarred by his manner of asking for alms, or by any other personal manifestation, we can take care of that outside the magazine. We need no commiseration for our connection with Mr. Pound.

We are not blind deficient children. . . . It is all very much only the outer-
most vibrations of discussions and replies" ("The Episode Continued"
36-37). Heap used her article as a means of asserting the editors' power as
distinct from Pound, as well as the extent to which they would go to
ensure the freedom of the artist, which had always been a crucial component of the *Little Review*. The sparse quantity of letters from Pound to the
editors after the "incident" suggests that he had little to do with the magazine for some time before the official notice of his resignation in May
1919 (Baggett 272).

In part, Pound's relations with John Quinn, the New York lawyer
who gave money to Pound to support *Little Review* contributors, helped
bring about the rift. Pound and Quinn often commiserated about the
editing of the *Little Review* and found particular cause for complaint during the most famous segment of the magazine's history: the editors' struggle
to print and distribute sections of Joyce's *Ulysses* during 1918-20 and the
subsequent court trial, for which Quinn served as their lawyer. The first
installment of the novel was printed in March 1918, followed by other
sections in 1919-20; these brought, as may be expected, a flurry of letters
from reader critics both for and against the book. Heap and Anderson
were clearly delighted by this particular controversy over the nature of
art, since *Ulysses* satirizes the kind of Victorian values and nineteenth-
century novelistic traditions that the avant garde found stultifying. The
attention took another turn, however, when the post office confiscated
the issues of January and May 1919—a reprise of the suppression of
Wyndham Lewis's "Cantleman's Spring Mate" in October 1917. In the
summer of 1920 another issue was confiscated for containing the
"Nausicaa" section of *Ulysses*, in which Gerty McDowell responds to
Leopold Bloom's prurient attentions at the shore, an expression of female
sexuality that directly tapped into the social anxiety over the sexual free-
doms represented by "New Women" (Baggett 243). An attorney whose
daughter received a copy of the magazine objected to this chapter, and his
complaint led the New York district attorney to urge John Sumner, head
of the New York Society for the Suppression of Vice, to prosecute. The
two women were accused of publishing obscene literature, a charge they
refuted on the grounds that "morality" should not constrict artistic ex-

pression—long an important tenet of the *Little Review*.[39] It became clear that men's disapproval of Anderson and Heap's personal lives were as much a part of the proceedings as was Joyce's book.

Baggett writes that throughout the hearings and the trial the fiercest invective against Anderson and Heap appeared in letters to Pound from Quinn, who was shocked into rage by his discovery of their lesbianism as well as by their resistance to his authority and who, as a result, helped turn the trial into a personal attack on the women (243, 249). Anderson's subsequent descriptions of one judge's objection to having the offending portions read in front of her and Heap not only points out the judge's woeful inattention to the case itself but also sharply characterizes just how old-fashioned his ideas about "protecting young women" seemed (*My Thirty Years' War* 219-21). As well, the judge's comment that Anderson did not know what she was publishing added insult to insult—all predicated upon the editors' gender.

Anderson and Heap, not ones to let such an opportunity pass, published comments about the charges during the hearings and again after the 1921 trial was over.[40] Heap was sarcastic about the irony of litigation—itself completely inappropriate to approaching a work of art—undertaken supposedly to protect the minds of "young girls": "So the mind of the young girl rules this country? . . . We are being prosecuted for printing the thoughts in a young girl's mind. Her thoughts and actions and the meditations which they produced in the mind of the sensitive Mr. Bloom. . . . To a mind somewhat used to life Mr. Joyce's chapter seems to be a record of the simplest, most unpreventable, most unfocused sex thoughts possible in a rightly-constructed, unashamed human being. . . . If there is anything I really fear it is the mind of the young girl" ("Art and the Law" 6). Heap's denigration of the "cream-puff of sentimentality" (an idealized young girl) being defended by representatives of a "noble manhood that could only have been assembled from far-flung country stores where it had spat and gossiped and stolen prunes" (5) made clear her view of the foolishness of a traditional (and in this case entirely male) system of authority trying to rule anyone's imaginative life.

Anderson herself was as unimpressed as ever by the lack of imagination that characterized these proceedings: "It is the only farce I ever par-

ticipated in with any pleasure. . . . perhaps one can be enlivened by specu-
lating as to whether [events] will swerve a fraction of an inch from their
predestined stupidity. . . . Ah—I shall make an effort to keep entirely
silent, and since I have never under attack achieved this simple feat, perhaps my mind can become intrigued with the accomplishment of it"
("'Ulysses' in Court" 22). Anderson's step-by-step depiction of the ses-
sion intersperses her own thoughts with humorous glimpses of the actions
that characterize the judges' complete lack of understanding about art. This
piece demonstrates the same boredom with authority and tradition that
gave her cause to start the magazine in the first place. Anderson also provides a clue in this piece to one notable aspect of the trial: the two women's
silence. Although during the trial Anderson and Heap were not allowed
by Quinn to speak, Quinn's restrictions would not normally silence Heap
and Anderson, so it is clear that they remained quiet by choice. At one
point, when Anderson writes that she wanted to leap up and tell everyone
"*why* I regard [*Ulysses*] as the prose masterpiece of my generation," her
language suggests two important reasons why she did not speak out:

"Let me tell you why"—I almost leap from my chair. . . . "Let me tell you what
it's about and why it was written and for whom it was written and why you don't
understand it and why it is just as well that you don't and why you have no right
to pit the dulness of your brains against the fineness of mine." . . . (I suddenly
feel as though I had been run over by a subway train. My distinguished co-pub-
lisher is pounding me violently in the ribs: "Don't try to talk; don't put yourself
into their hands"—with that look of being untouched by the surrounding stu-
pidities which sends me into paroxysms. I smile vacuously at the court.) ["'Ulysses'
in Court" 24-25]

Self-protection was only one reason to remain quiet; Anderson's amusement with Heap's droll expression suggests that their silence was a reprise
of the *Little Review* issue of September 1916, in which the blank pages
may be read in part as the editors' expression of interest in their own
society and as an obvious refusal to conform to social expectations. The
irony of publication and silencing seems at least to have given the editors
some pleasure amid the turgidity of proceedings that both seem to have
regarded as inevitable. Anderson's remark about smiling "vacuously" at

the court is yet another instance in which she utilized stereotypical "female" behavior ironically. In this case its use for distraction and disguise is so obvious that it emphasizes Anderson's previous deconstructions of sex-linked imagery.

The hostility or indifference of the male judges and lawyers led the two editors to remain silent for their own reasons, not only for self-protection but also as a means of acknowledging the irony of the situation. Certainly they were already planning what they would say in print later, under their own control. Baggett decides that through self-silencing the women were "symbolically repatriating themselves . . . from the rules of a society unable to come to terms" with what they represented (266). They were fined one hundred dollars and fingerprinted. Anderson added an ironic postscript in one article: "In this welter of crime and lechery . . . our appearance seemed to leave [John Sumner and the judges] without any doubts as to our personal purity. Some of my 'friends' have considered me both insane and obscene, I believe, for publishing Mr. Joyce" ("'Ulysses' in Court" 25). Anderson's language, juxtaposing "appearance" and "personal purity" with accusations of insanity and obscenity, clearly indicates her awareness of homophobic fears of the time; that the women personally had been on trial seemed to Anderson unquestionable.

Given these proceedings, it is not surprising that the two editors' private lives had been suffering strains, which were obvious by the time the *Ulysses* trial was finished. Their printed exchanges took a new turn in Anderson's short piece "Dialogue," published late in 1922.[41] Written in the form of a dramatic scene, it gives a brief and rather puzzling glimpse of Anderson and Heap apparently in editorial discussion. Its appearance after the long series of legal problems and the consequent loss of economic support for the *Little Review* dramatized for readers the weariness the editors felt, while paradoxically indicating both the strong connections between them and their fundamental differences of temperament. The piece utilizes the familiar stereotypes of Anderson as somewhat vain and flighty, Heap as wryly restrained. As "MCA" exhorts "jh" to action and creation, "jh" replies simply, "I know of no commandment to create," and as "MCA" exults in her own good looks and intelligence, "jh" has nothing to say. When the two reach a conversational "impasse,"

"MCA" finally asserts, "But thank heaven *I* can still get some ecstasy out of life!" Whereupon "jh" retorts, "Why limit me to ecstasy?" (24-25).

The passage clearly plays along with the public images these women created and also suggests the growing tensions in their private relationship. Even though the dialogue seemingly revolves around exhortations to "Art," its subject is intentionally vague and contains sexually suggestive language. This passage illustrates the indirection or "absence" through which lesbianism has often been treated in autobiographical writings, as Norine Voss points out.[42] Here, what is left out allows the reader to assume the "ecstasy" is aesthetic; what is left out also protects the speakers while still expressing an aspect of their personal relationship. The combined courage and self-assurance implied by this piece can allow compassionate readers to understand these women as real people walking the dangerous line of violating patriarchal norms.

If "Art," then, was the subject of the *Little Review*, there was also an art *to* the magazine. In explicit and implicit dialogues, Heap and Anderson ironically characterized their shared editorship, creating their public personae even while protecting their private selves. Such tension lies at the heart of a feminist revision of literary history and greatly increases the importance of taking a closer look at women's collaborative work in the modernist era.

The early 1920s brought a sea change for the magazine as well as for the editors. Anderson, wearied after the *Ulysses* trial and feeling the strain in her deteriorating relationship with Heap, left for Europe with her new lover, Georgette Leblanc, in the spring of 1924. Heap also visited Europe in the summer of 1924 before returning to New York and taking up the editorial work for the *Little Review* on her own, although she kept Anderson's name on the masthead.[43] Heap's particular interests are evident in the magazine's increasing attention to modern visual art during the 1920s. A few commentators have faulted Heap for this change in editorial attention, while some seem to believe that the *Little Review* ceased, in effect, after Anderson left. Heap's work ought to be evaluated on its own terms, however, since her many contributions to modernist art and letters extended well beyond the pages of the *Little Review*.

Some of Heap's plans and successes in promoting avant garde work included advances in the fields of art, architecture, and theater. While she retained the *Little Review*'s literary serializations and critical articles, Heap began to expand the magazine's coverage, particularly into visual art. She had strong ambitions both for the magazine and for related activities to promote new work in a number of media. One offshoot, the Little Review Gallery, was founded in New York in 1924; later, Heap helped develop the International Theatre Exposition (1926) and organized the important Machine Age Exposition (1927). She also "dreamed of, advertised, and never carried out" plans for an International Congress of Artists for America and an Inter-Arts Association.[44] The magazine itself articulated Heap's avant garde interests in two of the most influential—and controversial—contemporary European movements, Dadaism and Surrealism, offering theoretical articles, manifestoes, critical responses, and quantities of reproductions as early as mid-1920. In fact, the shift of emphasis in the *Little Review* demonstrates that Heap took on a broader editorial role years before the 1923 date that she cited in her retrospective comments for the final issue ("Wreaths" 63). Although the *Little Review* had occasionally presented reproductions of pieces by various artists, particularly photographs by Man Ray, the visual arts took firm hold from mid-1920 onward, with pages of work by Hans (Jean) Arp, Jean Cocteau, Giorgio de Chirico, Robert Delaunay, Charles Demuth, Max Ernst, Naum Gabo, Juan Gris, Hannah Höch, Fernand Léger, Joan Miró, László Moholy-Nagy, Francis Picabia, G. Ribemont-Dessaignes, Kurt Schwitters, Joseph Stella, and Theo van Doesburg, in addition to theoretical writings by Guillaume Apollinaire, Louis Aragon, André Breton, and Tristan Tzara—a gallery of names now indispensible to any discussion of modern European art. The *Little Review* served as a forum for the Dadaists during their later years of activity in France, and gave Surrealism strong support in the years prior to the first "collective exhibition of Surrealism" in Paris in 1925.[45]

Considering the scope of these plans and accomplishments, it is startling that Heap's energetic promotion of the avant garde has not received much notice from art historians. Heap knew that her contributions were valuable and, characteristically, was not reticent in pointing them out. In her comments for the magazine's final issue, for instance, she remarked: "In 1923 . . . Margaret Anderson threw up all active participation in the magazine she had founded and went to Paris to live. The Little Review was then carried on by 'jh.' Contacts were made with groups of the advance-guard everywhere, the scope of the magazine being extended to cover 19 countries" ("Wreaths" 63). She mentioned the Little Review Gallery as the only "gallery of its kind in America," pointed out that the Theatre Exposition presented "Russian constructivist stage-sets . . . in America for the first time," and called the Machine Age Exposition the first "exposition of its kind anywhere. First showing of modern architecture in America" ("Wreaths" 63). Not only does Heap delineate remarkable accomplishments but she expresses a clear note of pride in her work. It seems likely that Heap's tone, as well as her achievements, has been written off as another manifestation of the self-satisfied arrogance to be expected from the *Little Review*.

One art historian, Susan Noyes Platt, has discussed in depth Heap's contributions to the spread of avant garde art in the 1920s. Particularly in her book *Modernism in the 1920s: Interpretations of Modern Art in New York from Expressionism to Constructivism* (1985), Platt has identified the *Little Review* and its adjunct Little Review Gallery in New York as very important means for bringing the European avant garde to the attention of American art critics.[46] Platt finds that Heap's interest in the Dadaists, Constructivists, and Surrealists helped her to make "several major contributions to the introduction of modern art in America," through publishing "seminal" essays such as Léger's "The Esthetic of the Machine," van Doesburg's "The Evolution of Modern Architechture in Holland," and the 1921 Parisian "Dada Manifesto," as well as through arranging the International Theatre and Machine Age Expositions and preparing their exhibit catalogs (*Modernism* 12, 93-94, 116-17, 124). Subsequent to this exposure in mid-1920 and early 1921, one of New York's important groups of artists, the Société Anonyme, gained wide press coverage for its several "Dada" events that spring, and Dada was well launched, if not exactly understood, in the United States. Throughout, Platt notes, the *Little Review* did not fall into the trap of taking itself, or the movement, too seriously, because Heap enjoyed Dada; Platt goes so far as to suggest that "in its disorganized and humorous approach to art throughout the 1920s," the magazine "*was* Dada" (*Modernism* 97).

Platt suggests that American critics preferred the "clean hard-edged Machine Age art" (which also appeared in the *Little Review* thanks to Heap's interest in Constructivism) rather than Surrealism's obvious Dadaist features and its emphasis on the unconscious (*Modernism* 109). Heap was careful to enunciate how developments in Dada led to the experiments of the Surrealists, which was particularly important because American art critics tended to be suspicious of both movements. In the face of such discomfort, it is clear that Heap's careful articulation of fundamental Surrealist tenets, her astute and broad-ranging choice of reproductions, and her presentation of theoretical essays helped place Surrealism firmly in the history of the modern avant garde. No other editor was so well positioned to survey and select from European art for the benefit of English-speaking audiences and to promote this work in New York. Heap's *Little Review* work also prepared the way for the very important explorations that the Surrealists published later in *transition*.

Ultimately, Heap's publications of reproductions and theoretical documents influenced the "institutionalization" of modern art history, through the research and writings of Alfred Barr, the first director of the Museum of Modern Art. He put together what Platt identifies as the first cohesive history of Cubism and its related movements in the catalog for the 1936 "Cubism and Abstract Art" exhibition Barr assembled for the museum.[47] Barr's ideas had been formed in part through the series of translations of Apollinaire's "Aesthetic Meditations," which appeared in the *Little Review* in 1922, so that Barr "as a young art historian focusing on the scholarly approach in which he had been trained had literary sources on which to draw" (Platt, "Modernism, Formalism" 287). The legitimacy implied by Barr's research helped to promote the diffusion of post-Cubist aesthetics into contemporary thought. Apparently Barr, having found useful material in the *Little Review*, continued to pay attention to that publication, including Heap's special interest in theater and architecture, categories that Barr subsequently noted to be important adjuncts to abstract painting.[48] Heap's interest in modern art theory, as expressed in her editing of the *Little Review*, fed directly into the exhibitions and lectures Barr created at the Museum of Modern Art during his tenure from 1929 to 1936.

Thus, through her taste, effort, and support, Heap "played a crucial role in presenting the raw data of international modernism to America" (Platt, *Modernism* 12). This "raw data" included much influential new work in the visual arts and provocative pieces of literature and criticism. Her ventures outside the pages of the magazine had already demonstrated her energetic interest in modern innovations in a number of fields. Another aspect of Heap's continuing influence and interest in the world of modernist ideas is her labor on behalf of avant garde writing, most notably that undertaken for Gertrude Stein's long novel *The Making of Americans*.

This book had been in manuscript at least since 1911, and some sections had appeared serially in the *transatlantic review* before the entire book was published by Robert McAlmon's Contact Editions.[49] Working to place *The Making of Americans* is the one activity of Heap's that has drawn persistent attention; and several different versions of the story have appeared, most of which follow McAlmon's lead in casting Stein and Heap as having created problems by going behind McAlmon's back.[50] Archival evidence, however, suggests that Heap's efforts on behalf of *The Making of Americans* were intended to overcome McAlmon's resistance—a resistance that is hard to explain, given his position as publisher and proponent of avant garde writing, and that may account for the tendency of historians to criticize Stein and Heap in the matter. While Stein herself seems to have placed the book with McAlmon, Heap seems to have attempted to make the best of that situation once it became clear that McAlmon could not, or would not, give the book the send-off Heap felt it deserved.[51]

Heap had been a friend and supporter of Stein's for some time (despite the *Little Review*'s earlier connection to James Joyce, with whom Stein felt an artistic rivalry). The women's shared tastes in avant garde ideas, modern art, and stimulating talk certainly provided ample grounds for friendship; as well, they had literary acquaintances in common and knew many of the same members of the lesbian community in Paris. Heap believed in the value of Stein's writing, and besides soliciting portions of it for the *Little Review* she also tried to secure publication for some of Stein's books.[52] Placing *The Making of Americans* with a publisher was no easy task, since its bulk and style made most mainstream publishers wary.

Nevertheless, Heap wanted to find a publisher who could do a good job not only of the printing but also of the promotion. By the time Stein and McAlmon had reached an agreement to proceed with the Contact edition in 1925, Heap had already investigated the possibility of having *Americans* appear serially in the *Criterion*.[53]

While McAlmon proceeded with the publication of the book in Paris, Heap made concerted attempts to find publishers who would bind or distribute the book in England and America, which was desirable not only to reach those markets but also to secure copyrights. Having had refusals from The Dial Press and B. W. Huebsch, Heap tried the firm of Albert and Charles Boni, who for a time seriously considered the book.[54] Albert Boni had done *Tender Buttons* but had not made any money on it; however, as Heap wrote to Stein in 1925, he suggested with a laugh that Stein's books "ought to turn out well for me another time."[55] Another undated letter from Heap said that "Boni wants to do it" and was also considering an American edition of *Three Lives*.[56] It is odd that, after Heap had worked hard to interest the Bonis (at one point noting that she had "pestered Albert Boni about this contract on an average of twice a week all fall and winter"[57]), when McAlmon took over negotiations in London with a Boni representative, the deal collapsed.[58] Ostensibly, when McAlmon asked the Bonis for part of the payment in advance, they "'backed down'. . . claiming that their London representative had misunderstood the proposal" (Ford, *Published in Paris,* 66, Mellow 379). Stein and Heap doubtless felt some frustration at this turn of events, and may have begun to wonder about McAlmon's abilities, with this sort of follow-through on an agreement toward which Heap had worked for some time.

Nevertheless, Heap's work in interesting other publishers continued, extending to England, where she elicited interest from Stanley Nott's syndicate, which even considered taking other books of Stein's as well. This new expression of interest led to the most notorious aspect of the Contact publication of *Americans*. According to McAlmon, no problems had arisen until *The Making of Americans* was being bound, and Stein, claiming that Heap had received McAlmon's approval, went over McAlmon's head by ordering sheets sent to Paris in preparation for shipment abroad, whereas McAlmon had wanted to wait until he had a firm contract for distribution or payment of printing costs (McAlmon 206). This situation—whether disagreement, misunderstanding, or deliberate plan remains unclear—infuriated McAlmon, who threatened to destroy the entire edition.

Relating the incident in his memoirs, McAlmon mocked Stein by referring to himself in the third person, as Stein did in her *Autobiography of Alice B. Toklas*: "Miss Stein explained in a letter that Jane Heap had assured her that McAlmon would not object. McAlmon's anger did not cool when Miss Stein involved Miss Heap in the matter. Miss Heap had never been McAlmon's agent, she had no connection with his business, and he had not seen her while he was in Paris. Since Miss Stein so believed in her own genius, it occurred to McAlmon that she might sell a painting from her collection for fifty times what she had paid for it and pay her own printing bill" (206).

There are a number of reasons to doubt McAlmon's stated motives in this matter and to find in favor of Heap's diligence and persistence. It is clear that McAlmon suspected the two women of planning to take advantage of him, although his reasons for fearing their actions are not clear. His main charge against the two is that their intervention would force him into selling the printed sheets at a loss, but this charge seems insufficient when one considers Contact Editions on the whole. McAlmon's claim that he needed to recover printing costs is weakened by the fact that he lost money on a number of books; why then would this book suddenly require breaking even? The money with which McAlmon began Contact Editions had been given him, and McAlmon spent it as he pleased without paying much attention to the business side of publishing. His ungracious remark that Stein could pay printing costs if she sold one of her paintings is irrelevant and suggests rather that McAlmon's stated interest in new writing was qualified, having more to do with promoting people he found compatible (and with printing a number of his own books) than with his own discernment about modernist experimentation. His threat to destroy the edition demonstrates that his alleged motive in blocking a chance of broader distribution is a bluff, since destruction would guarantee a total loss. In fact, the possibility of loss on *The Making of*

Americans was exacerbated by McAlmon himself, who refused to help sell subscriptions to the book—his own publication—although a few years earlier he had enthusiastically gathered subscriptions for (and had done some haphazard typing for) Joyce's *Ulysses*, published by Sylvia Beach. Differences between Joyce's and Stein's works, of course, may account for McAlmon's response, yet the question remains why he would have agreed to publish *Americans* at all if he did not think it a worthwhile addition to his list. Also, since McAlmon had had trouble sending Contact books to the United States, one might expect him to have been grateful for Heap's attempts to secure a distributor there, which would work for McAlmon's own benefit as well as Stein's.

Certainly one explanation for McAlmon's actions over the edition may lie in his resentment of Heap's success in interesting other publishers, whereas McAlmon had not done much to promote the book, either before or after printing it. In his memoir, McAlmon indicates that Stein had prompted Heap to become involved, but this is not accurate since McAlmon had known of Heap's interest in promoting the book at least by the time of his meeting with the Boni representative in London. McAlmon may also have resented Heap's success because Heap and Stein were friendly with his wife, Bryher, whose father had given McAlmon the money for Contact Publishing Company and who provided some of the connections by which McAlmon accomplished his literary work. McAlmon seems to have viewed his publishing business as an interesting diversion that helped his own writing career and social situation, and he may have perceived the women's work as a threat to his business reputation as well as to his ego. The strength of McAlmon's resentment suggests that he had private reasons for putting obstacles in the way of *The Making of Americans*, for he would not easily have given up the prestige that accrued to small presses for having printed innovative and little-known work.

Concomitantly, there is an aura of businesslike dispatch in Heap and Stein, who, in contrast to McAlmon, were very interested in having *The Making of Americans* come out, which explains why they acted decisively without McAlmon at times. Heap and Stein had both been involved in literary publishing for years before McAlmon set up shop; they seem to have known about McAlmon's lax business habits and to have tried to protect the book by insisting upon contracts with specific terms and by looking for established publishers to handle distribution. At one point, in fact, Heap wrote Stein that she had "seen Bob several times, always drunk. When I talked to him about the book he cursed and said he knew nothing about it. . . . I had a short talk with Sylvia—Bob has told her that you are cheating him or trying to cheat him."[59] In another letter written during the negotiations with Boni, Heap reported that "Boni says that Bob has made him official agent for the big book [in New York]," and commented, "I said nothing, knowing that Bob can not dispose of [the] book after his first crack at it."[60] It is evident from these remarks that Heap felt McAlmon was, at the very least, not doing an effective job with Stein's book. Her many connections with other publishers, as well as her own experience, gave her a fairly good basis for comparison, which in turn guided her pursuit of options for the volume.

Ultimately, although hundreds of sets of sheets were printed, only a few copies of *The Making of Americans* were bound and sold. Despite this relative failure to distribute the novel in its whole form, Heap's efforts on Stein's behalf were not in vain, since by bringing Stein's work to the attention of a number of publishers she helped Stein through the period before the success of *The Autobiography of Alice B. Toklas.* Also, by introducing American art critics to Dadaism and Surrealism, Heap helped set the stage for acceptance and understanding of Stein's style, and thereby strongly encouraged the acceptance and dissemination of modern avant garde writing as well as art.

It is clear, then, that a broad knowledge of and interest in art and criticism informed the *Little Review,* and that the magazine's editors had more influence and did work of greater subtlety and social pertinence than has been previously credited, even considering the attention that the *Little Review* has drawn. The courage of their convictions, displayed both within and "without" the pages of the *Little Review,* demonstrates that Anderson and Heap's interests in contemporary literature and art, in social critique, and in artistic and intellectual freedom were hardly passing fancies, as some critics have characterized them, but aspects of a radical spirit the two women shared that deliberately created a forum for unconventional expression and "conversation" at a variety of levels. The *Little*

Review's antiauthoritarian opinions pushed the boundaries of what was acceptable both for women and for literary editors, of which the prosecution for printing "pornography" (*Ulysses* and "Cantleman's Spring Mate") is simply the most visible aspect. Promotion of such women writers as May Sinclair, Amy Lowell, Dorothy Richardson, Mary Butts, and Djuna Barnes in the magazine's pages also made a crucial contribution to modern letters, and even the editors' persistent interest in the Dadaist poetry of Baroness Else von Freytag-Loringhoven, considered by many to be insane, demonstrates the courage of Anderson and Heap's convictions about artistic freedom that allowed a remarkable amount of experimental art to reach an audience.[61]

As a result of the editors' beliefs and interests, the magazine's "conversation" was bold, humorous, subtle, ironic, and deliberately provocative. Even the inconsistencies in the kind of attention Anderson gave to her enthusiasms in print suggest that she particularly enjoyed conversation because it provided a chance to test and modify her ideas. The fact that she was willing to do so publicly in the pages of her magazine does not mean that she should be dismissed as flighty or muddleheaded, as some critics have done. Rather, one should keep in mind the eclecticism, even the confusion, of the ways in which social debate and change occur. In this sense Anderson and Heap's personal inclinations for debate were crucial factors in the *Little Review*'s agency in bringing together the kinds of ideas that shaped modernism. By the end of its run in 1929, the *Little Review* had not only presented many great works of literary and visual arts to the world but also had permanently changed the nature of literary periodicals. Its editors willingly courted controversy; they drew from a wide range of literary and critical voices while maintaining subtle control over the types and directions of critical exchanges; they deliberately and effectively resisted traditional "voices of authority" by presenting multiple perspectives—in short, the *Little Review* reflects and enacts many of the characteristics fundamental to modernism. In no other magazine of this era does one find the degree of critical interaction boasted (so to speak) by the *Little Review*, whose editors' innovative work significantly challenged theory and practice—that is, the parameters of modern aesthetics and of little magazines themselves.

4

TOWARD INTERNATIONAL COOPERATION

The Literary Editing of H.D. and Bryher

The activities of H.D. and of Bryher in literary editing and publishing during the rise of modernism deserve careful examination. Both women affected modernist thought in their contributions to the appreciation of cinematic art as well as through their support for avant garde literature. This chapter treats these two women in tandem because their long-term association led to work that was historically intertwined, from the early years of their collaboration for the Egoist Press through their attention to issues important to modern aesthetics in *Close Up*.

H.D.'s literary work during her first several years in London represents a critical period in her artistic development. During the years following her first appearance in *Poetry* (1913), H.D. became known as the "premier Imagist"; less well known, however, is the part she played in literary editing and publishing.[1] A good portion of H.D.'s time in England was spent planning the three Imagist anthologies of 1915-17, along with Amy Lowell and Richard Aldington, working with (and without) Aldington at the *Egoist*, and preparing the two Poets' Translation Series with Aldington for the Egoist Press. H.D.'s critical work, in reviews and in editorial choices, connected a sense of the artist's spiritual integrity with new investigations of form and helped to enunciate the parameters of modern thought.

Although Bryher published many critical comments and promoted other writers in a number of ways, her multifaceted support of publishing activities has been largely overlooked. She began her involvement by

Published the 1st and 15th of each month.

THE EGOIST

AN INDIVIDUALIST REVIEW.

Formerly the NEW FREEWOMAN.

No. 11. Vol. I.   MONDAY, JUNE 1st, 1914.   SIXPENCE.

Assistant (RICHARD ALDINGTON.   Editor : DORA MARSDEN, B.A.
Editors : (LEONARD A. COMPTON-RICKETT.   CONTENTS.

MODERN POETRY AND THE IMAGISTS.

By Richard Aldington.

LOOKING at the title I have written at the top of this page it seems to me that the readers of this paper, even though they are supposed to take more interest in the arts than the readers of the "Daily Mail," will probably turn the page and find something which interests them more keenly—Mr. Joyce's novel, or correspondence about sexual pleasures, or something like that. And this reflec-

Do you, most honourable reader, who are fed upon the works of Mr. Wells, and Mr. Henry James, and Mr. Bennett and Miss Sinclair and Mr. Cannan and Mrs. Barclay and Mrs. Humphry Ward and Mr. Max Pemberton and so on, do you take no interest in the works of Mr. Yeats, Mr. Sturge Moore, Mr. Bridges, Mr. James Stevens, Mr. Brooke, Mr. Flint, Mrs. Meynell and Mr. Pound? And the matter of Mr. Hueffer who has written

assisting with production and financial support for the Poets' Translation Series of the Egoist Press. Following her marriage to Robert McAlmon, she supported his publication of Contact Editions, which brought out Hemingway's first book and Stein's *The Making of Americans*, among other innovative works. H.D. brought Bryher to the *Egoist*, the Egoist Press, and other literary connections, and Bryher provided H.D. with years of financial support and an entrée into the world of cinema through *Close Up*. The articles that the two women wrote for that magazine during 1927-33 reflect the aesthetic, social, and political issues raised by the new cinematic art. The long association between the two allowed both to work as writers, editors, and critics helping to push forward the frontiers of twentieth-century thought.

H.D.'s connections with Amy Lowell and with the *Egoist* initiated an important segment of her career. At that time, H.D. was busy and influential within a significant circle of young writers in England. She shared in the spirit of comradeship that characterized the small group of poets in London including herself, her husband Aldington, Ezra Pound, F. S. Flint, and John Cournos. This sharing of mutual excitement over new forms and ideas carried through Lowell's visit to England in 1913 and the appearance of the anthology Pound had compiled, *Des Imagistes* (1914), which aroused some discussion in the United States, although it was less successful in England. Disagreement arose, however, between Pound and the others over what "Imagism" meant. The argument reached a breaking point during Lowell's return trip in 1914, when Pound provoked Lowell at a dinner party. Lowell and the Aldingtons, by this time good friends, preferred to continue in the spirit of sharing work rather than to reject such poets as John Gould Fletcher and D. H. Lawrence, as Pound would have done.[2] Therefore, when Lowell proposed another anthology based on more democratic ideas—each poet would help decide who would be included, with equitable space allotted to all—Pound refused to participate. As a result, H.D. and Aldington became the chief liaisons between the English group and Lowell.

H.D.'s correspondence during this time demonstrates the confluence of her personal and literary priorities: she was intent on preserving the spirit of collaboration intended for these volumes, she was stimulated by her exchanges with Lowell over possible inclusion and alteration of poems, and she trusted Lowell's judgment and discretion both to see to details of publication and to serve as H.D.'s surrogate in criticizing Aldington's work. In all of these functions, H.D. emphasized the democracy and cooperation that had been missing from *Des Imagistes* and that she supported despite her mixed feelings about the poems included in *Some Imagist Poets*.

Initially, H.D.'s distress over the contretemps with Pound caused her to urge Lowell to dispense with the word "Imagist" in the title of the 1915 anthology.[3] Pound earlier had made a similar suggestion, but from a desire to protect a movement he considered his own; his suggestion was that Lowell title the book *Vers Libre* in order to detach the term "Imagisme" from the work of people he did not consider deserving.[4] To H.D., however, the matter carried quite a different import. She wrote to Lowell in

December 1914 that she, Aldington, and Flint wanted to "quit" any association with Pound and offered a significant replacement title, *The Six*.[5] The letter shows impatience with the limitations implied by Pound's dictatorial definitions of "Imagism." To H.D., cooperative exchange was more important than the immediate recognition that might be gained by publishing a new book under the Imagist title. In fact, H.D.'s response suggests that she saw the dissent caused by Pound's authoritarianism as more inhibiting than any mutual criticism by the poets could be.

Since H.D. had no intention of being constrained or labeled by what she had written in previous years, she felt no possessiveness about the Imagist name. Indeed, part of the point of maintaining mutual contact between the poets was to help them all mature in their art. H.D.'s letters show her efforts to prepare and publish current poetry and to draw her friends together (especially after the disagreement with Pound) into a stimulating and supportive group. With Lowell back in the United States, H.D. began at once on the preparations for the 1915 volume, assembling materials, sending them to Lowell, and following up with comments and minor emendations.[6] By April 1915, she wrote Lowell that she was taking much pleasure in the book and expressed hope that the anthologies would continue; she was sending poems and articles by herself and Aldington, which Lowell tried to place in American publications while H.D. circulated Lowell's books among her friends.[7]

At one point, H.D. expressed regret over the distance between herself and Lowell, which prevented her sharing fully in the duties of their collaboration: "[It] is very hard arranging things, isn't it [*sic*], from both sides of the pond? . . . I wish we could share the burden of work, but this old pond does hinder."[8] Yet physical distance from the machinery of publication forced H.D. to leave some of those details to be resolved as Lowell thought appropriate, which suggests that H.D. had been designated to represent to Lowell the entire group of poets in England. In fact, the English poets may have felt the need to shield themselves from Lowell's powerful personality as they had from Pound's, despite the democratic nature of their undertaking. In this case, H.D. was their diplomat, faced with the delicate problem of making her own and the other London writers' intentions clear while preserving the mutuality of decision-making. When, for instance, H.D. deferred to Lowell the important decision about the final arrangement of H.D.'s poems in the 1916 volume, she indicated that she expected Lowell and Fletcher to work together—an urging apparently intended to preserve the cooperative nature of the volume, even if at H.D.'s expense.[9]

H.D.'s efforts in soliciting contributions and in smoothing the collaboration for the series of anthologies may be considered to account for the existence of the volumes at all. In 1914-15, certainly, the schism with Pound could have interfered with the publication of much good work had H.D. not acted as mediator. This mediation provided some of the important writers of that time a means of communicating among themselves as well as a way to reach a larger public, while the anthologies provided Lowell as well as H.D. with a means of staying in contact with literary developments that they both found stimulating.

In the meanwhile, H.D. had become involved with the *Egoist* through Aldington's position as assistant editor, which began in 1913. As Cyrena Pondrom notes, H.D. seems to have taken "an active part in the editing of the *Egoist* even before Aldington's departure for military service," sending Flint a review copy of Lowell's book *Sword Blades and Poppy Seeds* in November 1914 from the *Egoist's* editorial offices.[10] H.D. saw Harriet Shaw Weaver, the paper's editor, on a regular basis and certainly had been reading some of the submissions.[11] In fact, she solicited submissions for that magazine as she did for the Imagist anthologies. One result of H.D.'s assistance at the *Egoist* was the special number on Imagism that appeared May 1, 1915.

The combined boost of *Some Imagist Poets* and two special numbers of important little magazines helped to establish Imagism in modernist history, culminating more than two years of scattered notices more firmly than Pound's irregular association had. The March 1913 issue of *Poetry* had included two comments signed by Flint and Pound—Flint's brief outline of the history of Imagism, followed by Pound's well-known "A Few Don'ts by an Imagiste," which sketched the aesthetic tenets of the group. A few other mentions of Imagism had appeared before, for example, Alice Corbin Henderson's review of *Des Imagistes* in *Poetry* for October 1914. Mention of Imagism in the *New Freewoman* (precursor of the *Egoist*) in August of that year had been substantially a summary of the articles that had appeared in *Poetry*.[12] Imagism had gained more significant exposure through Lowell's acquaintance with Margaret Anderson, editor of the *Little Review*, which in July 1914 printed Charles Ashleigh's review of the "Des Imagistes" issue of the *Glebe*; subsequently, the *Little Review* published numerous poems by Lowell, articles discussing vers libre in November and December 1914 and April 1915, and Aldington's article about H.D. in March 1915.

The Imagist number of the *Egoist* for May 1, 1915, offered new poetry by Richard Aldington, H.D., F. S. Flint, D. H. Lawrence, Marianne Moore, and May Sinclair, and included a number of articles addressing the history, aesthetics, and poets of Imagism in more depth than in any previous publication.[13] The issue opened, however, with a lengthy philosophical editorial by *Egoist* founder Dora Marsden, and H.D., who had helped put the issue together, found herself again acting as mediator, this time by placating Lowell. Lowell had agreed to distribute the paper in America and had planned that the issue would coincide with the appearance of *Some Imagist Poets* and with a lecture that Lowell would give to the Poetry Society of America (Hanscombe and Smyers 202). Also, Lowell had arranged for the May 1915 issue of the *Little Review* to include pieces by various Imagists as well as her and John Gould Fletcher's collaborative review of *Some Imagist Poets* (under the pseudonym "George Lane").[14] After all her work to help establish Imagism in the United States, Lowell was upset about Marsden's article, which Lowell regarded (probably with justice) as a barrier to sales. H.D. attempted to alleviate Lowell's displeasure and redirect her attention to the positive force of the issue: "R. has done his best for that blooming old Egoist—though I know how disappointed you & Fletcher will be to see Miss M. on the first page. I assure you we both fought hard enough—but Miss Weaver runs the paper for Dora Marsden—swears by her—and R. is after all only sub-editor! He did work hard. I think the number a great success but for that!—Trust you will!"[15] By stressing the "great success" of the number, H.D. encouraged Lowell that the English side of the promotion was nevertheless continuing well. Considering that many of the Imagists were English, this was an important reassurance.

The Imagist number of the *Egoist* offered the first extended and collective examination of Imagism and amended what had gone before in several senses. All six of the poets appearing in *Some Imagist Poets* received detailed critical comment, which drew attention to their particular styles and thus helped to demonstrate the variety in this form of writing, as distinct from the directive tone of Pound's "A Few Don'ts." In addition, the issue included comments that were judicious in tone rather than directive or promotional, such as Harold Monro's substantial article placing Imagism's roots in "most of the more important English theorists of the past" as well as in the younger French poets, and located in *Some Imagist Poets* "a transitionary point in the Imagist movement," particularly for H.D.[16] The cumulative effect of the poetry and articles in this issue reiterated these writers' differences from Pound without homogenizing Imagism.

Lowell's continuing support for the Imagists "promised . . . that there would be a future," in Barbara Guest's phrase, and it is clear that H.D. appreciated the exposure that she and other writers stood to gain by book publication in America, whether or not Imagism itself continued after the anthologies as a viable concern.[17] H.D.'s reasons for continuing with the anthologies had less to do with her own personal success than with her hope that certain kinds of art would stand against the divisions of a world at war.

H.D.'s caretaking of much of the business for the anthologies in England included distributing some of the royalties, and in this point—seemingly a minor one—one sees an additional impetus for the work. H.D. felt great concern over the well-being of her friends and tried to provide for them through the means she had at hand. H.D. herself often was short of funds, like the others in her circle, yet in February 1916 she offered to share some of the money Lowell had sent her (calling it "royalties") with Flint and Lawrence, saying she had already given some of it to others.[18] In subsequent months, when Lawrence was suffering the effects of illness, discouragement, and censorship, she suggested that Lowell send money to the Lawrences directly.[19] Even when in 1917 H.D. agreed with Lowell that the anthologies had served their purpose, she punningly regretted the loss of the "*collective*" work."[20] Certainly Lowell's regular remittances cheered a number of writers, H.D. among them, during the privations of wartime.

The differences between writers who nevertheless worked in close contact emphasizes the sort of interaction H.D. wanted to promote. She was perpetually tactful in trying to preserve her good relationship with Lowell, even while letting the other woman know that H.D. as a poet intended to continue changing and growing in her art. H.D.'s letters to Lowell provide an interesting perspective on the younger poet during her years of association with the Imagist anthologies and with the *Egoist*; even as she revealed her growing self-confidence in her own work and critical judgment as expressed to a fellow poet, she also demonstrated what must have been a painful sense of ambivalence about Aldington's writing. She knew its personal significance to him and seemed to feel that some of the work had lasting value, but she objected to his methods and taste in several respects. At times H.D. asked Lowell to suggest changes in Aldington's poetry, which H.D., as Aldington's wife, felt she could not do. In November 1914, for instance, she wrote asking Lowell to criticize Aldington's work before putting it into the anthology, since Lowell was at a "safe distance" from which to offer such suggestions.[21]

H.D.'s requests for Lowell's criticism of Aldington seem to rely on a mutual understanding that developed during their association. Since H.D. could and did criticize Lowell's work as well as praise it, the implication that H.D. could not speak freely as a poet to her husband holds connotations that were probably not lost on Lowell. Yet H.D. also promoted Aldington's work. In 1914, for example, she defended "Whitechapel" as worthy of inclusion in *Some Imagist Poets*, and sometimes sent others of his poems to Lowell for placement in U.S. papers; later, while Aldington was in the service, she wrote that she tried on occasion to fashion something worth publishing from scraps of Aldington's writing.[22] This is an intriguing statement that qualifies H.D.'s later assertion that she wanted to keep her literary personality and Aldington's "absolutely distinct."[23] In fact, the letters to Lowell demonstrate that H.D.'s wish to express critical disagreement was in conflict with the need to protect marital harmony and to bolster Aldington's spirits during wartime.

H.D.'s vision of hope and mutual responsibility, expressed privately in her letters as well as publicly in her collaborative efforts to promote the Imagists, also appears in her three reviews of books of poetry for the *Egoist*. It is clear from these pieces for the *Egoist*—her first published comments about her aesthetic values—that she takes quite seriously the issue of the artist's responsibility to society as well as to beauty, clarity, and integrity. She expresses her belief that art can stand against the selfishness and waste of war. She also indicates her dissatisfaction with authoritative literary standards of the time. Her own interest in modern and avant garde work informed her readings of the modifications in imagery, language, form, and tradition she found in Marianne Moore, Charlotte Mew, and John Gould Fletcher, the subjects of her reviews.

Her first critical piece to appear in print was an appreciation of Moore in August 1916. This was the earliest full review to herald one of modernism's greatest poets, predating by nearly two years Pound's article about Moore in the *Little Review* in 1918, which has been called the first critical notice of Moore.[24] The two poets' reacquaintance when Moore sent poems to the magazine in 1915 led to years of friendship and artistic benefit for Moore, H.D., and Bryher, as these women eagerly read, commented upon, and tried to find publication for each other's work.[25]

From H.D.'s words in this article, it is apparent that she had already been gathering Moore's poems, as if in anticipation of preparing the volume *Poems* in 1921. It is also clear that she is a thoughtful reader of Moore's distinctive and elliptical verses: "I have before me a collection of poems. They have appeared for the most part in various American periodicals. And readers of *The Egoist* are familiar with certain of these curiously wrought patterns, these quaint turns of thought and concealed, half-playful ironies. . . . They have read Miss Marianne Moore's poems again and again, and questioned, half in despair—is this a mere word-puzzle, or does it mean something?"[26] H.D. includes the poems "Feed Me, Also, River God" (appearing in print for the first time), "He Made This Screen," and "Talisman" (both from Bryn Mawr publications), but does not provide a close reading of Moore's poems for her audience, instead using metaphors to suggest her own intellectual response to Moore's work. Since *Egoist* readers heretofore had seen only H.D.'s poetry or articles about her, this review provided her the opportunity to indicate her own critical approach. In this review, H.D. stresses the rigor of "perfect craft" and clarity, the appreciation of irony and the endurance of art and the value of "originality" in the sense of the ways in which artists make use of traditions.

H.D. begins the main portion of her discussion with the startling assertion that Moore might have been "laughing" at the audience, a statement that discards self-conscious seriousness and indicates the need to read ironically. "[If] Miss Moore is laughing at us," H.D. asserts, "it is laughter that catches us, that holds, fascinates and half-paralyses us, as light flashed from a very fine steel blade, wielded playfully, ironically . . . with absolute surety and absolute disdain" ("Marianne Moore" 118). What Gary Burnett calls a "battle metaphor—of fencing or sword-play—for a reading of Moore" (*H.D.* 19) clearly exists, but is not limited to being merely an image of battle. Rather, this linking of flashes of light with flashes of insight uses the familiar trope of artist as warrior, but in the context of fencing, suggesting a ritualized display of skill, perhaps for instruction—an effect quite different from that of real battle. Also, H.D.'s repeated use of blade imagery moves from war-making to skill and craft, using the images of a fencing instructor and a highly trained carver of a decorative screen. The degree of artistry in Moore's poetry, H.D. suggests, is as demanding as the greatest skill in swordsmanship or carving and stands in contrast to the destructive battle of war. As well, the metaphor of wielding blades symbolically represents fencing with patriarchal power. The fact that H.D. found in Moore's work a suggestion that the reader "shall not know that I [i.e., the poet] know you are beaten" evokes the indirection and "subversion" that women writers have had to use in order to accomplish their aims.

H.D.'s own poetic tastes show clearly in her assessment of Moore's accomplishment: "Miss Moore turns her perfect craft . . . to some direct presentation of beauty, clear, cut in flowing lines, but so delicately that the very screen she carves seems meant to stand only in that serene place of her own world of inspiration—frail, yet as all beautiful things are, absolutely hard. . . . The clear, flawless tones of Miss Moore's poetry come like bell-notes, like notes from some palace-bell carved beneath the sea" ("Marianne Moore" 118). The power of Moore's poetry, for H.D., lay in a "perfection" of form and thought that requires a new type of poetic understanding. H.D.'s praise for Moore reinforced her own advocacy of nontraditional art; at the same time, it exhibited H.D.'s concern with the artist's power to create brilliant surfaces that conceal meaning as well as reveal excellent technique.

Interestingly, while H.D. asserts her own poetic ideals in this review, she ends the piece by attempting to fit such a vision of beauty into the sordid world of war in which she wrote, as if to place this poetry in direct service to humanity, despite its place in a "serene" world of private inspiration. H.D. makes explicit the connection she sees between the war and the rampant commercial power that dominates the world:

Miss Marianne Moore is an American. And I think in reading Miss Moore's poems we in England should be strengthened. We are torn in our ambitions, our desires are crushed, we hear from all sides that art is destined to a long period of abeyance. . . . There are others here in England who do not for one moment believe that beauty will be one whit bruised by all this turmoil and distress.

Miss Moore helps us. She is fighting in her country a battle against squalor and commercialism. We are all fighting the same battle. And we must strengthen each other in this one absolute bond—our devotion to the beautiful English language. ["Marianne Moore" 118-19]

H.D.'s own "devotion to the language" can be found in her effort to guide readers through the difficulties of Moore's work. It was also a devotion with which H.D. would console herself in the difficult years to follow, through her extended work in writing, promoting, and publishing important new work.

Having found an individual avant garde sensibility in Moore, H.D. capitalized on the *Egoist*'s opportunity and asked Moore to send her critical articles. "The Accented Syllable" was printed in October of that year.[27] Just before it appeared, H.D. wrote in a letter of September 1916, "Miss Weaver, I think I wrote you, liked your article very much. So please do the comparison of Poe, Byron + Bacon. I do wish that the magazine could pay for contributions! It is very generous of you to send us your work."[28] Although the proposed article on Poe, Byron, and Bacon did not appear in the *Egoist*, H.D. continued to present Moore's work to other writers she knew and began exchanging ideas with Moore about the possibility of publishing a book of Moore's poetry. In the September 1916 letter, H.D. noted that May Sinclair, who had "a certain amount of influence," was interested in Moore's poetry, and that if John Cournos, another friend, failed in placing "the book," H.D. would pass the manuscript on to Sinclair; she also mentioned that Aldington wanted to write an article on Moore, although he could not "work at all now. . . . [He] wanted to write on you after he read the book."[29] These efforts on behalf of Moore's book were occurring at the same time that H.D. was working on her contributions for the first Poets' Translation Series and the Imagist anthologies with Amy Lowell, to say nothing of her own poetry and her critical work for the *Egoist*. H.D. continued to show her initiative and extend her experience by undertaking these promotional activities.

The other two critical pieces H.D. wrote for the *Egoist* appeared later in 1916. In a review of Charlotte Mew's *The Farmer's Bride* in September 1916, H.D. connected Mew's experiments in dramatic lyric with those of Browning: "Originality is now rare, if not extinct. That is why we overestimate it. But . . . even the most 'original' among us may take a sort of perverse delight in finding a new writer daring to discard his personality to follow, remotely or unconsciously perhaps, the tradition of an earlier generation."[30] Although admiring Mew's use of dramatic form, H.D. quietly suggests that such a style might enervate the writer's true "personality" and that the writer may not even know how her work is being shaped by tradition. H.D. herself, of course, was acutely conscious of her own use of various literary traditions. Nevertheless, her appreciation for the effects of Mew's poetry seems geniune: "When one reads of 'the white geraniums in the dusk,' one feels that [the heroine] has wandered in that same garden where the moth and the moth-kiss brushed the heavy flower-petals. . . . It is part of our pleasure in art these days to imagine such things, and the lines lose none of their poignancy, none of their personal flavour for this fine, subtle association" ("Farmer's Bride" 135). In noting the power of Mew's images to inspire the reader's imagination, H.D. shows appreciation for aspects of Mew's work that rely on evocative imagery and "fine, subtle association." The difficulty of making effective and not derivative use of poetic sources is an aspect of Mew's accomplishment that she finds intriguing: "Miss Mew has chosen one of the most difficult forms in the language—the dramatic lyric. She alone of our generation, with the exception of Mr. Hueffer and Mr. Frost, has succeeded in this form, has grown a new blossom from the seed of Browning's sowing, has followed a master without imitating him, has given us a transmutation of his spirit, not a parody of his flesh" ("Farmer's Bride" 135). The main issue H.D. raises involves the artist's integrity in using poetic tradition. Since this issue was one that H.D. faced in her evocations of Greek poetry and myth, this review gives an interesting edge to the development of her reputation at the time. She had been criticized for relying overmuch on Greek traditions to "escape" the contemporary world, but it is clear that her intentions concerned the recovery and distinctive use of beautiful elements from earlier poetic art.

Her final review appeared in December 1916, and treated John Gould Fletcher's *Goblins and Pagodas*. H.D. may have written this review as a favor to her collaborator in *Some Imagist Poets* and a regular contributor to the *Egoist*; at the same time, she may well have used the review as an opportunity to assert, in a subtle way, her differences with Fletcher, whose style was distinct from hers although he too was classed as an Imagist. The first paragraph of the review merely noted that "readers of *The Egoist* are already familiar" with some of Fletcher's poems from *Goblins and Pagodas*—as in the Moore review, a friendly gesture implying acceptance and familiarity for a new poet—and that "Fletcher presents with simplicity and directness a series of impressions."[31] Gary Burnett takes this comment to mean H.D. found that Fletcher "follows Pound's first precept, 'Direct treatment of the "thing" whether subjective or objective,'" and that she approved; in fact Burnett feels that her review intentionally sought out similarities between her writing and Fletcher's (*H.D.* 15). By this point in time, however, Pound and the other Imagists had long gone their separate ways, and there seems to be no good reason why H.D. would have reverted to Pound's delineations for Imagist writing, if indeed they were his; Cyrena Pondrom has demonstrated that the "precepts" Pound promoted were derived from H.D.'s poetry in the first place. Also, other portions of the review directly contradict the well-known Imagist precepts, and a close examination of H.D.'s language suggests that she was ambivalent about Fletcher's work.

H.D.'s praise of Fletcher's occasional success in "suggestion," for instance, occurs in a passage that evokes the difference between her poetry and his:

In the second part of his book, Mr. Fletcher deals with a more difficult and, when successfully handled, richer form of art: not that of direct presentation, but that of suggestion. . . . And as we come to a clearer understanding of the poet's method and his work, we are almost tempted . . . to say to the artist: the images so wrought upon the body of the vase—the maenad, poised for ever, quietly for all the swirl of draperies and of loosened head-band, or the satyr for ever lifting his vine-wreathed cup—are satisfying and indeed perfect. But how much more for the lover of beauty is the wine within the great jar beautiful—how much more than the direct image to him are the images suggested by shadow and light, the flicker of the purple wine, the glint across the yellow, the depth of the crimson and red? Who would stand gazing at a satyr and a maenad, however adroit the composition of fluttering garment and poised wine-cup when the wine itself within the great jar stands waiting for him? ["Goblins and Pagodas" 183]

The total effect H.D. ascribes to Fletcher's poetry, that it was "moving, whirling, drifting" like water or flowers, suggests her rejection of the "static" effect some readers had criticized in Imagism. Still, H.D.'s comments are equivocal. While praising Fletcher's images as "perfect" in one sense, she does not find the total effect of his work satisfying. She states that Fletcher uses images "as a means of evoking other and vaguer images" rather than creating a salvific or coherent vision and that his poems can "only be appreciated fully as a broad effect," an effect H.D. links to "grimmer moods" of artistic frustration, especially in the face of war: "[Through] it all, it is the soul or mind or inspiration of the poet, knowing within itself its problems, unanswerable; its visions, cramped and stilted; the bitterness of its own insufficiency. Knowing indeed not whence it cometh and whither it goeth, but flaunting in the face of its own ignorance, its own undaunted quest" ("Goblins and Pagodas" 184). Thus the "broad effect" of Fletcher's work is quite different from the precision and healing vision found in H.D.'s own Imagist work. Her review may be taken both as acknowledgment of the artist's essential frustration in attempting to elucidate her or his times, and as acknowledgment of the ways in which she found Fletcher's poetry unsatisfying. One also perceives her feelings of being trapped and limited by the war, which are not really mitigated by her final mention of the "undaunted quest." Nevertheless, H.D. ends the review by quoting the lines she found "most beautiful." In doing so, she again asserts an artistic ideal and an implied goodness in a world that at the time carried little evidence of them.

H.D.'s early literary editing and criticism may be read on several levels. On one hand, her collaboration with Lowell and the other Imagists continued to promote the spirit of exchange that had informed her first years in London. In this sense, H.D.'s publishing work may be seen as a means of self-assertion against the many troubles in her marriage and her life during wartime, as well as a positive expression of her aesthetic vision.[32] Most importantly, the different venues in which H.D. was able to present her aesthetic ideas enabled her to affect and effect modern writing in a number of ways. It was very important to her to be able to encourage and publish other writers, to share ideas and criticisms, to draw attention to writers whose work she thought worthy, and to elucidate her disagreements with other poets' writings. That she was so successful in presenting her own work and that of her contemporaries allows us to read H.D.'s critical and editorial work as an enactment of her vision of harmony arising from dissonance.

When the literary editorship of the *Egoist* passed to Eliot's hands in 1917, H.D. expressed little regret because her attention had been increasingly captured by war and personal problems. She left behind solid accomplishment in presenting and analyzing avant garde writing, and took with her several years' experience in editing, reviewing, and planning, which clearly informed her subsequent critical writing and publication.

The year after H.D. left the *Egoist*, she met Bryher. Already an admirer of H.D. and the Imagists through reading Amy Lowell's *Tendencies in Modern American Poetry* (1917), Bryher had obtained H.D.'s address through Clement Shorter, editor of Sir John Ellerman's the *Sphere* and husband of Bryher's friend Doris Banfield (Guest 105). When the two young women met in Cornwall in July 1918, one of their earliest topics of discussion was Lowell. Bryher became an enthusiastic reader of Lowell's poetry, and like H.D. entered into a correspondence with her that lasted until Lowell's death. Whereas H.D. appreciated Lowell's interest in her work, as demonstrated in the Imagist anthologies and *Tendencies in Modern American Poetry*, and kept Lowell informed of the plans for the Poets' Translation Series, Bryher carried on long discussions of literary matters in her letters to Lowell and sought her opinion about original essays and poems. Lowell, in fact, provided a foreword for Bryher's first novel, *Development* (1920).

Bryher's involvement with literary publishing and patronage reflected her consistent concern for high-quality, innovative writing. One of her early projects arose from her association with the Poets' Translation Series of the Egoist Press—a connection forged through H.D.—for which she was invited to translate Antipater of Sidon's "Six Sea Poems."[33] A few years later, Bryher helped subsidize the printing at least of Moore's *Poems* and of H.D.'s second book, *Hymen*, both in 1921.[34] Bryher also supported *Contact*, the magazine begun by William Carlos Williams and Robert McAlmon, after her marriage to McAlmon in February 1921, and later McAlmon's Contact Editions.[35]

Once Bryher and McAlmon were established in London, Bryher renewed her friendship with Harriet Weaver of the *Egoist*, and McAlmon's first book, *Explorations*, appeared through the Egoist Press in the winter of 1921. Bryher's publishing connections very likely provided McAlmon with the impetus and the basic knowledge that he later used to achieve his own reputation as a publisher in Paris.[36] His Contact Publishing Company was established there in 1922, and, in conjunction with William Bird's Three Mountains Press, brought out thirty-two volumes through 1929.

Literary historians have tended to give McAlmon credit for supporting, encouraging, and publishing a number of writers. Certainly McAlmon's memoirs were available earlier than Bryher's, and his lifestyle brought him greater attention through being mentioned in numerous other memoirs, but it is also clear that in this case Bryher became an "invisible" woman. Bryher's importance as supporter of the press has been treated merely as a convenience for McAlmon rather than as the source of vital connections and funds. The vicissitudes of McAlmon's work, in terms of both publishing and writing, suggest rather that Bryher's money was the only thing that allowed him to continue. Her status and previous friendships, as well, brought him into contact with many of the artists and writers who became his companions. Without these connections, the Contact Editions lists would have been extremely thin and might well have been limited to McAlmon's own books and Williams's *Spring and All*. Bryher has yet to receive proper credit for her support, while McAlmon's own lapses in his publishing work—for instance in the fiasco over Gertrude Stein's *The Making of Americans*, which Stein and Jane Heap finally tried to resolve without McAlmon—indicate that it may not have been a business in which he was entirely competent.[37] Even despite their subsequent separation, Bryher remained helpful to McAlmon, reviewing his *Portrait of a Generation* in *Poetry* in 1926 and later still publishing one of his stories in *Life and Letters*.[38]

The most celebrated early project with which Bryher was involved, however, was Marianne Moore's *Poems* of 1921. Bryher had met Moore with H.D. on their trip to America in 1920. They had become friends, although Bryher's sudden marriage of convenience to McAlmon just before sailing home had upset Moore very much. Still, their friendship endured that strain, and Moore may well have attempted to make amends later by claiming that McAlmon was one of the parties (along with H.D. and Bryher) involved in the publication of her *Poems*.

For many years it was said that Moore knew nothing of the compilation of her poems and was surprised when the volume was issued, but the evidence of Moore's collusion with H.D. and Bryher in making plans for such a volume has been clarified by Cyrena Pondrom.[39] Moore's response of surprise and consternation, which scholars have taken to imply that the publication was without her acquiescence, does not express "modesty" so much as strong feeling about editing and rewriting her own verse, as well as her personal preferences in selecting and arranging her verse, should she have done so herself. Based on the correspondence, one imagines that Moore's concern arose rather from a belief that her writing would be appreciated by only a few readers (H.D. and Bryher among them), that she disliked "public attention" to pieces that even she felt were highly individualistic, and that in fact she may have preferred to organize her first volume—perhaps at a later date—according to her own choices.

In general, the book seems to have been H.D.'s idea, as she had been collecting Moore's poems for some time, and Bryher's financial project, as she had the resources to see such a publication through; indeed, she had proposed to other writers that books of theirs should be printed under her subsidy. Bryher's efforts for Moore included assembly, support, and distribution, even at the expense of Bryher's own book, as is clear from a reference Moore made to Bryher's amusing "advance on the bookseller" on Moore's behalf; while Moore appreciated the support, she expressed regret that Bryher "did not have time to inquire for 'Development,'" Bryher's own novel.[40]

Bryher seems to have been less interested in giving herself credit than with providing other writers and artists with the means to present their works and with continuing to seek out new ideas and vehicles. An important example is the influential film magazine *Close Up*, which Bryher helped found and which was one product of the collaboration between Bryher, H.D., and Kenneth Macpherson during the late 1920s and early 1930s.[41] Bryher, who had divorced McAlmon and in 1927 married Macpherson, was again the financial backer, and for a while all three solicited work and engaged in editorial correspondence. The extent of Bryher's involvement in *Close Up* is reflected in unpublished correspondence far more than in the number of her articles alone.

During its six years of operation, *Close Up* gained thousands of readers and addressed many topics crucial to the development of film. Bryher provided capital for the magazine and wrote numerous reviews and articles; moreover, her work helped make *Close Up* the chief contemporary forum for debate about the social implications as well as the theory and practice of cinema. Bryher's articles for *Close Up* examined not only matters of technique and taste in film but also a range of cultural and political issues linking avant garde aesthetics to the practical concerns of Europeans. The art of the "silents," as Bryher put it, "offered a single language across Europe" (*Heart to Artemis* 246). She provided one very important means for teaching and sharing that language.

In an anecdote about how she became interested in film, Bryher expressed the connections she saw between cinematic art, critical thought, and psychological truth. She had found in film "no link with my particu-

C L O S E   U P

EDITOR : K. MACPHERSON
ASSISTANT EDITOR : BRYHER
PUBLISHED BY POOL
RIANT CHATEAU - TERRITET - SWITZERLAND

CONTENTS

Paris Correspondent : Marc Allégret.

SUBSCRIPTION RATES

ENGLAND . . 14 shillings per year.
FRANCE . . . 70 francs per year.
GERMANY . . 14 marks per year.
AMERICA . . . 3 dollars, fifty cents per year.

Table of contents for *Close Up*, vol. I, no. 2, August 1927.

lar development," until she recognized in "Joyless Street" "the unrelenting portrayal of what war does to life" and thereby realized how filmmaker G. W. Pabst's "consciousness of Europe" allowed him to "[see] psychologically" the truths behind human actions.[42] Bryher comments in her autobiography, *The Heart to Artemis*, that during the war "I had had to abstract myself from my surroundings in order to survive at all. To wish to create was a sin against the consciousness of the time. Yet I wanted things to be real" (183). One can thus understand the profound impact of Pabst's realistic film upon Bryher and her subsequent involvement with various aspects of cinema.

Close Up, from its inception, was clearly more than a journal meant simply to review new films and technical advances. It presented pieces by writers whose work reflected new ideas and approaches on a number of fronts—Sergei Eisenstein, Dorothy Richardson, Gertrude Stein, Robert Herring, V. I. Pudovkin, Andor Krazsna-Krausz, Paul Rotha, and Marianne Moore, among many others.[43] Rachael Low notes that most "serious writers" about film at the time "were connected with *Close Up*. . . . Its historical importance is very great despite its small circulation. . . . [It] enabled its readers to keep in touch with . . . important developments taking place in films abroad, especially in Germany, France and Russia. . . . [The] magazine undertook an important job which it did without compromise, that of building up a nucleus of cineastes devoted to the development of the art of the film."[44] The nucleus of readers that *Close Up* built was devoted to the free critical exchange of ideas, for reasons that extended far beyond the aesthetic inquiries of film art into issues of social and international cooperation.

Bryher's extensive role in producing and editing *Close Up* is not immediately evident from the tables of contents and is only hinted at in the tidbits about production and industry gossip she includes in *The Heart to Artemis*. Her characteristic modesty has deflected attention from her work; in *The Heart to Artemis* she states simply, "I kept to the business side of the magazine as much as possible and attended to much of the correspondence, but I was pressed into service occasionally to review educational films. . . . There were films to see and review because I was the only one of the *Close Up* group to speak much German" (245, 257). Studies of the magazine do not generally focus on the contributions of individuals; even Gillian Hanscombe and Virginia Smyers, while mentioning that Bryher financed, organized, and helped edit *Close Up*, do not specify the matters that Bryher investigated in her articles (195-97). Even a brief foray into her articles and papers, however, reveals that Bryher's activities for the magazine are far richer than she admits.

Bryher wrote reviews and articles, handled correspondence, solicited submissions, paid for submitted work, read proof, and helped plan layout and advertising. Although Bryher, Macpherson, and H.D. all worked on editorial and production matters for the magazine, many of the details of editing and producing *Close Up* fell to Bryher, especially as Macpherson's enthusiasm for the magazine waned when he turned to filmmaking. Mention of *Close Up* occupies decreasing portions of Macpherson's letters to Bryher during and after 1930, which, for the most part, concentrate on gossip and his detailed plans for Kenwin, their house in Switzerland. When Macpherson does mention the magazine, it is often in the context of discussing the use of photos, which he often selected while leaving placement and page design up to Bryher.[45] Macpherson was not particularly interested in the detailed preparations necessary to keep a magazine functioning smoothly month after month, allowing Bryher to "make final decisions on numbers, etc."[46] Bryher herself, who handled business matters well, remarked wryly in a letter to H.D. that Macpherson "says he doesn't like cold figures on paper. Idiot."[47] Nevertheless, while Bryher did handle much of the production work for *Close Up*, she clearly viewed her individual contributions to the magazine as far less important than its investigations into the art and social significance of cinema. Her life as well as her published articles expressed a belief in cooperative intellectual work that seemed particularly needful at that time and in that place.

Bryher's casual mention that she was the only member of the editorial group who spoke much German gains in impact when one considers the European context of the magazine. Bryher's coverage of German cinema for *Close Up* was vital, since Germany was a great consumer of films and the source of much experimental work. The number of movie theaters and production companies in that country had increased enormously after World War I, and in addition to importing films, "Germany produced more films during the 1920s and early 1930s than all other European countries put together."[48] Most of this activity was commercial rather than artistic, of course, but the sheer volume of such work coupled with the political possibilities of cinema made Germany a very important focal point. In Bryher's life, awareness of contemporary political activity merged with her interest in psychoanalysis and in cinema: "I went to [Hanns Sachs, the psychoanalyst] for an hour a day, during the rest of the time I saw films, attended to the business side of *Close Up* and shared in the extraordinary ferment abroad," she wrote in *The Heart to Artemis* (251). The "extraordinary ferment abroad" during the Weimar republic included an international intellectual community (with whom Bryher had contacts through Sachs and Pabst) who were interested in the democratic possibilities of film and who hoped that technological innovation would help alleviate social problems.[49] Bryher's sympathies allied her with this purview and helped her gain both readers and contributors for *Close Up* to participate in this discourse.

Because of her fluency in languages and her international connections, Bryher was able to solicit work from filmmakers and critics in Germany, Russia, and Czechoslovakia, and she regularly prepared translations. In fact, the roster of contributors to *Close Up* over the years features a series of international "correspondents," which eventually included writers from Paris, London, Berlin, Geneva, Hollywood, New York, Moscow, and Vienna. This wide-ranging conversation, quite obviously uniting nations formerly involved in World War I, suggests the success of the magazine in fostering a vital and serious climate of exchange.

Much of Bryher's critical work in the magazine involved the more important issues with which *Close Up* grappled: the problems of political dogma and censorship, the nature of public education and of the possible educational applications of film, the effects and disadvantages of using sound, and, especially, the relationship between film and psychology. As Bryher noted, film "offered occasionally, in an episode or single shot, some framework for our dreams," what she termed "an inquiry into the secrets of the mind" (*Heart to Artemis* 246, 251).

One of the "secrets of the mind" examined in the early numbers of

Close Up involved the problem of mass coercion used to promote war, which Bryher linked to the rote nature of modes of education. Her authorial stance in two articles examining several war films assumed that differences in point of view can, and must, successfully coexist, in politics as well as in art, although she was also careful to stress that this goal is not necessarily easy to accomplish.

In Bryher's discussion of the American movie "The Big Parade" in the first issue of *Close Up*, she praises the filmmakers for daring to express "so much scorn of war, so much stripping of what people in general like to regard as heroism[,] . . . the reckless unthinking plunge into an army, the actual dirt and horror and tyranny behind all warfare."[50] She makes clear that the potential of cinema to depict collective action for a mass market establishes that its social importance—for good or ill—is as great as that of the educational system: "[The] greatness of 'The Big Parade' was in the early opening scenes, the sweeping of everyone into something that they did not clearly understand, the enlistment through sheer mass hypnotism, the unthinking but definite cruelty of many women seeing war as romance instead of reality—the best lesson to those with eyes to read of the necessity of real education of people, instead of a standard fitting of a few facts and no real thought to hundreds of schoolchildren" ("War from Three Angles" 17). Bryher consistently links ignorance and sentimentality to "war fever," while redefining "courage" according to a veracity in art that faces the confusion of war rather than paying lip service to a spurious heroic "romance." "In a time of danger the 'We Want War' crowd psychology may destroy a nation," Bryher writes in another review. "By all means let us have war films. Only let us have war straight and as it is; mainly disease and discomfort, almost always destructive (even in after [*sic*] civil life) in its effects."[51] This insistence upon cinematic realism reappears in later articles, where Bryher equated using films as escape with ignoring the facts of actual "life in modern Europe," which, as *Close Up* neared the end of its run, included clear signals of the "storm" about to break.[52]

Bryher, an Englishwoman living in Switzerland, was under no illusions about the Great War having been the one to end all war. While she did make extensive specific criticisms about plot and technique in films, her deeper concerns clearly lay in asserting that cinematic art can transcend as well as depict political difference, thereby playing an extremely important role in the future. She insisted upon directoral skill, not nationality, as her standard, calling ironically upon the "English sense of justice" to refute English reluctance to face not only foreign films but also the alternative versions of truth they portray:

Perhaps in time [the English] shall make a film that combines the suspense of [the German film] "The Emden" with the swiftness and clarity of "The Big Parade," and without the concession to sentimentality and supposed crowd-desire, that crop up here and there in both these films. But this will not be until we have intelligent directors, camera men trained to use their equipment as the German and American photographer is trained, and until the idea is scrapped as utterly as worn-out machinery, that a film, because it is "English" must be praised. ["War from Three Angles" 22]

It is not simply the blind acceptance of "English films" that Bryher criticizes. Her reviews of war movies make clear the connections she believes cinema enacts between psychology and politics, and emphasize the persuasive importance of technical achievement. "Again no one has greater admiration than I for what the Germans have accomplished," she writes in October 1927, in a statement guaranteed to direct the attention of her readers toward her point: "They are far ahead of the rest of the world in cinematography. But it is idle to pretend that for some years [Germans] were anything else but enemies. Toleration there must certainly be but it is time that national affairs which involve thousands of lives and a future generation should not be brought down to the level of a football match nor that what was certainly and on both sides, a very bitter enmity, be reduced to the not too serious hostility of a couple of rival teams" ("War from More Angles" 47). Bryher refutes the easy stereotyping of the "enemy" in films by refusing to sentimentalize her call for international understanding. Also, while insisting on the sociopolitical significance of cinema, she asserts the integrity of cinema as art, able to portray certain emotional truths through the particularities of directoral skill. In this sense she reflects the neutrality of the "international" language of silent film, and links the vocabulary of aesthetic conversation to the vocabulary of social cooperation.[53]

Marianne Moore in 1932. Photo by Morton Dauwen Zabel, courtesy of *Poetry* Magazine. Zabel, editor of *Poetry* for a time after Harriet Monroe's death, was a friend of Moore's for many years.

Harriet Monroe at Agnes Scott College, March 17, 1921. Photographer unknown, courtesy of *Poetry* Magazine. Monroe grew up in a well connected family in Chicago and wrote poetry and reviews for years before founding *Poetry*.

Alice Corbin Henderson. Photo by Elizabeth Buehrmann, courtesy of *Poetry* Magazine. Henderson published her poetry as "Alice Corbin" and knew many leading artists through the connections of her husband, William Penhallow Henderson.

Jane Heap. Photographer unknown. Florence Reynolds Collection,
University of Delaware Library, Newark. Heap, an artist, came to Chicago to
study at the Art Institute and met Margaret Anderson through
Maurice Browne's Little Theatre.

Margaret Anderson. Photo by Man Ray. Anderson began her career as a book reviewer in Chicago before founding the *Little Review* in 1914.

H.D. (Hilda Doolittle), circa 1920. Photo by Man Ray. Carlton Lake
Collection, Harry Ransom Humanities Research Center, University of Texas at
Austin. This portrait suggests H.D.'s interest in the psychological reality of
mysticism as well as in the art of the camera.

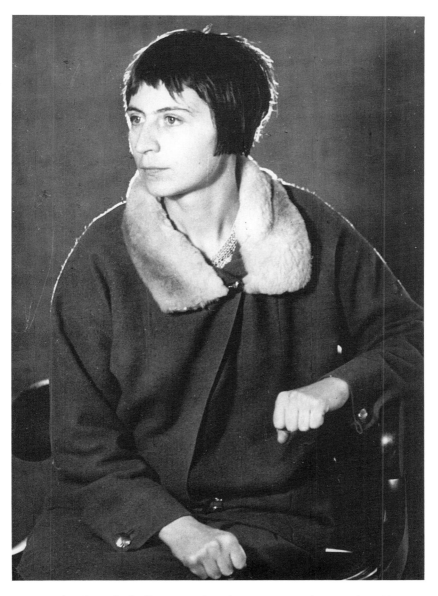

Bryher (Winifred Ellerman). Photo by Man Ray. Sylvia Beach Collection, Princeton University Library. Bryher, whose childhood included time spent in Europe and the Middle East, adopted the name of one of the Scilly Islands off the English Coast.

Left, Amy Lowell, 1916. Photo by Moffett Studio, courtesy of the Joseph Regenstein Library, University of Chicago. Lowell, relative of James Russell Lowell and Robert Lowell, usually rose late, entertained guests at dinner, and then wrote for most of the night. *Right*, Gertrude Stein, January 4, 1935. Photo by Carl Van Vechten. Fanny Butcher Papers, Newberry Library. Stein shared a long friendship with Van Vechten, who photographed her during a visit with Butcher, a Chicago journalist.

Ezra Pound. Photographer unknown. Alice Corbin Henderson Papers, Harry Ransom Humanities Research Center, University of Texas at Austin. This portrait captures some of the intensity that helped make Pound a striking figure in his early career.

Bryher's rejection of formulaic approaches to both political persuasion and cinematic art related to several other concerns she expressed in *Close Up*, for instance the larger social effects of public education. In August 1927, Bryher linked public fears about progress, especially mechanical innovation, with the strictures amounting to censorship that she perceived to be operating in educational systems. Bryher, herself very interested in mechanical progress, deplored the "complex of the machine," a defensive attitude in which "our parents and our grandparents resent . . . machines that have robbed them of a sense of power . . . and that have placed the young in a state equal with themselves."[54] Bryher uses the example of the typewriter, a means of learning to write that children would likely find efficient and enjoyable but that is scorned in favor of the painful old way of learning to write by hand. This "illogical" fear of progress, with its concomitant lack of imagination, Bryher declares, has created a situation in which affinity for "science, geography and history is killed in hundreds of children a year through dull methods of presentation and the failure to capture the interest—and the respect—of the child" ("Films in Education" 53-54).

As an alternative demonstrating her devotion to educational reform and her alliance with avant garde interest in the machine, she suggests that the judicious use of cinema as a teaching tool would not only compensate for any lack of good teachers but also generate immense creativity and satisfaction on the part of students: "There is for instance no reason why children should not write, direct, photograph and make their own films with very little instruction. There is hardly a subject taught that could not be helped by the cinema provided the film is prepared for first by a lesson and is then followed up by practical work. Where the classes are large it can make up for the lack of individual instruction. Where they are small it can speed up progress and open new possibilities" ("Films in Education" 54). The extent of Bryher's prescience about the possibilities of mechanical aids to education can be gauged only now, with the recent proliferation of computers and video equipment in schools. In fact, several of Bryher's articles mention her hope that new filmmaking equipment and materials coupled with lower costs could allow individuals to own their own prints of important films—another of her projections fulfilled after half a century.

Bryher's determination to "open new possibilities" to the public at large often took the form of pragmatic suggestions related to her concern over censorship. The issue of censorship informed a number of articles in *Close Up*. English blue laws caused imported films to be banned or mutilated, a practice that not only blocked the struggle to gain recognition for cinema as an art rather than as a mindless diversion, but also implied that censors had to protect an English public unable to face or understand certain films and ideas. To assist the English readership of *Close Up*, Bryher often included detailed descriptions of European and American films and gave specific information about current restrictions, urging readers to take responsibility for acquiring "the best" films in order properly to develop critical taste, for, she asks, "until we know what cinematography has already achieved how can we hope to evolve standards of comparison and criticism?"[55] Bryher qualifies her insistence upon ready availability by noting that this does not mean that all films are appropriate for children, but she specifies that it is a question of discernment, not of morals. "[There] are a lot of films that one would prefer a child not to see, just as there are bad forms of any art that one prefers they should escape if possible. . . ." she writes, "not from any point of view that their morals might be damaged, but because many great films treat of subjects outside their experience and many stupid films might blunt their discrimination."[56] It is clear that Bryher respected the rights of individuals to take charge of their reactions to challenging ideas and materials. Her objections to censorship entailed a specific rejection of the limitations implied in any legalized "moral guidance" intended to affect what people think.

In a series of articles published during 1928, Bryher gave directions for the creation of small independent film societies, stressing the importance of cooperative action and the necessity of access to proper equipment, including original uncut films.[57] Others of her articles urged English cinephiles to pressure Parliament to alter the heavy restrictions and tariffs then placed upon imported films.[58] Bryher's insistence on having movies from foreign nations readily available, in the versions originally intended by the directors, allied her call for individual technical excellence with her belief in free and open artistic expression.

Bryher's writings repeatedly averred that the individual carried responsibility for the actions of his or her nation, and that the collective action of small groups of informed people applied to the reform not just of film-showing habits but also of a nation's attitude toward its own problems and toward international cooperation. While Bryher did not foresee that film groups might be able to abolish all censorship in cinema, she suggested that they might be able to change the laws to permit private showings of films that would otherwise be ruined by cutting ("How to Rent a Film" 46-48). This action not only would preserve artistic integrity but also would honor the democratic nature of film itself, for—as she put it—"cinema belongs to the many." The emphasis on democratic action against autocratic censorship also carried significant social implications, which eventually overtook Bryher's other critical concerns as far more pressing issues intervened.

In her last major article for *Close Up*, Bryher abandoned the discussion of film in order to confront the deteriorating situation in Europe. During her trip to Berlin in 1932, Bryher writes, "I didn't go to cinemas because I watched the revolution." The growing ferment of Nazism had wrenched her attention from aesthetic matters.[59] The article outlines the bannings, boycotts, exiles, and lies that were clear signals of oncoming war. Bryher specifically reiterates the importance of collective action based on attention to what is real rather than to false images: "For the last fifteen years people have used the words peace and war so much that the sound of them means nothing at all. . . . very few have ever made a constructive attempt to prevent the months of 1914 from being repeated on a larger and worse scale. I do not think a pacifism of theories and pamphlets is of any use. . . . If we want peace, we must fight for the liberty to think in terms of peace, for all the peoples of Europe" ("What Shall You Do" 190). "Do not let the lessons of the last war be lost," Bryher continues. "Make your decision now while you have still time to work for whatever you believe" (191). But the tone of the piece hints that, by 1933, Bryher already knew that the aesthetic investigations of *Close Up* would soon be superseded by war. The magazine itself endured only until December of that year; by that point, Bryher had joined a group dedicated to helping Jews escape Germany (*Heart to Artemis* 275). Although in *The Heart to Artemis* Bryher suggested that the advent of sound ruined the experiments of avant garde filmmakers and led to the demise of *Close Up* (262), it is also apparent that Bryher had decided to put her energy into war resistance. *Close Up* had done its work in creating an international discussion concerning the art of film; but Bryher, who had done so much to make this possible, had to take action in another field.

Bryher's work for *Close Up* added explicitly to the quality of debate that made the magazine a vital forum for the avant garde during a particularly important historical period in Europe. The seriousness with which *Close Up* treated cinema as art gained from Bryher's insistence on technical skill, good equipment, widespread dissemination of ideas, and the importance of film as an educational tool that could be used for political and social as well as academic aims. The magazine itself deserves much more critical attention, coming as it did during those crucial years when cinema made the transition to sound—a change Bryher deplored as compromising the psychological qualities of cinema—concomitant with the escalating changes in Europe during the later Weimar republic. Bryher herself anticipated the importance of the ideas and issues she had examined in the early thirties; in *The Heart to Artemis* she wrote, "We believed that if we stated facts without comment, moral or otherwise, mankind must see its follies and revise its laws. It was a vain and idle dream and yet, looking back at it after forty years, how much that we created in the way of thought is accepted now as valid and desirable" (204).

H.D.'s critical contributions to *Close Up*, quite distinct in form from Bryher's, were no less important to avant garde thought, and are particularly interesting in light of her experiments using cinematic techniques in writing and her knowledge of psychoanalysis.[60] During 1925-27, prior to the founding of *Close Up*, she had written a number of short critical reviews for John Middleton Murry's magazine, the *Adelphi*.[61] In these unsigned paragraphs, H.D. treated books written about various aspects of classical cultures and art, in the process demonstrating her continuing aesthetic concerns. These included spare language, sincerity, and a non-romanticized, carefully imagined Hellas, utilized not for dramatic impact but for what H.D. saw as the psychological reality of mythic connections. She was also learning about the art of film, through Bryher's agency and perhaps also through the discussions of cinematic art that had begun to appear in the *Dial* under the editorship of her friend Marianne Moore. Thus, when H.D. began to appear in *Close Up*, she was ready with thoroughly thought-out analyses of the psychological and aesthetic possibilities of this young art.

Of H.D.'s editorial work in soliciting material for the magazine, some evidence exists in unpublished correspondence. On June 6, 1927, H.D. wrote to her friend Viola Jordan: "I am now intensely interested [in film]. . . . In fact am doing a little critical work for a new very clever movie magazine, supposed to get hold of things, from a more or less 'artistic' angle but not the highbrow attitude. . . . It is to be called, CLOSE-UP, a splendid title I think. . . . I feel [film] is the living art, the thing that WILL count but that is in danger now from commnerical [*sic*] and popular sources. . . . [Write] us an article for our movie paper. (I can't guarantee its being printed but will offer it with suavity to the editor.)"[62] H.D.'s involvement in the editorial work for *Close Up*, through soliciting contributions but particularly through her critical reviews, helped to place that magazine in its important position as avant garde organ of modern artistic thought. While her articles for *Close Up* are difficult—circuitous, impressionistic, and as resonant as her poetry—H.D.'s criticism looked both outward to the cinematic matériel and inward to her own continuing artistic concerns.

A few critics have begun to examine H.D.'s critical work for *Close Up*.[63] Charlotte Mandel, asserting that "film art was peculiarly adapted to H.D.'s mode of perception," has discussed some aspects of H.D.'s writing style that show the poet's affinity for film and its aesthetic effects ("The Redirected Image" 44). Mandel asserts that changes in H.D.'s poetic style between early lyrics and later epics can be ascribed to H.D.'s involvement with cinema and mentions several cinematic techniques that appear in the poems "Projector II (*Chang*)" and *Helen in Egypt*. Among the examples she cites are language that imitates or evokes montage and dissolve, use of "close-up" visual details, juxtaposition and transformation of images and scenes, cinematic "structuring" via altered line and stanza breaks, and particularly, the sense of "dual levels of consciousness—the view dictated by the camera lens [interacting] with our conscious awareness of the self as onlooker" ("The Redirected Image" 40-41, 37; "H.D.'s 'Projector II'" 43,

44). Mandel finds that "mystical or mythic realities" affect the form of H.D.'s poetry and the importance her experiments hold for her aesthetic thought. Mandel does not examine in detail H.D.'s critical pieces for *Close Up* but does describe generally H.D.'s approach in these articles: "H.D. as a film reviewer does not tell us *about* the film; instead, she places us within her own perception, so that we re-enact her experiences as she perceives them and simultaneously perceive her thoughts as she watches those images" ("The Redirected Image" 38). In listing H.D.'s contributions to *Close Up*, Mandel links the nontraditional style of the poet's critical articles to the episodic nature of cinema itself:

During the period 1927 to 1929, H.D. contributed eleven articles of film review and commentary to *Close Up* and two poems, 'Projector' and 'Projector II (*Chang*).' . . . The articles in *Close Up* prove H.D.'s knowledge of film editing to be sophisticated and in touch with new trends. Even more, the style of the essays provides direct access to H.D.'s thoughts and impressions. She writes conversationally, openly expressing feelings of admiration, puzzlement or distaste. The films are described through the perceptions of the writer, almost as though she is writing a memoir. For H.D., cinema was an exciting new source for expanding the boundaries of art, and she wrote these articles at the moment of her experience. ["Garbo/Helen" 127-28]

Mandel's investigations provide necessary ground from which to examine more closely H.D.'s incorporation of cinematic techniques and effects, which give the impression that films and processes of thought unreel in similar ways. When Mandel claims, however, that H.D. presents her filmgoing experiences in an episodic manner ("at the moment of her experience"), she does not assess the reconfiguration of raw material into essay presentation, and so does not analyze the actual structure of H.D.'s articles in their refusal to follow traditional essay forms. Anne Friedberg, also, mentions only briefly H.D.'s use, in poetry and prose, "of cinematic metaphors of light/focus/superimposition/projection" in her discussion of H.D. as an emblem of "problematized" history, a writer encoding "a privatized form of reception, of viewing." Friedberg does not systematically examine the style and contents of H.D.'s critical articles that evoke such cinematic techniques ("On H.D." 30, 29).

H.D.'s pieces for *Close Up* displayed a more experimental form than she used in the *Egoist* and showed suggestive development of her aesthetic ideas. The articles and reviews discussed the need for "classic, ancient Beauty," which H.D. identified with "the good" and with "reality," a beauty constituted in integrity, authenticity, subtlety, a sense of proportion and restraint, and the harmony of body and mind.[64] Achieving these qualities in film, H.D. stressed, required good cinematic techniques and, above all, artistic intellect. Her own use of cinematic techniques in writing, particularly montage and dissolve, create in her essays the sort of psychological reality and immediate critical perception of beauty that she called for as the true goal of film art.

The series of three articles H.D. wrote treating "The Cinema and the Classics" together form an oblique statement of her artistic demands both of literature and of film. These articles for *Close Up* expressed her complex perception of beauty and of psychological and spiritual truth, and implemented a radical critique of standard critical approaches through her adaptation of cinematic grammar.

Her first piece for *Close Up* deliberately engages the question of what is "classic" in art; the essay elaborates her own aesthetic viewpoint while it helps recuperate the reputation of cinema—just as Bryher had tried to do in her writings. At the same time, H.D.'s article itself calls "classic" standards into question by refusing to follow traditional expository form. Thus her advocacy of the avant garde was enacted in an innovative context that gave the impression of cinematic montage and dissolve in order to evoke and commingle the processes of viewing and thinking:

I suppose we might begin rhetorically by asking, what is the cinema, what are the classics? . . . Classics. Cinema. The word cinema (or movies) would bring nine out of ten of us a memory of crowds and crowds and saccharine music and longdrawn out embraces and the artificially enhanced thud-offs of galloping bronchoes. . . . boredom, tedium, suffocation, pink lemonade, saw-dust even; old reactions connected with cheap circuses, crowds and crowds and crowds and illiteracy and more crowds and breathless suffocation and . . . peanut shells and grit and perhaps a sudden collapse of jerry-built scaffoldings. Danger somewhere anyhow. ["Cinema and Classics I" 22-23]

Although H.D. opens by suggesting she will offer a definition, in fact what she offers is not an analytical but an impressionistic response in a style that functions like montage, moving quickly between images in order to create certain linkages in the reader's mind. The effect of what Mandel calls being placed within H.D.'s "own perception," that is, of experiencing the film along with the reviewer, is enhanced by juxtaposition of descriptive and evaluative comments. This stylistic experiment is borne out in the intellectual contents of the article, in which H.D. explicitly identifies her aesthetic ideas with the avant garde, corrects what she sees as the current misapprehension of beauty in cinematic art, and proposes a radical vision of spiritual reality within the simplicity of daily life.

In this first article, H.D. deliberately aligns her critical purview with "the fortunately vast-increasing [sic], valiant, little army of the advance guard or the franc-tireur of the arts, in whose hands mercifully since the days of the stone-writers, the arts really rested. The little leaven" ("Cinema and Classics I" 23). She suggests that the avant garde are those who can lead the public (which she wittily calls "the lump") to become educated about film art, the better to recognize the simplicity of the beauty around them and so to resist the censorship that can arise when beauty is distorted. Her resistance to Hollywood's portrayal of the female beauty (Greta Garbo turned into "a Nice-carnival, frilled, tissue-paper rose in place of a wild-briar") underlies her insistence that "Beauty brings a curse, a blessing, a responsibility. Is that why your Ogre, the Censor, is so intent on disguising it, on dishing it up as vamp charm[?]" ("Cinema and Classics I" 27, 33). By rescuing beauty, therefore, one can restore integrity, simplicity, and spiritual truth to modern life. H.D. calls on "the duty of every sincere intellectual to work for the better understanding of the cinema, for the clearing of the ground, for the rescuing of this superb art, from its hide-bound convention" (28). In this sense, H.D.'s alignment with avant garde ideas—her rejection of traditional, purportedly "moral" conventions—carries a political as well as a spiritual dimension, a vision of life in which an educated public could appreciate the intellectual and psychological expression offered by film art.

Having established the grounds for her defense of cinema, H.D. in her next article (subtitled "Restraint") discusses the reasons for her own particular taste in cinematic design: simplicity, careful choice of detail, suggestion rather than embellishment. In these qualities one sees the persistence of Imagist doctrine, which had never served H.D. as a guideline but rather arose largely from her own severe aesthetic. "[To] present the 'classic' it is not necessary to build up paste board palaces, the whole of Troy, the entire over-whelming of a battle fleet," H.D. remarks. Rather,

[the] "classic" as realism could be better portrayed by the simplest of expedients. A pointed trireme prow nosing side ways into empty space, the edge of a quay, blocks of solid masonry, squares and geometric design would simplify [and] at the same time emphasize the pure *classic* note. . . . A Greek interior should be simple, cold and chaste, with one blocked in doorway, not a vista of ten. . . . We should be *somewhere* with our minds. . . . It is preconceived ideas that destroy all approach to real illumination. *What* do you know of beauty, of life, of reality should be the first questions that a manager or a producer asks his scenic artist. ["Cinema and Classics II" 30, 32, 37]

H.D. stresses the importance of concentration or intensity, the "real illu-mination" that reveals meaning within material reality. This mystical sense of immediacy appears again when H.D. describes why well-chosen preci-sion is more important than a general effect: "I am concerned here chiefly with attempts at more subtle simple effects; they so often fail for lack of some precise and definite clear intellect at the back of the whole, one centralizing focus of thought cutting and pruning the too extraneous un-derbrush of tangled detail. . . . The classic then . . . is a point of view and 'restraint' is a classic virtue which means simply tact and intuition and a sense of the rightness and the fitness of things in their interrelation" (33, 38). The real danger, in poorly made film art as in life itself, H.D. sug-gests, is "satiety." Cinema in particular offered a versatile and suggestive medium that could continually remind viewers of the mystical possibi-lities of psychological reality: "Here is our medium, as I say here is the thing that the Elusinians [*sic*] would have been glad of; a subtle device for portraying of the miraculous. Miracles and godhead are *not* out of place, are not awkward on the screen" (36). Ultimately, H.D. decides, "Light speaks, is pliant, is malleable. Light is our friend and our god. Let us be worthy of it" (35).

H.D.'s language provided a sense of mystical appreciation for film, an almost primitive belief in its ability to transform the human soul. Her

conviction that beauty lay hidden within everyday life had obviously deepened in the interval since the *Egoist*, and her writing for *Close Up* was
further informed by her perception of the connections between film technique, psychoanalysis, spirituality, and mysticism. These prose pieces, written during a period in which H.D. published almost no poetry, clearly
set out what Sandra M. Gilbert and Susan Gubar see as H.D.'s self-trans-
formation "into a spiritual poet, indeed into a deeply revisionary theolo-
gian" who had found "the spiritual source of her authority" through a
pagan mythology, which eventually led her to create the female deity, the
"Lady" or "Maia, Mary, Mother" of *Tribute to the Angels* (*Letters from the
Front* 171, 193-97).

H.D.'s other articles in the series show the development of her "cinematic" prose style as she explores the idea that cinema expresses a shared
vision. In a review of "The Student of Prague," her writing style helps
express her belief that cinema can facilitate communication for all people—
a belief Bryher later echoed in her comment that film offered "one language" for Europe.[65] The cinematic influences shown in this article arise
particularly from juxtaposed sensory impressions rhythmically intercut
with critical statements:

A small room, a stuffy atmosphere; a provincial Swiss lakeside cinema; the usual
shuffle and shuffle and the unaccustomed (to the urbane senses) rattle of paper
bags. Crumbs. "Mlle. must not smoke here." Of course I might have known that,
I never smoke in these places, what made me this time? Something has been
touched before I realise it. . . . The horses filing again, in obvious procession,
mean something. They are going to spell something, make a mystic symbol across
short grass, some double twist and knot and the world will go to bits. . . . something is going to happen. ["Conrad Veidt" 34-35]

H.D.'s style allows her audience to participate as she teaches herself to
"read" the film, thereby demonstrating that cinema could indeed become
"a universal language, a universal art open alike to the pleb and the initiate,'" through its ability to engage the imagination ("Conrad Veidt" 44).

The third essay in the sequence discussing "The Cinema and the Classics" appeared in November of that year and dealt with cinema's move
into sound.[66] H.D. disliked this change because it enervated the capabil-

ity of film to suggest, evoke, and symbolize mystical reality. She questioned whether the possibility of achieving "perfection" in the medium was worth the loss of "vision" such contrivance entailed: "It seemed to me, astonished as I was at both (beauty of face and mellow finish of song) that each in some diabolic fashion was bringing out, was under-stressing mechanical and artificial traits in the other," she writes. "Each alone would have left us to our dreams. The two together proved too much" ("Cinema and Classics III" 21). This quotation reiterates H.D.'s resistance to capitalistic machinery in her *Egoist* articles, despite her later comment that "Peace and love and understanding and education could be immensely aided" by the development of cinematic sound ("Cinema and Classics III" 26). The real problem she identifies is that mechanical perfection distracts from cinema's great possibilities to provoke spiritual understanding—a point somewhat different from Bryher's objection that cinematic sound destroyed film's psychological structures.

H.D. extends the artist's responsibility of creating a redeeming vision for society to the filmgoer, who must be wise enough to accept and interpret the spiritual "vision" offered by film. "Isn't cinema art a matter . . . of inter-action?" she asks. "We sang, so to speak, hymns, we were redeemed by light literally . . . watching symbols of things that matter, accepting yet knowing those symbols were divorced utterly from reality. . . . Into this layer of self, blurred over by hypnotic darkness or cross-beams of light, emotion and idea entered fresh as from the primitive beginning" ("Cinema and Classics III" 22-23). While affirming that "[some] of us will grow in outer and in inner vision with the help of this invention," she nevertheless concludes that "Too mechanical perfection would serve only[,] I fear, to threaten that world of half light," the "mystery" that could occur (27, 31). H.D.'s response to mechanical development in cinema was qualified, for even though film was a medium that by its nature could depict and provoke an altered sense of reality, it also carried the possibility of destroying the mystical imagination that was a vital part of H.D.'s artistic vision.

These three articles set the tone for H.D.'s other pieces for *Close Up*, as she continued to assert the spiritual importance of integrity, clarity, and imagination in cinema as in any art. By seeing art as "religion," H.D.

allied her affinity for visual and linguistic clarity with a synchronic truth that allowed her mind to transcend a reality fettered by convention.[67] Her articles can be read as emotionally accurate lines of thought by which H.D. worked out her responses to film art and its implications for the mind. Her pieces for *Close Up* offer a context for the blending of cinematic techniques, religious vision, and mythic imagery found in her later poetry.

The writing H.D. and Bryher contributed to *Close Up* demonstrates two aspects of the thinking that engaged the modernist avant garde. One finds in Bryher an insistence on changes in human perception and values that could be brought about through educational reform, as well as an inclination toward psychological analysis of social problems, particularly as related to, and expressed in, the cinema. H.D., on the other hand, offered stylistic experimentation that suggested the mutual influence of poetry and film on each other, while insisting upon the spiritual qualities that can be suggested and encouraged by the flexibility of film art.

Both H.D.'s and Bryher's work for *Close Up*, then, can be seen to have added explicitly to the quality of debate that made the magazine a vital forum for the avant garde. The seriousness with which *Close Up* treated cinema as an art gained from Bryher's insistence upon technical skill, good equipment, widespread dissemination of ideas, and film's possibilities as an educational tool. H.D.'s film criticism, on the other hand, incorporated such elements of film grammar as montage and repetition to create a new critical style, and provided an emotional, affective dimension against the more standard expository and technical articles in the magazine. The role of the magazine itself, coming as it did during those critical years when cinema made the transition to sound, deserves additional research and evaluation; this must occur in terms not only of film history and theory but also of art history, art theory, and the social history of cinema in education and propaganda during the crucial years between the wars.

Finally, it is clear that both H.D. and Bryher affected the development of modernist art and thought in a number of significant ways. Each gave generously of time and money as well as writing; each strove to make connections between people, to publish important new work by herself and by other writers, and to work against the despair of wartime as well as the stagnation of outmoded ways of thinking. They were outspoken in their resistance to two world wars, and between them wrote creative and critical pieces presenting their hope that art might help heal humanity's spiritual and intellectual wounds. Together, they refused to accept the imposition of conventional standards on their writing and their lives, and opened the way for much that was new in the world of modernist thought.

5

THE IRONIC
"EDITORIAL WE"

Marianne Moore
at the *Dial*

Marianne Moore's work as editor of the *Dial* during 1925-29 has garnered only modest attention in studies of her life and art and in critical
examinations of the magazine itself, partially because of Moore's own
claims that she did nothing to violate the editorial dictates set out for the
magazine before she joined its staff.[1] *Dial* historians Nicholas Joost (*Scofield
Thayer and* The Dial [1964]) and William Wasserstrom (*The Time of* The
Dial [1963]), for example, have explored the roles of Scofield Thayer and
James Sibley Watson, whose collaboration provided the intellectual, aesthetic, and financial bases that helped the magazine become one of the
most influential periodicals of its day, but their histories fail to enumer-
ate any real differences between the men's accomplishments and those of
Moore. Although a few more recent scholars have found that Moore indeed put her mark on the *Dial*, the cumulative effect has been an uncritical acceptance of Moore's own "*The Dial*: A Retrospect," in which Moore
presented herself in low profile as simply a member of the editorial team,
conferring regularly with Watson and Thayer and doing nothing to upset
the *Dial*'s established line of development—a stance that has persisted
even among those writers who found fault with Moore's particular editorial procedures (Wasserstrom, "Marianne Moore" [1963]; Parisi 146, 165-
66 [47n]).

 Yet such insistence upon Moore's perpetuation of an existing editorial line misrepresents Moore's private perceptions of her situation as well
as the extent of her hard work and influence during this busy period of

her life. Moore's responses to *Dial* traditions and to the opinions of Thayer and Watson reflected her own strong opinions about order, decorum, and duty, which provide the moral thread traceable throughout the pattern of her work. Her editorial tenure with the *Dial* gave Moore immense enjoyment as an outlet for her critical writing, an opportunity to correspond about and arrange for the appearance of new works, and a chance to offer publication and critical attention to writers whose work she found crucial to the development of modernist literature and modern aesthetics. Just as important, Moore's position with the *Dial* allowed her to help her friend Thayer cope with the grave problem of his emotional illness: privately, Moore acted as confidante and mediator for a man she deeply admired, even as her tastes and connections helped to bring important modern literature to the public eye, under the guise of editorial collaboration.[2] Moore, in fact, wielded influence over the editing of the *Dial* even before her editorship officially began.

Moore was associated with the *Dial* by 1920, after she met Thayer at a party and he asked to see some of her work. Her poems had already been rejected by the *Dial*, but she complied, and "Picking and Choosing" and "England" appeared in the April issue (Stapleton 29). Moore's interest in this lively, eclectic magazine can easily be understood; she was a subscriber before her own work appeared there, and, well before her own editorship, she mentioned the magazine in her letters.[3] Her other early contributions to the magazine included book reviews and articles as well as poems. Thayer and his managing editor, Alyse Gregory, found Moore's work congenial and soon began to rely on her for periodic contributions.

It has proven easier to examine the stylistic affinities between Moore's poetry and prose than it has to determine the nature of her work behind the scenes at the *Dial*. Moore herself had much to do with this incomplete perception, as her editorial comments and published reminiscences offer little help in clarifying the policies and procedures of her position with the *Dial*. Rather, they seem deliberately to mute, or avoid, the question of what innovations she may have made during her tenure.

In her reminiscence "*The Dial*: A Retrospect," Moore indicated that she conferred regularly with all members of the staff throughout her association with the magazine. Her opening assertion seemed to promise an

THE

DIAL

NOVEMBER 1925

VOLUME LXXIX   NUMBER 5

50 cents a copy

analysis of editorial policies but then retired into the anecdotal structure that characterizes the piece: "As growth-rings in the cross section of a tree present a differentiated record of experience, successive editorial modifications of a magazine adjoin rather than merge; but the later *Dial* shared, or thought it shared, certain objectives of its predecessors. It is that *Dial* which I know best, and when asked about it recollections spring up, of manuscripts, letters, people."[4] Moore deflected attention onto her anecdotes and "recollections"—the "compacted pleasantness" of the building with its decorative details and its street vendors calling; the various contributions of W. B. Yeats, William Carlos Williams, Wallace Stevens, Thomas Mann, T. S. Eliot, H.D., Charles Sheeler, Georgia O'Keeffe, Padraic Colum, Maxim Gorki; correspondence from D. H. Lawrence, Paul Valéry, A.E.; and the personal and authorial characteristics of staffers Kenneth Burke, Henry McBride, Paul Rosenfeld, Gilbert Seldes, and Alyse Gregory. "There was for us of the staff," she wrote, "whatever the impression outside, a constant atmosphere of excited triumph; and from editor or publisher, inherent fireworks of parenthetic wit too good to print" (*Predilections* 105). Moore added that these "fireworks" also involved the *Dial*'s correspondents: "Rivaling manuscript in significance were the letters," she noted, "indivisible as art in some instances from their authors' published work."[5] This deliberate impression of lively exchange underlined the importance of the *Dial*, so that even as Moore effaced herself by posing as merely part of the staff, she asserted the magazine's importance within a contemporary exchange of ideas.

Of course, such exchange often means disagreement, but Moore avoided any suggestion of anger or schism by suggesting that the aesthetic concord was consistent:

Misunderstandings were with us in most instances, like skepticism that "doubts in order to believe"; and anything in the way of ill-wishing fulminations was constantly neutralized by over-justice from other quarters. . . . Those of us employed at *The Dial* felt that the devisers of the organization we represented could do better than we what we were trying to do, and we shall ever feel their strength of purpose toward straightness, spontaneity, and usefulness. "If," as has been said, "*The Dial* had rough seas to navigate because it chose to sail uncharted zones, structure was the better tested"; and I think happily of the days when I was part of it.[6]

Despite this conclusion, Moore evaded describing her own particular "part of it." In fact, although the concise characterizations in the essay are delightful, the "Retrospect" offers little evidence of daily practices at the *Dial* and specific information about Moore's particular editorial dealings is hard to extract.

"*The Dial*: A Retrospect" served to fill out an illusion that Moore had already designed. During her time with the *Dial*, Moore had kept Thayer on the masthead as "editor" until January 1926—well after she had taken up duties—and as "adviser" thereafter. She had also maintained the convention of referring to the editorial staff in the plural, at the end of the "Comment" section (whether or not she had written it, as was usual), and in almost all of her magazine-related correspondence, in which Moore sometimes mentioned editorial consensus as the reason for particular decisions. In all, the illusion of staff harmony in the *Dial* was preserved throughout the 1920s, in the magazine's pages and in communications with contributors; no overt acknowledgment of controversy or upset appeared in the *Dial*—although regular readers may have detected some disturbing nuances in Thayer's occasional letters from abroad, which Moore published regularly, as she did his poems.

While critics agree that Moore's comments and reviews are intriguing adjuncts to her poetic, no one has described how Moore took control of the editorship. Despite the fact that Moore had been associated with the *Dial* for five years before officially assuming the editorship, most scholars subscribe to the notion (derived from the appearance of mutual decision-making) that Moore was somewhat unsure of herself editorially. Charles Molesworth asserts that Moore depended on consultation with Watson and Thayer and did little to change their procedures, writing that Moore "was in a somewhat precarious position, because while Watson and Thayer obviously trusted her editorial judgment, she doubted herself. At least she felt that she had continuously to consult the two men on major decisions, such as those concerning major authors who were past contributors to the magazine" (217). A few pages later, however, he asserts that her decisions were important for the magazine and expressed her own ideas, and states that "Moore's decisions were crucial at *The Dial*; it was only with Watson that she would occasionally consult" (223).

Celeste Goodridge, also, writes that "[one] reason editorial decisions cannot be attributed to Moore alone is that many of the decisions seem to have been discussed in the office or were made in consultation through the mail with James Sibley Watson" (138 [17n]). This observation is qualified by Goodridge's earlier statement that "Moore . . . avoided giving the appearance of directly and publicly promoting her critical enterprise. This reluctance may be seen in part as a way of compensating for her extraordinary ambition; it can also be seen as another version of her desire to vacillate between concealment and disclosure in her art."[7] Goodridge does not apply this observation to the question of Moore's actual decisions in editing the *Dial*, despite her assertion of Moore's "extraordinary ambition." Rather, she characterizes Moore's editorial tenure at the *Dial* in a few sentences:

Although one might be tempted to link what *The Dial* published while Moore was editor with her own critical values, the linkage is not smooth; for Moore's own daring, experimental, eccentric, yet catholic criticism stands in contrast to much of the criticism published during her tenure as editor. . . . As editor of *The Dial*, Moore supported and did not try to change what was finally a conservative journal. In a letter to Saintsbury in 1926 Moore remarked, "Fortunately for The Dial I have only half power in decision, and often decline to use the whole of that." Since Moore was, by her own admission, somewhat detached from the editorial decisions made at *The Dial*, it is dangerous to assume that *The Dial*'s values were her own. [4-5]

In making these statements, Goodridge does not refer to the nature or implications of the unpublished correspondence between Moore, Watson, and Thayer, but bases her assertions on Moore's "own admission" in this matter—despite the fact that Goodridge pointed out Moore's reticence, indirection, and deliberate "self-effacement." The very fact that editorial decisions did not seem to be arbitrarily Moore's raises a much more interesting question of the reasons she collaborated (or appeared to collaborate) in editing the *Dial*.

Taffy Martin believes that Moore used the *Dial* to advance, in the contents, organization, and "Comment" in each issue, her idiosyncratic vision of American modernism (45). Far from assuming that Moore simply followed Thayer's dictates, Martin contends that, "in spite of Moore's own self-effacing accounts of her editorship, she rapidly assumed a position of authority that she used in assembling each issue" (47). In general, Martin decides that "Moore's method and her reinterpretation of *The Dial*'s mission is so subtle that it has eluded even Nicholas Joost. . . . Moore's 'Comments' were a far more imaginative and creative undertaking [than Joost believes]. In them she deliberately reversed the defensive and argumentative tone of the early 'Comments' [under Thayer]. Moore conducted by enacting in her essays the multiplicity and disparateness of the world around her. Moore's essays present . . . positive judgments that accept and mirror rather than attempt to diminish the fragmentation of the modern world" (47). Martin asserts that Moore "imposed her personality" on the *Dial* by adding her playfulness and "wit" to Thayer's editorial guidelines and by expressing her sense of modernism in the "Comments," and concludes that "Moore's quaint facade serves as an ironic cover for Moore's prophetically postmodern sensibility" (45, 48).[8] Her influence over literary history, according to this viewpoint, lies in her particular vision of modernism as expressed in the makeup and editorial comments of the *Dial*.

This opinion, while useful in revising the assessment of Moore's influence, nevertheless leaves unexplained certain of Moore's individual decisions as editor and her response to the power of that position. Moreover, it does not engage the reasons underlying Moore's self-effacement on the subject of the *Dial*, an especially interesting question in light of her later affinity for the public eye.

Examination of unpublished correspondence between Moore, Watson, and Thayer reveals that Moore's reticence was certainly not the kind of "modesty" by which R. P. Blackmur characterized her poetic persona. Her reticence resulted from professional and private convictions that together influenced her aims in editing the *Dial*'s pages. Moore manipulated information about her years with the magazine because she had decided to create the illusion of harmonious collaboration, which offered protection and freedom for herself and others, not only for Thayer in his illness but also for reviewers who helped to shape the *Dial*'s critical opinions. The history of Moore's association with the magazine involves more than the important modern works that appeared in print; it involves the indirect manipulation of power that often marks women's literary production. Her ironic fiction of collaboration has acted as a foil to disguise her decisionmaking, as if it were subservient to men's interests, when in effect she was promoting critical literary thought at the *Dial* almost single-handedly.

When Moore sent Thayer poems for the *Dial*, she had already gained notice in the *Egoist*, *Poetry*, *Others*, *Contemporary Verse*, and *Chimera*. The point at which Moore was considered for critical work for the *Dial*, however, is not easy to fix; her previous lack of success in marketing her reviews has been attested to by Laurence Stapleton (52-54). Stapleton asserts that Thayer had already asked Moore for a review before Ezra Pound suggested her in 1918 (241 [4n]). In her "Retrospect," Moore credited H.D., already a contributor to the *Dial*, with suggesting that Moore offer work, too (*Predilections* 105). Moore's critical appearances in the *Dial* began in January 1921—with a long, idiosyncratic review of a biography of Jacopone da Todi—and occurred fairly regularly thereafter. From 1920 through 1924 Moore appeared in the *Dial* with ten signed book reviews, two articles, eleven poems, and no fewer than twenty-one unsigned comments in the "Briefer Mention" section (Abbott, *Marianne Moore*; Joost and Sullivan, The Dial, *Two Author Indexes*; Zingman).

The earliest surviving letters from Moore to Thayer, which proposed *Dial* pieces by and about Bryher and H.D., indicate Moore's strong feelings about drawing attention to friends' writings that she admired, and link her emergence as a *Dial* critic to the development of H.D.'s and Bryher's reputations in America. It appears that Moore felt sure of Thayer's interest in new work and his trust in her own judgment. In 1920, for instance, Moore wrote to Bryher: "I should submit to *the Dial* with assurance, anything that I was thoroughly interested in and be sure of its being welcomed and read with enjoyment whether it were used or not. I am a little in doubt as to the exact nature of the editorial policy. I have not met any of the editors but Scofield Thayer but he is enthusiastic and I think he is sincere in not wishing to miss anything good."[9] In this same letter Moore mentioned other possibilities, such as the *Yale Review* and the *Bookman*, to which she felt she might send work. This sense of assurance Moore felt belies the tone of a letter to H.D. in 1924 in which Moore wrote, "I wish I could review Bryher's TWO SELVES but I haven't an undisputed welcome anywhere and just don't know the art of ingratiatingly confronting an editor."[10] Since later that year Moore reported that she had been able to review *Heliodora* for the *Dial*, one finds again that Moore's deferential tone about the *Dial* cannot be taken at face value.[11]

Archival letters indicate that Moore had certainly begun to do production-related work for the *Dial* in February 1924. A letter from Alyse Gregory in February 1924 demonstrates that the *Dial* staff relied on Moore for editorial work, as it shows Moore was familiar with decisions about content and make-up for the magazine more than a year before she took on the editorship: "We are writing you in extremis having just failed to reach you on the telephone, to know if you can help us out by writing two advertisements for The Dial. I am certain that you could completely outdo Tappe if you would. Do come to the make-up meeting tomorrow (Wednesday) at 11:30 o'clock. It is there that we decide the contents for the next issue of the magazine, and you could then look over the material and thereby get some idea of what to feature. You could also take our portfolio containing all the old advertisements."[12] A few days later, when Gregory sent Moore the April table of contents and "a rough list of our material on hand," she remarked, "You are our comfort and mainstay."[13] That Moore's work for the magazine went beyond creating advertisements into editorial consultation is further apparent from one of her letters to Gregory, in which she commented, "I have had two letters and two visits from Mr. Wrynn respecting the work which he expects to submit to The Dial. He hopes that I will 'not think him weakly procrastinating'! He has written another story different from the one which he first brought over and he has in preparation, several very pleasing poems."[14] Apparently, by the middle of 1924, Moore was perceived to be an integral part of the *Dial* staff, not only for her regular reviewing but also for her knowledge about the editorial tastes and procedures of the *Dial*.

By the time Thayer and Watson asked her to take over the editorship, Moore had been regularly reading for and engaging in correspondence for the magazine.[15] Moore accepted the offer but stipulated that she did not want to begin before January 1925. A letter of March 1925 shows

Moore's ambivalent feelings about taking over the editorship in a time of stress occasioned by Thayer's illness; even as Moore showed her pleasure at the men's expression of "confidence," she nevertheless claimed that her "most [was] not enough" to meet the rigors of the position.[16] Moore's hesitation at taking on what she knew to be a demanding job arose in part from the fact that Alyse Gregory, feeling pressed for personal time, had announced she would not continue as managing editor; therefore the clerical demands on Moore would be greater than usual, and her collaboration with Gregory would be lost.[17] Even as she expressed doubts, however, Moore continued to participate in the editorial debates at the *Dial*, offering her opinion about a submission by Ernest Hemingway over which Thayer, Watson, and Gregory disagreed.[18]

Moore had clearly taken up duties by mid-1925. One of her letters to Thayer (who had gone to Europe) in May of that year indicates the relative amounts of work in the hands of Moore and Thayer at that time:

I am delighted that you should have decided to use in the July Dial, Counsel to a Young Man. . . . Dr Watson suggested our using the Coppard story and said I might write to Mr Coppard that we consent to allow his indebtedness to us, of $37.50, to stand until he should be able to cancel it by offering further work. . . . I have declined with a letter, the manuscript which you sent me in care of Mr Burke. . . . I have written to Mr Piccoli, to Mr y Gasset, and to Dr Mann, speaking of our pleasure in their former letters and asking for further comment . . . and am writing today to Maxim Gorki. . . . Mr Colum and Joseph Campbell called at The Dial one afternoon, I asked Mr Campbell if he knew the origin of the phrase, "the creeping Saxon.["][19]

Obviously Moore was working regularly in the *Dial* office, looking after financial dealings and engaging in editorial correspondence and solicitation in preparation for her "official" debut in the July 1925 number. Moore's ascendance resulted in editorial changes that were both subtle and extremely important to the *Dial*'s lasting reputation as a preeminent forum for modern work.

Moore was generally compliant with Thayer and Watson's precedent in terms of such minor matters as the physical appearance of the *Dial*; she also preserved the impression of equilibrium among the editorial board and staff, writing to Thayer of the importance of maintaining "unanimity."[20] While unanimity implies agreement, it also suggests that Moore wanted to head off any disruption of her editorial control. In matters of policy and direction, unpublished letters reveal that Moore's concern for Thayer and her own ideas about the magazine affected her editorial activities even as she resisted Thayer's demands on a number of occasions.

Although Thayer had gone abroad for rest and treatment, his illness proved to be a continuing trial during Moore's editorship, but Moore was able to maintain cordial and respectful relations with him despite the strain he caused. She asked him for suggestions about reviewers, praised his selection of artwork for the frontispieces, and complimented his poems, asking that he offer them for publication each month. In fact, Moore performed a balancing act, trying to spare Thayer worry about operating expenses and personnel by writing to him confidently that *Dial* operations were proceeding as usual, while at the same time trying to help him feel needed by asking his opinions on minor matters and by assuring him that his office remained exactly as he had left it. The extent of Moore's overall control, however, is clear in her reply to Thayer after one of his offers to resign: "You had no more labour before than you will have now, and we shall now have no more than we had."[21] Meant as reassurance, the statement also asserts the extent to which Moore had taken over the post of editor-in-chief.

Moore continually assured Thayer that his opinions and contributions were welcome, but some of his actions upset Moore so much that by late 1925 she had already thought of resigning.[22] Of the problems Thayer presented during Moore's editorship, the most upsetting for her involved his abrupt accusations about certain staff members and his demands for their dismissal, due to his suspicions of incompetence and "disrespect." The turmoil brought on by these actions created an in-house crisis at the *Dial*, during which Moore acted decisively to reinstate and placate office staff members in defiance of Thayer's express wishes. Moore explained to Thayer that her main desire was to spare him the embarrassment and the negative publicity that could result from his actions, and she again stressed the need for staff unity in order for the *Dial* to continue. This appeal

Thayer could not gainsay without refuting his own involvement in the magazine, an involvement that at this point represented one of his few links to regular life. By appealing to Thayer's pride—the wounding of which had occasioned the situation—Moore disguised and protected her own ambitions by keeping Thayer calm and the office in good order. Her concern for Thayer's reputation seems to have stood alongside a concern for the efficient pursuit of her own editorial and intellectual goals for the magazine.

Moore was also well aware of the importance of keeping Thayer's name attached to the *Dial*, since his editorial predilections and connections had helped to establish the magazine's respected position. Moore may have feared that, if Thayer were to withdraw from the *Dial* (as he had considered doing, having gone so far as to offer to resign in a 1926 "Comment"), the magazine might fold. At one point, Moore wrote, "Do withhold in your December comment, any mention of your threat to withdraw your name, for we do need it. It is very hard when contributors come to the office, to 'quiet' them as Mr Burke would say—with respect to your complete absense [*sic*]. What will happen if you really withdraw the prestige of your name, I dare not contemplate. I feel that the magazine is going well and that a collapse would be insupportable."[23] Thus, in addition to legitimate concern for her friend, Moore's letter expresses oblique concern over the threat of losing work with which she was thoroughly engaged. At the same time, Moore's decision to protect Thayer's name publicly, which extended even to excuses she made to office visitors, involved the use of indirection by which neither Thayer's problem nor Moore's stake in the issue was declared.[24]

Another of Moore's letters casts interesting light on how she perceived her role in reference to Thayer: "[Your] name alone is support to us and if you gave not a single direction we should still enjoy as present lustre, the writing and other thought devoted by you to the magazine heretofore. . . . Our only incentive to continuing without your name is a belief that you will before so very long restore it to the Dial. I have no doubt of myself as a faithful ally, but I am not an *editor*. I shall most willingly write to Yeats and only wish I were able in some way to really diminish the hindrances you suffer, in not having a secretary."[25] By using the word "secretary" while explicitly rejecting "editor"—despite the extensive and decisive editorial action she took on behalf of the magazine—Moore expressed deference to Thayer, yet her remarks about Thayer not giving "a single direction" and being (literally) only a nominal collaborator point out the control Moore maintained. Moore's apparent deference, therefore, was in fact a form of self-assertion that helped her to manipulate Thayer.

Thayer's illness may have had additional spin for Moore because of her own father's experience of a nervous breakdown. One suspects that Moore's persistent conference by mail with Thayer and Watson was intended not only to keep the two men informed of *Dial* proceedings but also to help maintain Thayer's feelings of importance while indicating solidarity on the part of Moore and Watson. At one point, Moore noted to Watson that she intended to reassert "tranquillity," saying, "I shall be in nothing combative; but gentle and conciliatory"—a policy she was already pursuing.[26] It may well be that, confronted with Thayer's situation, Moore's response was to try to provide what she could in terms of reassurance and rationality, not only to help Thayer but also perhaps to assure herself on a deeply private level that she had faced the problem of another's mental disturbance as well as she could. In this sense, the *Dial* may have presented Moore not only with Thayer's problem but also with the means by which she could act to allay her anxiety.

Not that Moore was necessarily compliant with Thayer's wishes. A case in point involved "Leo Arrogans," a satirical poem Thayer wrote and demanded to have published. "Leo Arrogans" was part of the *Dial*'s extensive dealings with Leo Stein, described in detail in Wasserstrom's *The Time of* The Dial; the poem was one of Thayer's salvos against Leo Stein's ideas. The exchange over this poem demonstrates the process by which Moore made decisions in the face of disagreement with Thayer. In a carbon of a letter from Moore to Watson on April 29, 1926, Moore expresses dismay over Thayer's demand that she use the poem, to which she objected on several counts. The sequence of events described in this letter show in capsule form the process of her dealings with Thayer, from courteous disagreement through appeal, to insistence, and finally to decisive action. Moore wrote, "After Scofield cabled insisting that Leo Arrogans be used, I cabled asking him to omit stanzas 7 and 8. He cabled requesting that they be used. I telephoned Ellen [Thayer] yesterday, asking that she cable: 'Marianne begs that you make that one concession. Ellen.' But I did not ask that it be signed Ellen and it went without a signature. Scofield cabled today: 'Desdemona begs that you will make this one concession.' (No signature) I replied: 'Cannot publish 7 and 8. Marianne Moore.'"[27] Despite her sincere efforts to accommodate Thayer's wishes, Moore saw no reason to publish stanzas she thought inappropriate to the sort of intellectual exchange she was working to perpetuate in the *Dial*, and acted firmly to protect her ground. On the back of this carbon is another, dated April 29, 1926, in which Moore told Watson the upshot of her contretemps with Thayer about the poem, and also indicated how she had evaded Thayer by pitching her argument toward his concern over *Dial* expenses: "His stipulating the order of his poems and our arranging to have a great many pages intervene between the two sets of cuts necessitated an uneconomical make-up. He cables: 'I defer to you as acting editor. Please run dotted line indicating omission also footnote stating two stanzas have here been omitted.'"[28] Moore's appeal to the economic side of the issue allowed her to act decisively without embarrassing Thayer, by excising the offending portions and substituting dotted lines. The return of Leo Stein as a contributor in 1927 testifies to the success of Moore's actions.

In sum, the combination of compassion, firmness, and subtle persuasion that Moore used with Thayer demonstrates her concern for the reputation of her friend and benefactor, the depth of her own commitment to the *Dial*, and the need to protect her self-interest. Her actions toward Thayer carry quite a different meaning than the deference and acquiescence that *The Time of* The Dial asserts.

Moore's editorial relations with Watson were more standard; in fact, his courtesy and droll wit probably provided Moore with welcome relief and balance against Thayer's emotional outbreaks. Moore often tested her ideas on him, and Watson frequently offered his thoughts about contributions and topics. In addition to making suggestions about possible book reviewers and about editing to be done on his own pieces, Watson appears to have assisted with the physical processes of publication on some occasions. The press of work for Moore—who, as Joost and Sullivan note, initiated the practice of keeping accurate records of *Dial* business—sometimes led her to ask Watson to read proof.[29] Watson, however, generally stayed at his home in Rochester, New York, making only occasional visits to New York City, which precluded close attention to daily minutiae; his distance insulated him against the office drudgery and the countless daily decisions with which Moore was involved full-time.[30]

Taffy Martin finds that Watson's letters "quickly [became] merely informal notations of Moore's editorial decisions to which Watson simply added his approval" (48). As a consultant, Watson offered few surprises and a good amount of reinforcement. His relaxed attitude allowed Moore to maintain the polite fiction of editorial collaboration while running the magazine according to her own wishes. One letter to Moore, in which Watson suggested that Moore should not take his comments very seriously, demonstrates the difficulties that arise when editorial communications take place over distance and reinforces the impression that Watson's contributions to general editorial work were minimal: "I feel guilty to read that you had accepted the Cowley, which you quite properly put no on. I expect it is really nothing but imitative, and merely expressed doubts to give him the perhaps added advantage of your even more careful consideration. Maybe you did like it better, but I fear you didn't; and anyway please don't pay much attention to these question marks in future."[31] Watson made it clear that he expected Moore to do the careful reading and make the final decisions. Moore's apparent willingness to set aside her own judgment in favor of Watson's does not devalue her judgment but rather seems a gesture of respect, possibly tied to practical necessity in finishing out an issue. Coupled with his surprise over the amount of time Moore spent in editing the journal, and Moore's own remark to Bryher about Watson's being "permanently absent" from New York, these comments indicate that Watson viewed his own involvement with the *Dial* as advisory.[32] At one point, he even remarked, "As for me I proved long ago by a series of really bad mistakes that the editorial panel was not for me. . . . Would 'publisher' be better than 'president' [as his masthead title]? If it must be something."[33]

Watson also provided Moore with a safety valve for her worries about Thayer, and reinforcement when she decided effectively to abandon seeking Thayer's approval while maintaining the pretense that he was still involved in matters of publication. In one letter of 1926, she observed that Thayer seemed unable to stand being "thwarted in every direction": "It has seemed to me that Scofield did not receive well when he was in America, adverse criticism from me, invariably made in his interest, of things which seemed to me a little egotistical. . . . However, perhaps from this on, we ought to take him at his word and if he invites criticism, ought honestly to give it."[34] This letter points to the sea change in Moore's relations with Thayer that resulted from his attempts to fire office staff. Moore's previous decision to spare Thayer agitation was revised in favor of diplomatic honesty and a determination to do what she thought appropriate. Her explanation to Watson, however carefully worded, betrayed not only her frustration but also her decision not to rely on having Thayer's approval. Watson supported Moore in this decision; early in 1927 he wrote, "Why not run the Dial as we think best, giving as much consideration as possible to Scofield's wishes when he cares to express any. I got the notion that he is perhaps not so *close* to the situation as he appears to be, that he is more indifferent to fate than his language, always so definite, would suggest."[35]

Despite the continual exchange of suggestions among the three, then, it is clear that Thayer had little directive effect on *Dial* operations during Moore's editorship, while Watson served at a distance as a sounding board, source of ideas, and confidante. As Moore noted in a letter to Pound, "Mr Thayer has for some time withdrawn himself from social and literary obligations—has not been well enough to participate in them—and Dr Watson, living away from New York most of the time as he does, is not available. . . . My enslavements are self-imposed, but from inability to transfer them or ignore them, work for me is practically continuous."[36] Moore herself oversaw the bulk of the work of editing and production, which (despite the demands suggested by her reference to "enslavement") seems to have suited her desires exactly. Certainly she worked far longer hours than would be warranted by a part-time position, which the *Dial* editorship was intended to be—Watson's surprise over her diligence suggests that he had did not think of the *Dial* as requiring more than part-time involvement. He acknowledged the extent and individuality of Moore's work as early as mid-1925, when he wrote to her, "Never has [the *Dial*] been as 'creatively' edited."[37]

Her particular form of creativity manifested itself in distinct ways, notably in the increase of poetry and avant garde aesthetics that she arranged to publish. Her particular contributions to the *Dial* include gaining important submissions and publishing a higher proportion of fiction and poetry than had previously been done; her more subtle achievements include what Martin outlines as the expression of Moore's own version of American modernism, as well as Moore's manipulation of opinion and emphasis in calling attention to work that was setting the standards of twentieth-century literature.

As an influential position in the domain of literary opinion, the *Dial* editorship could scarcely be bettered, and Moore was well aware of and stimulated by the power she wielded over the presentation of new thought and letters. Moore's achievement in balancing diplomacy, intellectual variety, and a sharp taste for the avant garde is evident when one considers her editorial successes with central modernist figures whose favor she had to court: Ezra Pound and Gertrude Stein.

Moore's success in mending relations between the *Dial* and Pound, who had been dismissed by Thayer years before, was achieved through a series of small steps by which Moore overcame Thayer's distrust and Pound's resentment toward the magazine. Initially, Pound had written several items for Thayer and Watson, including the *Dial*'s Paris letters, but a lack of empathy between Thayer and Pound was exacerbated when Thayer refused to publish some of the *Cantos* because he neither understood them nor liked their method. The severe break occurred when Thayer fired Pound as the *Dial*'s Paris correspondent in 1923; later, however, Thayer claimed that the arrangement with Pound had been temporary from the beginning.[38] Watson regretted the break, although with his customary reluctance to speak ill of or disagree with Thayer, he once suggested to Moore that the fault was his own.[39]

When Moore took over the editorship she saw the opportunity to recover Pound as a contributor to the magazine. Moore had been in sporadic correspondence with Pound for years, ever since his initial inquiry about her work following her submission to the *Little Review* in 1918, and doubtless felt his contributions would add to the quality of inquiry at the *Dial*. She had indicated as much in a 1921 letter, which told Thayer that she had been so pleased with Thayer's article on Joyce that she had sent a copy to Pound.[40] Accordingly, in 1925 she apparently broached to Watson the idea of retrieving Pound for the magazine.

Watson, who had earlier decided to follow Thayer's lead in this matter despite being generally amiable toward Pound's work, expressed some caution in these proceedings. In a letter of October 1925, even as he told Moore that he himself would be willing to offer Pound a virtual carte blanche, he did suggest that Moore not request anything she would not be willing to accept without changes—as if to say that Watson himself were unwilling to participate in, or explain, such editorial alterations.[41] During this period other letters between Watson and Moore discuss asking Pound to write some reviews.[42] At any rate, Moore clearly decided to take the necessary action, and her negotiations resulted in the return of Pound to the *Dial*.

Scholars have referred to these negotiations as if Moore had entered into them naively, suggesting that, when Moore wrote to Pound asking for critical reviews, she "apparently did not know that Pound had argued with *The Dial*'s editors concerning the rejection of some of his cantos and that Thayer subsequently wrote Pound terminating his position as Paris correspondent for *The Dial*" (Martin 48). Surviving evidence, however, indicates a slightly different situation, as Patricia Willis suggests when she notes that Moore "persuaded Pound to write again for the magazine," although Willis does not outline the process by which Moore achieved this aim ("American Modern" 315). On October 15, 1925, Moore wrote Thayer about the upcoming *Dial* award to Cummings:

Dr Watson will write the award January comment and I am to review the poems. We wished of course, to cable Ezra Pound in accordance with your instructions, but I had written to him with Dr Watson's approval, asking him to review the complete Stendahl and had just had his reply which was that even if his relations with The Dial had not been terminated some time ago, he wished (1) to leave the writing of prose to younger men; (2) that Stendahl was not in need of an introduction. Therefore I felt prohibited from cabling, but wrote as persuasive a letter as I could and submitted it to Dr Watson. He gave me permission to send it, but said he thought that Ezra Pound would not find the suggested task congenial and that he really was very anxious that I should write on the book—XLI POEMS,—(and mention the green spotted book); so I am to do it. We are willing not to refer to you in comment if you so direct, and scrupulously to maintain your incognito.[43]

Moore's reference to Thayer's "instructions" has no clear antecedent in the two main archives. In the absence of unequivocal documentation, one may surmise that Moore was referring to Thayer's directions to Watson in 1923 that all materials sent by Pound, which he presumed would be classed as "European" submissions, should be sent to Thayer for approval, while Watson would approve "American" submissions; Thayer's subsequent incapacity invalidated this plan.[44] Thus, two years later, Moore's reference to "Watson's approval" deflected the appearance of her power as the new editor, even as she took steps to reinstate Pound. The letter indicates that Moore did know about Thayer's argument with Pound, and her preservation of Thayer's "incognito" suggests Moore knew that mentioning Thayer's name might trigger Pound's refusal as well as prove an embarrassment for Thayer. Her mention that she would write a review provided further diversion so that her solicitation could continue.

In writing to Pound, Moore needed to be even more disarming, approaching the topic of contributing to the *Dial* from the flank and showing that Moore was well aware of a strong rift between Pound and the *Dial*. It is clear that she chose to meet the problem by appealing to Pound's dedication to promoting others' writing as well as to his continuing work on the *Cantos*:

The "fashion["] of R. C. Dunning's poems in the April number of POETRY is very pleasing and we might care to publish something of his, but we should care yet more to publish some of your own poems. . . . I wonder if you would not be willing to send us, to be published in connection with work by Dunning, an article upon him, or upon him and the work of others? . . . [If] you positively wish not to write for The Dial, we can but acquiesce; but I build upon the hope that your lack of interest is not fundamental.

The need for doing importantly, important work, has frequently brought you to my mind; Dr Watson was pleased last June when Mr Wescott asked if he might write upon your Cantos; and Mr Thayer wrote from Germany some time ago, suggesting that we ask you to write for us. (He had not known of Dr Watson's and my having asked if you would review for us, the Stendahl.) If our suggestion that you write for us a criticism of Ralph Dunning, of Ralph Dunning and others, or merely of others, is uncongenial to you, is there not some other subject of aesthetic import—of Italian or general interest—upon which you will write for us? It seems to me as hazardous to entrust prose to "younger men" as it is to entrust to them, verse.[45]

Moore evaded the issue of discord between Pound and the *Dial* by implying that Watson and Thayer not only agreed to but also hoped for Pound's return as a "guide" for "younger" writers, thereby deflecting Pound's ire and indicating that his work would be accepted. With small chance of Pound hearing directly from Thayer, hers was a calculated risk.

As Martin repeats the story, Pound did not answer for a year and then wrote an angry reply, in which he asked Moore if she had any idea about why he had split with the *Dial* (48). Despite the indications of her earlier letter to Pound, Moore's later answer disclaims knowledge of any specific problem between him and the *Dial* and reiterates the assurance of harmony on the magazine's part anent Pound's work:

In answer to your letter of February 9th, I may say that I have no precise knowledge of past correspondence between you and The Dial. Nevertheless I feel that the invitation that I extended to you was entirely supported by interest on Mr Thayer's part when he was in New York for a short time last fall, upon my proposing that we request poems from you. And before that, upon my coming to the office, Doctor Watson expressed interest in your poetry, and not long ago when he was in town, was again quite positive in his friendliness—from an editorial point of view.

Perhaps I am criminal in liking some things better than others—even by an author for whose work I have unqualified enthusiasm; and I feel that individuals may sometimes publish what magazines may not. But I have always read your work with delight. Accordingly to have none of it to publish since I have been associated with The Dial has been to me a real hardship.[46]

Having exchanged letters with Watson about Pound since the summer of 1925, Moore was reasonably acquainted with the situation, and her decision to disclaim "precise knowledge" may have been intended to deflect attention away from pointless debate over personalities and back onto the business of literary inquiry. Her reiteration of Thayer's interest in Pound affirmed that the situation had changed.

Moore's campaign at last resulted in the return of Pound to the *Dial*'s pages. In 1927, "apparently at Moore's suggestion," Watson offered Pound the *Dial* award, which could be given only for work that was published in the magazine during that year (Martin 48). The promised award, coupled with Moore's longstanding interest in Pound's work, provided a good reason for Pound to relent; he sent part of Canto XXVII, which Moore printed in the issue for January 1928, along with a critical piece by T. S. Eliot on Pound's *Personae* and the announcement of the award.

Once Pound was back in the fold, Moore extended to him the same editorial policies that she did to others, asking for changes where she thought they were needed, refusing certain submissions and saving others for appropriate placement, and (in answer to Pound's inevitable criticisms) calmly defending her choices in reviewers and selections, claiming that "we have no policy other than that which is apparent. . . . [We] are not willing to displace certain contributors that we have, and in respect to new ones, feel we cannot refuse or accept work until we have seen it."[47] Her reference to "consultation" as the basis for editorial decision-making served both to reinforce the image of harmonious collaboration and to reassure Pound that he was still in the *Dial*'s good graces, despite the occasional refusals of work he submitted for himself or for others, as demonstrated for example in this letter from Moore: "We are most sorry to be returning THE CITY. Arriving at our decisions as we do by consultation, and being predisposed to publish anything you might send us, we were loath to find THE CITY not really homogeneous with our plan. . . . The Lermontov we are keeping with the understanding that we be permitted to defer publishing it for a long time. . . . Please speak of anything that it would be congenial to you to review. We are assuming that it is your feeling as it is ours, to give space only to what is valuable."[48] That Pound's work was part of what was "valuable," Moore made clear throughout her correspondence with him as well as in the *Dial*'s pages.

During the last two years of the *Dial*, Pound appeared in almost every issue, with translations of Cavalcanti and Orlando, selections from two Cantos, two articles, and two reviews. In addition, the index of materials used for clipsheets shows that Moore selected passages from Pound's work several times after his return, to advertise the issues for January, March, July, and November 1928, and January 1929 (Joost and Sullivan, The Dial 47). It is clear that Moore appreciated Pound's work and did not pass up the chance to advertise his return to her *Dial*.

The retrieval of Pound demonstrates Moore's diplomacy in psychological maneuvering around the mercurial natures of Pound and Thayer. Moore, like Pound, knew what she wanted for the magazine, and one of the things she wanted was input from this important literary figure. Her persuasive talents allowed her to keep Pound interested as a contributor to and solicitor for the *Dial* without compromising Moore's editorial standards. Her mediation directly improved Pound's visibility on the American literary scene during the late 1920s, providing him with an audience and a small but regular income.

Another example of Moore's mastery of editorial tact and determination can be found in her requests for work from Gertrude Stein. Stein's difficult and expansive writing style had been misunderstood by many, yet in her work Moore recognized qualities truly important to the development of modern literature. Stein, like Pound, possessed a personality that demanded a careful approach, and her appearances in the *Dial* demonstrate once again Moore's successful plan of taking a series of steps designed to appeal to her target, especially since Stein, again like Pound, apparently had no particular affection for Thayer.[49]

Moore began by reviewing *The Making of Americans* in 1926; in fact, she had asked to review the book for the *Dial* as early as 1924, anticipating its publication.[50] Having prepared the ground, she asked in a letter to Stein later that year whether the magazine could publish "Composition as Explanation" in the November issue, and requested material for a contributor's note. The final paragraph of this letter shows Moore's particular skill in carefully phrased praise, here used to prepare the way for soliciting work from Stein in the future: "The Letter which I received from you was a very great pleasure. The reading of THE MAKING OF AMERICANS was one of the most eager and enriching experiences that I have ever had and uncontent as I was with my comment upon it that the review could at all meet with your acceptance enhanced the pleasure which I already owed to you."[51]

Moore built on the appreciative tone of her earlier exchange with Stein in another letter, dated March 4, 1927:

It is good of you to be willing to have work of yours in *The Dial* and in thinking back to *The Making of Americans*, I cannot but wonder if you have some pages you could give us, at all analogous to those descriptive of the Hersland's home and their hedge of roses, or of Philip Redfern at Earnham College? If I seem too particular in my appreciation, I hope you will pardon the enthusiasm of one who greatly admires *The Making of Americans.*

We are just now, not at liberty to offer very abundant space; neither are we willing to set a limit on anything you might wish to give us. That you may see the length of our prose pieces, I am sending you a representative issue of *The Dial.*[52]

Moore was familiar not only with Stein's writing but also with the vicissitudes of publication that Stein had suffered—and promulgated—up to this point in her career. She was well aware of the problems that had attended publication of *The Making of Americans* and was clearly balancing both the exigencies of the *Dial* and Stein's feelings. From this letter, one may decide that Moore, like other editors, was concerned about the length and style of some of Stein's pieces; her admiring phrases about one section of Stein's magnum opus suggest, in a reasonable manner that could hardly give offense, the type of contribution that would be acceptable. By creating a positive atmostphere toward a certain type of work, Moore obliquely directed Stein away from making a contribution Moore might have to refuse.

Despite her genuine appreciation for Stein's work, however, Moore had no intention of altering her editorial parameters if a piece did not seem usable either in terms of taste or of space. A letter to Stein written a month later demonstrates Moore's diplomatic firmness:

It is a happiness to us indeed, that you should grant us these pages of *A Long Gay Book.* Have you sufficient patience with magazines to know that this delight is genuine, and yet that we can wish to omit a portion? Is it out of the question to suggest that you allow us to stop on page 2, with the sentence, "It is something to have a baby come into the world through them. It is nothing just to be one." and continue on page 6: "In this book there will be discussion of pairs of people and their relation,"? I am hoping that you have a duplicate of the manuscript, that you may see just what we are asking? We should willingly send to you the copy that we have.[53]

Pitching her letter to the character of its recipient, Moore began with the praise that Stein (according to some commentators) demanded, before moving into editorial suggestion using only positive language and avoiding any statement that would give a critical reason for the excision. As well, by pointing to certain passages, Moore suggested her own tastes in this sort of experimental writing. By asking for changes Moore demonstrated her editorial prerogative in making the *Dial* exactly what she wanted, with each piece—however distinctive—showing the best writing possible while maintaining the magazine's range of interests.

Moore's successful handling of Stein is apparent in Stein's several appearances in the *Dial*, as well as in the continued cordiality between the two women, which allowed Moore to solicit another piece from Stein in one deft letter in 1928: "We hesitate to ask you to send us pages of *Lucy Church Amiably*, since we feel we must, even in the instance of highly perfected art, select. If these pages are analogous to those in *An American Family* about 'roses at the Herslands', 'the Dehning house', or 'a college of the west', I can scarcely support such deprivation as their loss is, to me personally."[54] Moore wrote as if asking a favor for which she could barely hope. The balance between praise and editorial assertiveness once more directed Stein gently toward offering the sort of writing Moore felt was appropriate to the *Dial*.

Moore's success in wooing Stein for publication was notable considering the appearance in the *Dial* of "Leo Arrogans." Although Gertrude Stein did not get along well with her brother, she could not have missed this exchange, coming as it did in the midst of Moore's efforts on her behalf. Moore's insistence over "Leo Arrogans" relates to the firmness and initiative she showed in actually editing submissions. Moore's decision to suggest alterations in contributions by Pound and Stein, as by other writers, reflects her treatment of her own writing and her affection for precise detail. These suggestions point to the perpetual editorial dilemma between encouraging artistic freedom and serving as an indispensible reader through whom any writerly imprecisions might be caught. Moore's decision to presume meant that she intended to rely on editorial skill and taste, and, as Martin notes, "sometimes led to genuine thanks from the authors in question" (44). Moore's choices, in fact, resulted in the acceptance of material for the *Dial* that might otherwise have gone unpublished, and are an obvious aspect of the power she assumed by manipulating the magazine's contents.

When Moore suggested certain alterations to Pound in 1928, for example, she "indicated to him the exact cuts by mail, with an opportunity
to improve," as Molesworth puts it. "Since the piece was slated for the
July issue, it is safe to assume she thought he would agree with her
recommendations" (221). The short time frame indicates not only that
Moore thought he would approve but also that she used her prerogative
boldly. Moore's editing of submissions, in fact, was probably the most
obvious change in "policy" and shows her taste for precision and control;
it also clearly indicates that Watson and Thayer's status was advisory. In
fact, Moore's mention that the two men had disposed of rather than altered submissions before her tenure suggests that their shared editorship
had been based on cautious consensus rather than serious engagement
with the materials. At one early point, Thayer wrote Moore that he felt
she "should treat the contributor and his contribution—once accepted—
more *cavalierly*."[55]

Moore's decision to intercede also represents a dialectic between
Moore's artistic self-assurance and her sense of an individual's integrity.
In a 1926 reply to Robert Hillyer, who had cited Moore's "very careful
editing" of his work, Moore claimed to want to maintain the "standard
and style of writing" espoused by Watson and Thayer but also said that
"they decline contributions rather than request changes, [and so] I am
exceedingly unhappy in harassing contributors, and in certain instances,
close friends of theirs" (quoted in Wasserstrom, "Marianne Moore" 254).
The term "harassing" may reflect more of Moore's demands on herself
than her requests of contributors, which her own taste suggested and which
were, in their eloquent politeness, far from what Moore terms "quarrel-
some." Certainly Melville Cane depicted himself as grateful for the time
and attention indicated by Moore's editing of his submissions, but Cane's
voice has not carried the weight of Hart Crane's famous invective (Cane
316-21; Wasserstrom, "Marianne Moore" 252-53). It is symptomatic of
gender bias in perceptions of literary history that Moore's editorial suggestions have been seen as odious "meddling," while, for instance, Pound's
far less circumspect opinions have been taken as evidence of the acute
judgment necessary to goad writers into doing their most effective work.

Moore sometimes even refused or suggested alterations in pieces by her friends. In a letter to Bryher in 1926, for example, even as she discussed her interest in H.D.'s work she avoided an uncritical acceptance of Bryher's comment:

I am eager to see Hilda's book. Your preface—if it *is* your preface—I shall present to other magazines if we cannot have it for The Dial. I sent it to Doctor Watson and knowing our limitations was tempted to ask if we might ask alterations but my conscience tells me editors deserve nothing, if they cannot be thankful for what they get. . . . In meeting Ernest Hemingway who was here some time ago, I remember saying to him that I tend to be a bad editor for I am innately a nepotist and so keenly feel the disappointment of not publishing sometimes, the work of my friends and notices of books written by my friends.[56]

Her hedging about the preface was accompanied by the generous offer to place it elsewhere, if the *Dial*'s "limitations" (which were generally under her control) meant a refusal.

All told, Moore's decision to suggest varying degrees and types of changes in submissions, or to refuse certain pieces without suggesting changes, seems based on her thorough engagement with the submitted matter. She respected the work, offered praise and censure, and by suggesting alterations invited the contributor to participate in her response, which could range from delighted acceptance to polite but firm dismissal. The range of her suggestions—from changing a name to excising a stanza or even a large portion of a work—demonstrates that Moore was not working from any received policy of accepting or rejecting work without making alterations, despite her later claim to Donald Hall (67). This engagement allowed Moore to shape aspects of the *Dial* that had not previously been affected by Thayer's or Watson's editing, the better to demonstrate her idiosyncratic tastes and opinions—the magazine would reflect what she wanted and what she thought was valuable, like it or not.

Another way Moore effected her editorial power was through the use of anonymity both for herself and for others in the magazine, notably in the "Briefer Mentions." Moore could comment on current publications without seeming to impose only her own views; she also used anonymity to deal with reviewing the work of friends. For example, when Glenway Wescott turned down the offer to review Williams's *In the American Grain*,

Moore made sure the book was given notice by writing the review herself.[57] In some cases, Moore's anonymous contributions nearly filled the *Dial*'s review pages. While this fact may merely reflect the dearth of material at deadline time with which many editors have to contend, it also indicates the subtlety of Moore's power and effects upon literary history. Moore's manipulation of anonymity in the book reviews was a very real aspect of the power she wielded, and it allowed her to influence opinion without providing ammunition for charges of favoritism or tendentiousness in her choice of reviewers. Anonymity also serves, as Rachel Blau DuPlessis points out, as a narrative strategy that can "suggest a mediation between the poles of individual assertion and group similarity," as part of the "group protagonist" or shared consciousness that some women writers have used in order to break traditional sequences of expectations (*Writing Beyond the Ending* 173). There is a provocative relationship between the disruptive narrative strategies DuPlessis identifies in some modern women's writings and Moore's own manipulation of a purportedly collective editorship in which her real power took several guises.

Moore's general attitude about her *Dial* years, as privately expressed, seems notably different from that shown in her public memoirs. Her "Retrospects" depict a cheerful office full of intellectual excitement, while her private letters reveal the reasons for the diplomacy Moore employed and the strain she sometimes felt. Molesworth finds that Moore was wearied and frustrated by her time at the *Dial* (231–32). Nevertheless, she was also intensely interested in a broad range of ideas, and actively sought out contributors whose work she thought important. In a letter of 1932, apparently in reply to Pound's urging that she find a forum in which to continue her editorial work, she mused over editing in general in a way that reflects back on the *Dial*, in terms both of editorial policy and of design: "A magazine exists: to innovate or exceedingly emphasize. The editor should know how to keep contributors from becoming sharks in the net and should be able to actuate them to do better for him than they do for others. And it should pay for contributions unless it is the unique specimen."[58] In a later letter to Pound, Moore asserted herself in a way at variance with the self-effacing persona she would later create for her *Dial* retrospects in *Life and Letters To-Day*:

I feel cooperative if one has anything to present toward making art great, or keeping it unmuddied. . . . Every clear thinker and sound worker that we have, is committed to the procedure. You, for instance, have been untiring in producing best work. So has Mr. Zabel, and though I should never have thought to say so independently, I have myself—by intention at least, and it seems wasteful to let production be hindered by taking time to analyze the negative aspect of progress. . . . [A] dilemma that I am very conscious of is our dependence on publications that are less than perfect. An absolute chivalrous necessity compels the continuing to keep faith with a publication to the degree one showed it by consenting to appear in it.[59]

The "chivalrous necessity" that Moore herself demonstrated while editing the *Dial* more than kept faith with the magazine and its literary community. Her assertions and her silences, the "lexical restraint" that Marilyn Brownstein finds characteristic of Moore's poetic (327), provided protection and freedom for Thayer, for other *Dial* writers, and especially for herself. The cost of this chivalry—a cost Moore embraced—was the subsequent misapprehension of her truly extensive influence in the modern world of letters.

Brownstein notes, "Intentionality, marginality, and restraint constitute the moral principles of Moore's feminist politics" (328). Moore worked long hours and postponed her own poetry in order to achieve these qualities in the *Dial*. Above all, it was this idealistic aesthetic that guided the private morality behind the public forum over which Moore presided for four years.

It is clear that Moore had private reasons for obscuring her particular accomplishments during her years as the *Dial*'s editor. Her own penchant for understatement, especially in regard to herself, has often been viewed as a humbleness amounting to self-abnegation and has rarely been analyzed for its ironic or tactical qualities. Moore's own complicity, however, in the publication of her *Poems* (1921)[60] calls attention not only to the quantity of information heretofore overlooked in archives but also to the interplay of sincerity and calculation in Moore's correspondence. The suggestive new light that has been shed in recent years proves that traditional interpretations of her methods and intentions must be expanded upon in order fully to address the scope of Moore's life and work.

Moore's work as editor of the *Dial* involved public and private issues, both subtle and broad-reaching. One must take into account the evidence of Moore's manipulation of *Dial* history, which served to protect Thayer from harmful gossip even as it protected Moore from either gaining or suffering in stature at his expense. At the same time, Moore's experiences and artistic accomplishments, as manipulator on several levels of all kinds of texts, were affected by her acting simultaneously as editor, writer, and friend. Her impact on modernist literary history expresses her genius, for those who understand it, in an extremely satisfying way.

6

A DISTORTING LENS

Ezra Pound
and Literary Editors

Any study of modern little magazines and their editors—especially if those editors were women—must assess the influence of Ezra Pound and the mythology surrounding his many involvements with publications. Literary historians often presume that Pound was the most important editorial force behind little magazines, which is understandable given Pound's high visibility during early modernism and the subsequent influence of his pronouncements about what was significant at the time. But such a presumption simplifies and distorts the evidence of the many interactions of editors, contributors, publishers, and patrons that affected the development of these little magazines over time. Such neglect is particularly telling when the editors were women. Pound made numerous attempts to control the editorial directions of little magazines headed by women, and his statements about such magazines in articles and correspondence form an extreme expression of a male-oriented viewpoint through which modernist women's editorial and critical activities have often been viewed— or ignored. Pound's frequent use of stereotypes or gender-based personal criticisms has greatly influenced treatments of Harriet Monroe and Margaret Anderson, among others, in literary history. In fact, Pound has been credited with some important accomplishments that actually belong in whole or in part to women, including the editorial procedures of some magazines. Although the misogyny shown by Pound and other men has been generally minimized or even overlooked as a crucial factor in the politics of modernism, Pound's example demonstrates the prevailing ethos in which women editors had to work.

Of course, Pound's treatment of editors in general shows some similarities to his treatment of women. He expected editors (and women) to act according to certain roles helpful to literary men, roles in which either editors or women would provide money and encouragement for male writers, appreciation for men's critical and creative activity, and labor for the tasks of publication. Pound's treatment of those who assisted in publishing and supporting writers suggests that he thought all such tasks were of "lower" status and that persons performing them might benefit from his instructions but were unlikely to show better editorial judgment than his. While Pound certainly was not alone in having these opinions, his high profile in modern literary history requires scholars to look closely at the effects of such opinions on literary publishing.

Pound was occupied with many important publishing concerns, especially small magazines, during his years in London and Paris (1908-25), which encompassed the most active period of literary modernism in English. In the years following his arrival in England in 1908, Pound allied himself with, among other periodicals, the *English Review, Poetry Review, Fortnightly Review, New Age, New Freewoman* (soon to become the *Egoist*), and *Poetry and Drama*; among American periodicals, he was associated with *Literary Digest, Current Literature, North American Review, Forum, Smart Set, Poetry*, and the *Glebe*. Even a glance at Donald Gallup's *Bibliography* or the recent collection of Pound's *Contributions to Periodicals* reveals the range of his involvements.

Pound's actions as agent for small independent publications are especially telling because of the quantity of noteworthy pieces he helped to place and because of the unprecedented importance little magazines took on at that time. Since many of the ideas expressed in Pound's writings have been integral to an understanding of modernist aesthetics, his other types of statements about modern work have been persuasive to many historians. Pound was not shy about promoting his own influence. A typical passage, purportedly describing the "emergence of modern literature from the war years," appears in his piece "Date Line": "Emerging from the cenacles; from scattered appearances in unknown periodicals, the following dates can function in place of more extensive reprint: *Catholic Anthology*, 1915, for the sake of printing sixteen pages of Eliot (poems

Ezra Pound

12

Ezra Pound. (During the little Review's early years. Letter ████ undated).

Dear M.C.A.

The Little Review is perhaps temperamentally closer to what I want done ??????
DEFINITELY then (:)
I want an "official organ" (vile phrase). I mean I want a place where I and T. S. Eliot can appear once a month (or once an "issue"), and where Joyce can appear when he likes, and where Wyndham Lewis can appear if he comes back from the war.

DEFINITELY a place for our regular appearance and where our friends and readers (what few of them ████ there are), can look with assurance of finding us.

I don't know quite how much your pages carry. I don't want to swamp you.

I must have a steady place for my best stuff (apart from original poetry) which must go to "Poetry" unless my guarantor is to double his offer. Even so I oughtn't to desert "Poetry merely because of inconvenience.

(I have only one quarrel with them. Their idiotic fuss over christianizing all poems they print, their concessions to local pudibundery, and the infamous remark of Whitman's about poets needing an audience).

As to policy, I don't think I am particulary propagandist. I have issued a few statements of fact, labelled two schools an there has been a lot of jaw about 'em. But an examination of files will show that I have done very little preachy writing.

L a t e r . Dear editor, the one use of a man's knowing the classics is to prevent him from imitating the false classics

You read Catullus to prevent yourself from being poisoned by the lies of pundits; you read Propertius to purge yourself of the greasy sediments of lecture courses on "American Literature", on "English Literature from Dryden to Addison"; you (in extreme cases) read Arnaut Daniel so as not to be overawed by a local editor who faces you with a condemnation in the phrase "paucity of ████████ rhyme".

The classics "ancient and modern", are precisely the acids to gnaw through the thongs and bulls-hides with which we are ██ tied by our schoolmasters.
They are the antiseptics. They are almost the only antiseptics against the contagious imbecility of mankind.

Edited typescript by Margaret Anderson of selections for *My Thirty Years' War* from Ezra Pound's letters to the *Little Review* (Library of Congress).

later printed in *Prufrock*). Criticism of Joyce's *Dubliners*, in *Egoist*, 1916 [*sic*: 1914], and the series of notes on Joyce's work, from then on. Instrumentality in causing Joyce to be published serially and in volume form, *Egoist*, *Little Review*, culminating with the criticism of *Ulysses* in the Mercure de France, June 1922."[1] In this retrospective passage, Pound points out his own critical and publishing activities as being crucial for fixing the "emergence of modern literature." A letter of May 1934 reiterates this belief, describing "*The Egoist*'s having been necessary to print Joyce, W. Lewis, Eliot and a lot of my stuff" (*Letters of Ezra Pound, 1907-1941* 259), as if the *Egoist* had come into being for this aim, rather than having its own prior, independent purpose as a forum for feminist, socialist, and philosophical matters as well as literary ones.

Pound's inaccuracy with such details as dates can be found throughout his articles and published letters. While accuracy is difficult after many years, his errors are frequent enough—and occur often enough in favor of his assertions—to cause readers to wonder about the effects of wishful thinking. His own "instrumentality" would have meant little without the existence of little magazines and independent publications such as the *Egoist* and the *Little Review*. This passage gives no credit to the people who carried out the difficult work of keeping those magazines in operation, whose belief in the vitality of contemporary writing was as strong as Pound's, and whose opinions, efforts, and capital were derided by Pound even while he used them as extensively as possible.

As well, Pound's focus on male modernists presupposes that it was men's creative work that was important. His orientation toward what he considered masculine literary power is especially clear in the language he uses in a letter to John Quinn; he writes that in Wyndham Lewis's art he perceives a modern impulse representing the "vitality, the fullness of the man[,] . . . beauty, heaven, hell, sarcasm, every kind of whirlwind of force and emotion. Vortex. That is the right word, if I did find it myself. Every kind of geyser from jism bursting as white as ivory, to hate or a storm at sea. Spermatozoon, enough to repopulate the island with active and vigorous animals."[2] The language expresses Pound's recognition of an overwhelming—albeit chaotic—masculinity that he envisions "taking over" England, if not the literary world. Such language also seems to indicate male anxiety over changing sex roles, which some scholars believe produced a "sex war" between men and women. Whether Pound thought in terms of a "sex war" or not, the emphasis of his writings falls on promoting the writing and art of certain men he thought important, and paying little positive attention to women or to editors and publishers who were directly involved in presenting such work to the world.

In this context it is useful to consider briefly Pound's relationship with a particular male editor: Ford Madox Hueffer, later Ford Madox Ford, who edited the *English Review* (1908-10) and the *transatlantic review* (1924). Pound and Ford had a long, friendly association, which began when Ford helped introduce Pound to the London literary scene during 1908 by publishing the first of Pound's poems to appear in a recognized periodical and by providing him with connections and funds.[3] Pound did his part by directing new contributors Ford's way, and was one of the small group of friends who continued to visit Ford during his liaison with Violet Hunt, a loyalty that Ford reciprocated in longstanding support for Pound. Both professed admiration for each other's writing and achievements, and each published and disseminated work by the other. Brita Lindberg-Seyersted notes that their relationship included a shared dislike for academicism, an interest in cosmopolitanism, a passion for Mediterranean culture, and unceasing "promotion of writers and writing" (*Pound/Ford* viii-ix). Pound was influenced by the older man's ideas about using common language and writing about modern life, and may have picked up some of Ford's linguistic mannerisms and clichés; he certainly shared Ford's preoccupation with the lack of money that besets so many artists (*Pound/Ford* viii, xi-xiv). Their interactions were generally cordial, yet Pound's treatment of Ford also displays characteristics that illuminate Pound's attitude toward editors who were women. Pound's relations with Ford reflect a belief in masculine literary authority and a disdain for certain duties in literary production that seemed to be linked with "women's roles" in general.

Pound early in his career looked to Ford as an example of the ideal "man of letters" who wrote and lived in the thick of London's literary society. Ford knew a number of established writers, including G. K. Chesterton, Joseph Conrad, Thomas Hardy, Henry James, and H. G. Wells, and was able to solicit enough good material to make a very impressive debut as editor of the *English Review*. Although Ford's career there spanned just over a year, Pound admired Ford's ability to attract fine writing to the journal and his ability quickly to detect such work—as with his legendary acceptance of D. H. Lawrence's "Odour of Chrysanthemums" after only a brief glance. Pound also proposed Ford as one of the judges for a yearly poetry prize that Pound had suggested Amy Lowell should institute (*Letters of Ezra Pound, 1907-1941* 121-22). It seems clear that Pound took a lesson from Ford's many useful literary connections and believed, as did Ford, that the editor's position should command respect and confer power in the literary community.

Pound's attitude toward Ford was, nevertheless, a complicated matter. Despite his admiration, Pound could be dismissive and critical of Ford, writing equivocal reviews of Ford's writing and saying unpleasant things about him behind his back. Lindberg-Seyersted notes that Pound made fun of some of Ford's characteristics (*Pound/Ford* 22); in his correspondence, Pound called Ford "Fat Madox Hueffer" in a 1919 letter to William Carlos Williams and complained to John Quinn that "Hueffer on [Henry] James spatters on for 45 pages of unnecessary writing before he gets started" (*Letters of Ezra Pound, 1907-1941* 145, 137).

Pound was more interested in Ford's influence and ideas than in his poetry and prose; his reviews of books by Ford in *Poetry Review*, March 1912, and the *New Freewoman*, 15 December 1913, made it clear that Pound had mixed feelings about Ford's writing. Years later, in 1937, Pound made several comments in his letters that revealed his ambivalent attitude toward Ford and, at times, placed Ford's value implicitly in terms of his connection to Pound. In a letter to Ronald Duncan in January of that year, Pound noted Ford's accomplishment in having coordinated several "stratified groups" to provide the intellectual basis for the *English Review* but also remarked that he was "unbusinesslike" (*Letters of Ezra Pound, 1907-1941* 287). The following July Pound wrote to Michael Roberts that Ford had been the "man who did the *work* for English writing" in the *English Review,* but went on:

The old crusted lice and advocates of corpse language knew that *The English Review* existed. You ought for sake of perspective to read through the whole of *The Eng. Rev.* files for the first two years. I mean for as long as Ford had it. Until you have done that, you will be prey to superstition. You won't know what *was*, and you will consider that Hulme or *any* of the chaps of my generation invented the moon and preceded Galileo's use of the telescope.

Don't think that I read *The Eng. Rev.* then. I did *not* lie down with the Wells or read *Tono Bungay*. Nothing to be proud of, but so was it. [*Letters of Ezra Pound, 1907-1941* 296]

This recommendation of the *English Review* seems predicated not upon Ford's accomplishment in bridging the Edwardian and modernist literary periods but upon Pound's idea that the magazine would be useful as instructional material showing the revolutionary nature of writing done by "chaps" of Pound's "generation"—a reading that basically calls attention back to Pound. Pound's admiration for Ford's editing may have arisen from his perceptions of Ford as an editor who wanted to shake up London's literary scene by helping to promote new styles of writing with which Pound was involved. Ford's success, in short, was useful to Pound's own ambitions and those of other literary men.

Pound tried to make Ford useful to his own aims in other ways. At one point in 1913 during Pound's volatile relationship with *Poetry*, for instance, he resigned and suggested that Ford should take his place. While this act may be read as deference to someone whose ideas and editorial acumen Pound admired, it may also be seen as Pound's attempt to break free of his obligations to *Poetry* while still retaining an authoritative masculine voice (with whose ideas Pound was in sympathy) to deal with Monroe and Henderson—Ford in effect taking care of Pound's business. Ford wrote Harriet Monroe a good-humored letter fending off the proposal of his succession, noting rather tellingly that if he did accept, "that energetic poet [Pound] would sit on my head and hammer me till I did exactly what he wanted and the result would be exactly the same except that I should be like the green baize office door that every one kicks in going in or out" (*Pound/Ford* 21). Clearly Ford had some reservations of his own about his relationship with Pound.

Pound also helped Ford found the *transatlantic review* because he apparently "was eager to secure a dependable and tolerant outlet where he could publish at will" (*Pound/Ford* 73, 75), an outlet he had tried to find several times before. Pound was not the only important contributor to the magazine, which published Djuna Barnes, John Dos Passos, Ernest Hemingway, James Joyce, Gertrude Stein, and William Carlos Williams. Aside from offering work, Pound did not do much to help the magazine after it was launched despite the fact that he was one of its directors. He may have lost interest in the review because Ford essentially continued to support an older literary tradition that did not appeal much to Pound. Ford himself was pleased to resume the prestige of editorship and enjoyed being in the thick of Parisian society for a time. But scanty finances plagued this magazine as they had the *English Review*, and Ford's correspondence with Pound asking for advice and empowerment to act betrayed impatience with Pound's absence; Pound himself wrote wryly to his father not to invest any money in the *transatlantic review*, which folded at the end of 1924 (*Pound/Ford* 75-78). As with the *English Review*, Ford's editorship ended ingloriously in a welter of financial problems, from which Pound no doubt drew another lesson.

Both men apparently believed that an editor ought to be an arbiter of ideas who should not be deflected by mundane matters of production, including any difficulties posed by funding deficits. Both men desired the recognition and power attached to editorship and looked for other people (often women) to deal with running magazine offices, doing setup and proofreading, providing operating funds, handling correspondence, and so forth. Arthur Mizener notes that Ford, in editing the *transatlantic review*, hoped to reestablish himself as "the Master" of current literary activity and mistakenly assumed that the American expatriates in Paris "would be delighted to do the magazine's boring chores while the Master designed its policy" (329). Ford disliked the physical minutiae of publication and asked other people to find office help for the magazine while he pursued contributors; Pound, whom Ford had asked for help, met a woman named Marjorie Reid and suggested she might work as Ford's secretary.[4]

Marjorie Reid, in a letter to Bernard Poli, recalled that

I was on the staff, at first I *was* the staff, from the time when the Review was only an idea in Ford's mind. One of my first parts as such was in bringing his plan to the attention of those who might participate either intellectually or financially and, specifically, with advance contracts for advertising space. Later on . . . my role was expanded to include everything from routine matters of copy and proof readings, make-up etc. to receiving some of Ford's colleagues, critics, publishers' and distributors' representatives and others when he could not or would not be available. One occasion when he was not available, I remember, was when he learned that he must comply with a system of detailed records and accounts with books open for inspection and audit. . . . I . . . set up the books . . . [and] sometimes wrote book reviews or brief comments . . . [and] made contacts with printers or contributors when occasion arose. [Poli 28-29]

In fact Reid "did anything from deciphering James Joyce's hand-corrected proofs for the printer, to discussing with a couple of French lawyers the ways in which [the magazine] might be breaking corporation laws, or making . . . afternoon tea on the office gas jet" (Poli 29). The movement of Reid's responsibilities between discussing corporation laws and making tea is suggestive; on the one hand, the fact that Reid made tea places her in the sphere of "women's work," which has often been discounted, while on the other, Reid's knowledge seems to have been vital to the legal and financial status of the magazine and its persistence in general.

Mizener's treatment of the situation in his biography of Ford implicitly validates Ford's and Pound's attitudes that the details of magazine production could be delegated to women: "Fortunately Pound . . . turned up a really efficient secretary, Marjorie Reid, who produced such order in the affairs of *The Transatlantic Review* as there was; it was not a great deal. 'I had,' as Ford said quite as if he had not contributed his share to making it necessary, 'to edit [the *Transatlantic*], put it to bed, see it packed in boxes, and delivered. The problems of running a magazine in Paris are certainly numerous. There are no efficient young men to manage things'" (329). Ford's lament over a lack of "efficient young men" effectively ignored Reid's ongoing and pervasive contributions. In fact the very range of Reid's contributions has been used against her, as the less important factors of her office work are assumed to be representative while more important matters of production are passed over or assumed to have been part of Ford's accomplishments.

Ford himself was no businessman; his dependence on financial backers, including his mistress at the time, Stella Bowen, affected his editing of the *transatlantic review*, which nevertheless failed as his poor management took its toll. Ford's attitude toward financial matters was predicated upon distaste for business details, a distaste that limited the duration and nature of his editorships. The problems Ford had with his magazines show some resemblance between his use of other people's money and his reliance on women's editorial assistance, a linkage one also finds with Pound.

In sum, it seems that Pound found Ford to be a congenial representation of masculine literary authority who also proved helpful to Pound's own career. Pound's retrospective comments about the "chaps of [his] generation" specifically link Ford's success as an editor with promoting male accomplishments. Ford's role as exemplar of editorial "presence" and high critical sense seemed to Pound to provide a good example of what literary men ought to do—enjoy the authority and privileges of editorship but delegate to other people the drudgery of production and the dreary responsibility of dealing with finances. Production work and running an efficient office, both Ford and Pound thought, were of lesser status and therefore appropriate to subordinates, especially women.

Most critics have either ignored the evidence of Pound's attitude toward women or have lumped it together with other evidence of Pound's irregularities and temper as an example of the eccentricities of genius. For instance, Noel Stock's *The Life of Ezra Pound*, like many other books, gives the impression that Pound was the most important figure in any venture with which he was associated, while Hugh Kenner has gone so far as to propose that the early twentieth century was *The Pound Era*. James Laughlin also has attempted to soften the perception of Pound's autocratic behavior in literary history. Over the past few decades, Laughlin's work in republishing Pound and other writers in easily available editions by New Directions has proven an invaluable service to twentieth-century letters; at the same time, Laughlin has attempted to account for Pound's treatment of colleagues and editors by presenting it simply as a harmless aspect of the man's brilliance.

In a collection of essays and lectures, *Pound as Wuz*, Laughlin briefly mentions Pound's editorial interactions, excusing them as evidence of "Pound's Pedagogy."[5] While Laughlin admits that "Pound usually tried to gain control of the editorial policy of the reviews for which he acted as advisor or foreign editor," the context indicates that Laughlin is apologizing for Pound: "His letters to Harriet Monroe, telling her whom to print are merciless. But Harriet's letters to Ezra show she was not intimidated; she gave him back as good as she got. In the end Pound gave up trying to 'eggerkate' Harriet. He moved on to Margaret Anderson at *The Little Review*. Here the pattern of the correspondence is about the same, though Margaret printed more of what Ezra recommended than did Harriet" (40). This is a reductive reading of what obviously were complicated editorial relationships. Laughlin does not offer a close look at any of this correspondence, nor does he refer to manuscript evidence in the *Poetry* and *Little Review* collections. Laughlin suggests his readers ought to assume an objective (and benign) context for Pound's work. It is precisely this attitude that accounts for the dearth of critical studies in which Pound's interactions with editors, particularly women, are examined closely, for good or ill. One must turn to the correspondence itself in order to assess the effects Pound had on the particular intentions of women editors.

There are some pragmatic factors—particularly the relative availability of certain letters—that apart from sheer literary power help account for the extent to which Pound seems to have controlled the critical narrative of the literary history of modern little magazines. Pound was a prodigious correspondent. Recipients saved his letters; hundreds of his letters have been published, and scores more survive in various collections. In contrast, with many correspondents Pound rarely returned the favor. For example, only a few of Monroe's letters to Pound can be found in the Ezra Pound archives at the Beinecke Library of Yale University, the earliest of which is dated 1918, well past the time of their most volatile engagements. Ellen Williams's book relies on copies kept in the *Poetry* archives in order to reconstruct Monroe's side of the exchanges. The gleanings of letters to Pound from other women editors are also skimpy; several from Moore to Pound also survive at the Beinecke, and Ira Nadel includes nine letters from Henderson to Pound in his recent edition of *The Letters of Ezra Pound to Alice Corbin Henderson* (1993). Such an incomplete record of direct evidence hampers the efforts of any scholar interested in exploring the development of these women's editorial sensibilities and inevitably invests Pound's opinions and actions with authority. Consequently discussions about Pound's interactions with women editors have generally relied on Pound's point of view.

Under pressure by these many factors, Pound's interactions with women editors have come to be seen in a light favorable to Pound, or to other literary men, at the women's expense. In part, of course, the prevailing cultural bias accounts for this situation; in part, Pound influenced those around him. One finds evidence of a defense of Pound's methods and a patronizing attitude toward women in other materials at the time. In 1913, for instance, Richard Aldington wrote in a letter to Monroe: "Of course it's no business of mine, but you know Ezra Pound does actually *know* more about poetry than any person in these islands, Yeats not excepted. Of course, he will insult you; he insults me; he insults Mr. Hueffer; he insults everybody; most of us overlook it because he is American, and probably doesn't know any better. On the other hand he is certainly the cleverest man writing poetry today, so you'd better do what he says."[6] Aldington, whose poems Pound had sent to *Poetry* for publication, stood to benefit from advancing Pound's reputation as someone who knew "more about poetry than any person in these islands." Yet his letter also testifies that Pound dealt with both men (specifically Ford) and women through "insults" arising from Pound's pride in his own knowledge, the same preference for instruction and pronouncement seen in Pound's comments about Ford. Pound's attitudes seem to have influenced Aldington to condescend to Monroe as a woman editor who should "do what [Pound] says" because he is "the cleverest man writing poetry today." The insult to Americans, incidentally, indicates the provincialism against which U.S. editors and artists had to struggle. The cumulative effect of such attitudes shaped not only the reception of women's work but also publication history and the nature of editorial debates over what was to be valued in modern writing and art.

Pound's attitudes toward women appear often in his published letters. In the *Letters of Ezra Pound, 1907-1941*, for example, he persistently refers to Monroe, one of his most important early publishers, as a "bloody fool," as "an old maid," "too old to learn" and in need of his own strong guidance, and as a "silly old she-ass" "with the swirl of the prairie wind in her underwear" (26, 138, 147, 157, 124). This attitude reappears in Pound's comment to Joyce about the printing of *Ulysses* in the *Little Review*—"in general the editrices have merely messed and muddled, NEVER to their own loss"—a comment that seems bleakly ungracious when one recalls the financial and emotional punishment Heap and Anderson took in printing as much of *Ulysses* as they could.[7] Pound was also contemptuous of women's editorial and critical writings. He dismissed H.D. by saying that she could not write criticism—although as it happened her sensitive and knowledgeable critical appreciation of Marianne Moore predated his brief review of Moore by two years.[8] Although Pound respected Moore's poetry and suggested to Monroe at one point that Moore was the only person capable of taking over the editorship of *Poetry* should it become available, he nevertheless qualified his praise by asserting that "Marianne has got the brains to edit (all sewed up in a bag)" (*Letters of Ezra Pound, 1907-1941* 238). Pound's exchanges with Wyndham Lewis show the men's feeling of superiority over the women upon whom they were, from a practical standpoint, dependent for publication—a factor especially important in providing Lewis with hope during his military service in World War I.[9] On the whole, Pound's attitudes indicate a belief that women seldom had solid critical or editorial capabilities, yet might prove useful as sources of publication or money for Pound and his chosen companions. Given such opinions, it is not surprising that Pound made numerous attempts to control the editorial direction of women's literary magazines.

When Pound was "literary editor" of the *New Freewoman*, for example, with responsibility for a page of work per issue, his ambitions led him to ask Amy Lowell early in 1914 and later John Quinn, the American lawyer, to provide some financing so he could increase his control. Dora Marsden worried that Pound wanted to take over the magazine and edge her out; Harriet Shaw Weaver had agreed to assume the editorship in part to avoid that possibility.[10] Ronald Bush finds that Pound approached the *New Freewoman*, through his connections with May Sinclair and Rebecca West, "with no little thought to his own agenda," a situation that demonstrated Pound's "will to power" (354-55). This "will to power" clearly emerges in Pound's relations with Harriet Monroe and Alice Corbin Henderson at *Poetry*, which have often been cited, although not usually with an eye to their true complexity. At the very least, two prongs of the

Poetry/Pound relationship have long been evident: Pound's many important contributions, offered in the context of giving "instructions" to Monroe, and Pound's unpleasant remarks about Monroe in his letters to her and to others. The criticisms of Monroe, examined at length by many scholars and evident in *Letters of Ezra Pound, 1907-1941*, utilized personal denigration as the vehicle for expressing disagreement with some of Monroe's actions and opinions. He did not make such personal remarks about Henderson and in fact treated the two women differently in his correspondence. He often told Monroe what he wanted done, whereas he would ask Henderson to do him favors. In both cases, Pound treated the women's editorial functions as a service to his own interests.

From the earliest months of his relationship with *Poetry*, Pound set out to stir things up. Interestingly, although literary history has usually ignored the collaborative nature of *Poetry*'s editorship, Pound saw Monroe and Henderson's interaction as a means by which he might wield influence. Sometimes he wrote to Henderson asking her to intervene with Monroe on his behalf, particularly in terms of restoring goodwill. He wanted Henderson to help keep lines of communication open while he continued to send bullying directives to Monroe. "I have just written a violent epistle to Miss Monroe, on the sins of American poetasters," he wrote one day.[11] "I entrust the negotiations to your care.—Do tell me when she gets really tired of tirades." This request was not, however, accompanied by a concomitant decline in the "tirades" that formed a good portion of Pound's letters. These included the assertion that what "Chicago really needed was *me* in some chair or other at the University or the Art Institute," and the instruction to "See that you get some more things from Miss Widdemer. And make her stop using the word 'pulsed' all your rotten contributers [*sic*] 'pulse' at least once to each page" (*Letters of Pound to Henderson* 8).

No doubt Pound's letters amused editors; even after many years his sharp observations and jokes retain their wit. Yet Pound's unflattering remarks about *Poetry* often appeared in the same breath as his requests that Henderson mend fences for him with Monroe. Pound was not above encouraging disagreements between the two; he flattered Henderson at one point by suggesting that she ought to "look after the [magazine's] style."[12]

Pound clearly knew he risked going over the line but was determined to push as far as he could without breaking the connection to *Poetry*, one of the few paying venues for new work. What Pound evidently wanted was for Henderson to smooth the road for him and maintain his profitable relationship with *Poetry*—in effect to serve as mediator—without his having to modify his acknowledged "tirades."

In his first letter to Monroe, Pound had promised to provide *Poetry* "exclusively" with "such of my work as appears in America" (*Letters of Ezra Pound, 1907-1941* 9)—a promise that would be hard to keep, as the evidence in the bibliographies for those years makes plain. Pound's intentions seem somewhat different in later letters. Sometimes he asked Henderson to place things for him in magazines other than *Poetry*, or offered work to the magazine on terms that were difficult to accept. In one early letter to Monroe, which she passed along to Henderson, Pound suggested that he should write a series of monthly articles on French poetry and asked whether Monroe knew "any Chicago paper or magazine that would print 'em," quoting his asking price of $100 each, or twelve for $1000, knowing full well that such sums were beyond *Poetry*'s parameters for payment.[13] This activity can be viewed as the natural inclination of a writer to use connections in seeking remunerative outlets, yet Pound's suggestion that he would send work elsewhere if he were not paid more seems to tease the women by asking them to place items that *Poetry* might wish to print but could not afford, and thus in effect to work against *Poetry*'s interests. This action suggests that Pound thought of Monroe and Henderson in terms of his own concerns, not as editors who were deeply invested in providing the first substantial paying venue for new poetry and poetics in America.

In 1915 Pound solicited work and advice from Henderson when there appeared to be a "faint chance" he would get a weekly. If he did, he wrote Henderson, "[What] can I count on from Chicago? . . . Mind I shall have the voice of Chicago if I can possibly get it. I shall make a paper where the two sides of the Atlantic can at last really converse. Do get me an answer as soon as you can."[14] This letter indicates that Pound felt capable of providing an international venue that would also, paradoxically, display the "voice of Chicago"—as if *Poetry* could not, although Monroe and Henderson had been actively publishing poets from "both sides of the Atlantic" for two and a half years.

Pound's determination to have publications reflect his own interests took several forms. Often he wanted an item to appear in the magazine without delay—without, in fact, the necessary lead time in which to set up, read proof for, and print an issue. Late in 1913, for example, he wrote to Henderson directing her to approach Monroe to "suggest that she print" in *Poetry* work by several poets he had just sent "*at once*. it would make a fairly decent number. There will be some *me* in April. & some Yeats in May. & possibly some Sturge-Moore. . . . The Lawrence will do for Feb. if it aint in before then. And thereafter what I send over marked definitely to go in. will appear within two months."[15] This disregard of lead time (and of the women's ideas about the make-up of these issues) is the more striking since Monroe had told Pound about the long backlog of materials she had for *Poetry*, which sometimes caused delays of many months before an item appeared in print.

Pound wanted his ideas put into practice with little regard for Monroe and Henderson's own plans for the magazine. A letter of January 1914 expressed Pound's private, grandiose hopes for *Poetry* in terms that disregarded its editors' intentions and feelings by suggesting that his discernment and abilities, not theirs, would raise the magazine above others: "Dont worry about the other poetry journal. There is no other. WE *Are*. . . . Now I must get on. to that Ars Poetica. I advise you to print it in *Poetry* . . . and then to have 50000000000 copies of it separately printed on thin paper and insert one in each returned msss. for the next decade. . . . I have no modesty [about] my belief in our usefullness. We can become so authoritative that *no* periodical will be able to refuse the work of a man whom we praise . . . and we can quite well afford to insult any one we like."[16] Pound viewed his own "Ars Poetica" as fundamental to *Poetry*'s accomplishments—indeed, as the best means to promote new writing. The extent of his egotism is clear in that he seems to have thought that the editors of *Poetry* would agree with his authoritarianism. That was not the sort of editorial stance, however, that Monroe and Henderson had in mind or had expressed all along in their editorials and articles. As for Pound's combativeness, it was certainly not Monroe's style to insult or overpower other people or publications; Henderson, on occasion, did use satire. *Poetry* never intended, though, to aggrandize itself through name-calling, even for the good of the art. Monroe wanted all kinds of good new work to find a home there, not just things that met a particular "Ars Poetica."

This letter in particular demonstrates the connections Pound saw between his own achievements and the importance of little magazines with which he chose to associate. He continued:

[There] simply is no one in America (or here either), who writes, and who has made anything like the study of the laws of the art. the fundamental eternal etc. in ten languages that I have. . . . DDDD——n it [I] can speak, not merely give a fuzzy impression of whether a poem pleases me or not, but I can speak with something vaguely resembling authority.

And this critical position can *stand*[,] *entirely apart from* anybodys like or dislike of what I happen to produce[,] in the way of original composition. . . . Simply I've got the artillery. You may—being on the spot—be able to arrange the position better, *much better* than I can from here, but in your campaigns and diplomacy, you can take a certain assurance.

There are probably, any number of greater poets in the U. S.—mute, inglorious, etc.—but in a matter of dialectic. I can take on the lot. and I jolly well know it.

I admit it ill becomes me to say so. [Letters of Pound to Henderson 20]

Pound's claim to have "the artillery" to "take on the lot" demonstrates considerable self-confidence about his own knowledge of poetry (notwithstanding his professions of humility), whereas his comment that Monroe and Henderson could "arrange the position better" hints that he preferred they deal with the production aspect of the magazine. It is apparent that his belief in the magazine's influence rested on the combination of his discernment and the women's support.

The gender-linked aspects of Pound's comments to these women and to Margaret Anderson lie in the distinction between Pound's desire for authoritarian editorial power and his distaste for a large portion of the work that necessarily accompanies editing. Pound made clear that his desire to exercise editorial control encompassed only certain activities. He disliked being "smothered" in what he considered to be such mundane "executive functions" as typing business letters and mailing back issues.

He refused to help with certain day-to-day duties even when a task would have been easy and logical for him to do. After a few desultory attempts he did not try to arrange advertising exchanges between the magazines with which he was associated, which would have saved them some much-needed money and which could have helped to foster goodwill and a sense of literary community. At one point Pound told Henderson, "For heaven's sake make your own exchanges direct with the English periodicals," despite the fact that he was in England, serving as *Poetry*'s foreign correspondent and making professional use of the magazine's stationery—and had written in the summer of 1913 and in January 1914 that he would arrange exchanges between *Poetry* and the *New Freewoman*.[17]

One quotidian responsibility Pound did undertake was that of collecting subscriptions and arranging for issues to be mailed (often at no charge) to certain people. He expended considerable effort in sending Margaret Anderson lists of names of those whom he thought should receive the *Little Review* because some of them might become subscribers or benefactors of the magazine; he directed that copies on "extra fine paper [be sent] to a certain sort of person," mentioning for instance Lady Cunard.[18] Subscription money was important to the *Little Review*, which operated on a shoestring, but although Pound liked acting as a magazine's representative he disliked the time it took to collect subscription money because it took him away from the work he wanted to do—writing and soliciting material.

Pound was interested in per-page costs and circulation figures as they related to editorial remuneration. He may indeed have had "great respect for anyone who [could] adequately finance a literary journal" (Benstock and Benstock 76), but his respect seems to have involved persistent attempts to increase his own influence over the spending of journals' money. He wrote to Henderson, for instance, early in his association with *Poetry*, asking about gross sales and suggesting that back numbers could yield some revenue. This inquiry underlay Pound's personal (and unrealistic) desires for the magazine, as is seen in one letter: "In two years we'll expand the critical section into what the *Mercure* thinks its 'revue de quinzaine' is, only we'll be really efficient, and we'll all be drawing fat salaries from a paying concern. Je rêve? Mais non. Ca va venir.. But never any more poetry per month. Higher rates yes"[19]—as if what *Poetry* paid for contributions could easily be increased. Pound also proposed that Margaret Anderson should try to arrange for the *Little Review* to make a profit from which he might be paid—as if Anderson had not already tried to make the magazine profitable (*Pound*/The Little Review 7). These grandiose proposals about quantities of funds had appeared before in his offers, to Marsden and Weaver, of John Quinn's money in exchange for more editorial control (Garner 138).

Pound's main interest in the financial outlay of small magazines was centered on what the magazines could pay their contributors, including himself as "foreign correspondent." Despite his reputation as an avant garde leader, Pound himself was always in financial distress. Although he acted tirelessly in writing and soliciting new work, he scarcely made enough to live on during his London years. His resultant attempts to extract more payments for himself, other writers, and artists were understandable, yet demonstrated little empathy with the actual financial instability of most small magazines. Pound persistently underestimated the economic stringencies faced by editors and became upset when they could not offer him more money. This situation probably encouraged him continually to seek new magazines with which to associate; it also created friction between him and editors, even those sympathetic to his aims.

During his association with the *Little Review*, for example, Pound had arranged with John Quinn that Quinn would provide a certain amount of money for Pound to pay "his" *Little Review* contributors. Despite Margaret Anderson's request, Pound refused to arrange a direct subsidy, although the magazine was continually in need of cash. While Pound's demurral may have arisen from his intention to protect payments to writers, his position displays less concern for the *Little Review* itself than for maintaining a certain amount of leverage. One of his letters to Anderson and Jane Heap during this time gives an idea of the frustrations editors faced when dealing with Pound over finances. He wrote in 1917, "Will send you £5 to cover subscriptions etc. as soon as I hear it {part of my fund} has been put in my American bank. [Quinn] says it will be on his return from Washington."[20] Having assured Anderson and Heap of his goodwill, Pound suddenly confessed, with the glee of a successful flea-market shopper, his sudden acquisition of a quantity of books from a London bookstall. "Staggered home with four huge folios in a burlap sack yesterday, result of walking about with 'subscriptions' loose in my pocket. Cubic capacity 10 by 16 by 10 1/2, weight uncertain, and no busses running. 1/4 inch leather boards, and about 4000 pages. *Some* raid." Besides the fact that Pound had vowed earlier, "All money from new subscriptions to go to you," he was proud of his finds and didn't blush to tell his (cr)editors.[21] Few fans of literature would begrudge him the joy of finding good books; nevertheless, Pound's decisions sometimes made life more difficult for those with whom he worked.

Despite his many suggestions to editors about the contents of their magazines, including urging them to squeeze as much work as possible into their pages (*Pound*/The Little Review 44-45), Pound was not interested in promoting or even reading most writers, whom he considered to be minor and who consisted for the most part of nearly everybody except himself, W. B. Yeats, T. S. Eliot, Wyndham Lewis, and James Joyce. In 1913 he informed Alice Corbin Henderson, "I think that *Poetry* should print all the Yeats and all the me it can get, and when it gets us. I think it should fill in [with] people whom I can take seriously, or who are at least trying to do honest work. En effet W.B.Y. and myself seem to have been shove[d] in with a lot of shisters and amateurs. at least that's the general effect. and provincial shisters at that."[22] To Margaret Anderson he complained, "CRRRRHist JHEEZUS when I think of the hours of boredom I have put up with from people MERELY because they have in an unguarded and irrecoverable and irresponsible moment committed a good poem, or several!" (*Letters of Ezra Pound, 1907-1941* 121). These examples represent a recurring theme in Pound's letters to *Poetry* and the *Little Review*—an impatience with a great deal of writing and experimentation that formed an indispensable part of the avant garde.

This lack of interest in most other writers is reinforced by Pound's belief that only the materials he had chosen could represent writers properly. He sometimes implied that, if he had not recommended a piece, it was not worth the editors' bother. At other times, he sent work about which he was lukewarm, admitting for instance to Henderson that work by Richard Aldington that Pound had sent was not particularly good:

"I'm not so stuck on this lot, I only think it is better than what we have been getting, or are likely to get from others," he wrote in August 1913, adding that *Poetry* "may as well use some" of it anyway.[23] Pound's attitude suggests that he expected editors to accept what he sent but does not give much credit to their independent judgment.

Pound also figured that magazine editors would take care of such literary housekeeping as responding to those who criticized his work, writing to Henderson that "I cant be bothered replying to the small fry tho' I was on the point of asking Prof. Alden [of the *Nation*] to please explain why he thought my stuff would appeal to 'the frankly licentious' rather than to those who were licentious without being frank about it."[24] In this case, Pound's humor somewhat disguises his refusal to engage the criticisms of "small fry." In other instances, Pound made it clear that he preferred not to stop to take account of criticism.

Interestingly, the women themselves would come to Pound's defense; Bonnie Kime Scott has noted that women's defense of men often occurred in the modernist literary world (11). Harriet Monroe of *Poetry* often wrote—sometimes in her own pages, sometimes to other magazines—on Pound's behalf. For instance, she defended Pound against an outpouring of criticism about his use of the word "dolts" to refer to the public in his poem "To Whistler, American," on the grounds of literary freedom of expression. Again, when Pound's hurriedly written "Contemporania" appeared in *Poetry* for April 1913 and generated protests, Monroe wrote to the *Dial* supporting Pound (*A Poet's Life* 305). Even Pound's public defection to become "foreign editor" of the *Little Review*, which was the last straw for Henderson, did not cause Monroe to castigate Pound or remove him from *Poetry*'s pages in subsequent issues, despite his very pointed remarks about *Poetry* in the *Little Review* of May 1917. In this case, Pound's appearance in another magazine to express his quarrel with *Poetry* is a matter quite different from his reasons for maintaining a variety of publishing associations, and betrays a lack of concern for Hender-son's and Monroe's feelings and their editorial purposes.

The editors of the *Little Review*, once Pound had joined their fold, also defended him. At one point, Anderson and Heap ran a section headed "Ezra Pound's Critics," which featured several passages praising Pound, including one taken from Jean de Bosschère's article about Pound that had appeared in the *Egoist*. Over the course of several years, Anderson and Heap printed a number of letters supporting Pound in the *Little Review*, as did Monroe and Henderson in *Poetry*. In fact, these editors' generosity toward Pound extended for years after his most active relationships with their magazines. In the first volume of her autobiography *My Thirty Years' War*, Anderson included portions of his letters to her—a practice Monroe also followed in her autobiography—by way of demonstrating the liveliness he brought to the magazine.

The women's defense of Pound was not unequivocal, though. Both *Poetry* and the *Little Review* included letters and articles critical of Pound, most notably Professor Hale's response to "Homage to Sextus Propertius" in *Poetry* in 1919 and Monroe's and Heap's responses to Edgar Jepson's criticism of *Poetry*, which Pound had arranged to be reprinted in the *Little Review* in 1918.[25] By printing both positive and negative materials about Pound, Monroe, with her patience and her "open door" policy, and Heap and Anderson, with their love for "conversation" embodied in the *Little Review*, emphasized the spirit of critical dialogue in their magazines in ways quite distinct from Pound's didacticism.

One of Pound's letters to John Quinn conflated this didacticism with disdain for women's literary aspirations and, by implication, for patronage per se. Pound obviously viewed patronage as useful but not as evidence of discernment or knowledge on the patrons' part: "I hope you aren't going to be offended by my remarks on artists and patrons in the editorial I sent direct to Miss Anderson. I was wroth with the editorial in *Poetry* on the same topic. H. Monroe seems to think that if her Chicago widows and spinsters will only shell out she can turn her gang of free-versers into geniuses all of a onceness. . . . I may have phrased it a bit crudely. But I think what I said is so" (*Letters of Ezra Pound, 1907-1941* 109). Pound here was trying to smooth the feelings of his own patron Quinn while at the same time denigrating Monroe, to whom he owed at least as much for publishing him frequently. In fact, Monroe's assistance to Pound in providing him with a forum for his work and his "finds" had helped build Pound's reputation so that he could later serve as agent for Quinn and build the roster of good contributors to the *Little Review*. Pound viewed money and pliability as the most important attributes of a patron; taste, it is clear, Pound could provide to "widows and spinsters" if it seemed worth his while.

It is also pertinent to note that Pound's expressions of derision for women are couched in the same language that he used about the United States of America—a language often utilizing gendered imagery in censorious terms. These examples attest to Pound's belief that his own ideas were crucial to the development of modern literature and that "America" (like Monroe, Anderson, and women in general) needed to be instructed by him. At one point, Pound commented to Quinn, "It still seems to me that America will never look *anything*—animal, mineral, vegetable, political, social, international, religious, philosophical or ANYTHING else— in the face until *she* gets used to perfectly bald statements" [emphasis added] (*Letters of Ezra Pound, 1907-1941* 138). Pound's willingness to provide "perfectly bald statements" ignored others' feelings and was often deliberately incendiary or provocative. While this provocation may indeed demonstrate Pound's position as an avant garde critic of cultural institutions, his message is diminished by its reliance on personal attacks.

Pound saw himself as trying to enlarge the audience and means of production for new literary work, but his actions in so doing created problems for editors. Monroe, Henderson, Heap, and Anderson in particular had to deal with Pound as a contributor whose diligent work in acquiring new writing was accompanied by equally diligent attempts to direct their magazines according to his own views, which did not take into account the women's own preferences and which to varying degrees enlarged or restricted these editors' work. As a result, Pound's intentions were often at cross purposes even with those editors willing to give him considerable latitude and defend him in print.

From the nature of Pound's attempts to direct women's literary magazines, it is clear that Pound thought of women as subordinates who could offer money, hard work, and approbation in support of literary men. Pound wanted to enjoy the benefits and prestige of editorial control without having to deal with the numerous less glamorous duties that necessarily accompany it. He wanted someone else to take care of quotidian activities so that he could more easily act as author, literary procurer, and pedant; this attitude indicates why Pound was interested in sending sample issues of magazines to, and in soliciting new subscriptions from, wealthy and influential people. In general, Pound's relationship with editors demonstrates his desire for control over the magazines, over literary movements, and over the public whom he railed against and continually tried to instruct. Though such attitudes are certainly not exclusive to Pound, he consistently indulged his urge to claim as his own much of the groundbreaking work actually done by women. Literary history has tended to pay less attention to the mechanical and psychological barriers that must be met in publishing, yet the encouragement of genius requires pragmatic results (the printed page) as much as a discerning mind in order to make a difference. The short life of Pound's own periodical, the *Exile* (1927-28), seems to have brought home to Pound the difficulties of blending an idealistic editorial agenda with the continuing demands of publication and the scarcity of reliably good new work. Humphrey Carpenter's discussion of the *Exile* captures the idiosyncratic and somewhat confused tone of the magazine that ultimately rendered it undistinguished (*A Serious Character* 458-59).

It is also apparent that a number of women's achievements have been credited to Pound in whole or in part. H.D. made the first real critical comments about the poetry of Marianne Moore, and Moore credited H.D. with suggesting that Moore write prose for the *Dial*—both activities that have been attributed to Pound.[26] Cyrena Pondrom has demonstrated that H.D. also created the poetic style that became known as Imagism and was the artistic locus of the movement.[27] H.D., and especially Amy Lowell, played central roles in disseminating Imagism through the *Egoist* and the anthologies of 1915, 1916, and 1917, and through Lowell's many lectures in America. Literary histories, however, often give Pound full credit for the development and promotion of Imagism. Although Pound early on gained a high profile through his and Flint's articles in *Poetry* as well as through *Des Imagistes*, the anthology was not well received and Imagism received its great boost in America from Lowell (Hanscombe and Smyers 200-202). In addition, many of the poems used in *Des Imagistes* had been printed earlier in *Poetry*—which emphasizes its importance as a forum during that time of experimentation—but Pound neglected to give credit to the magazine (Carpenter 211). As well, the numerous discussions of vers libre and Imagism in *Poetry* and the *Little Review* relied on many writers other than Pound, including editors Monroe, Henderson, Heap, and Anderson, and such women as Lowell, May Sinclair, and Eunice Tietjens, to deepen and extend that important dialogue. Pound's comments in "Date Line," as in other retrospective passages, suggest that his own efforts caused Joyce "to be published serially and in volume form" but ignore the dedication of Harriet Shaw Weaver of the *Egoist*, Anderson and Heap of the *Little Review*, and Sylvia Beach, publisher of *Ulysses*, all of whom at various times dealt with the extensive demands of getting Joyce's works into print—revisions, legal problems, printers' resistance and all.

Nevertheless, many literary histories persist in using Pound as the single lens through which to view modernism and its constituent publishing history. Such an attitude makes it difficult to imagine the likelihood that women editors of such forums as the *Egoist*, *Poetry*, the *Little Review*, and the *Dial* also were effective agents in that literary world, who in fact made use of Pound's services to assure a flow of avant garde writing to their magazines for their own particular reasons.

Pound's behavior has carried heavy consequences when he wielded it against women editors, whose serious purposes—not to mention livelihoods—have been misunderstood as a result. Such antagonism, or "male self-certification" as Sandra M. Gilbert and Susan Gubar have called it, is typical of modernist patriarchalism on the whole (*War of the Words* 154, 236). In this sense Pound's relationships with women editors substantially reflect the nature of gender differences in modernist literary history.

Although the postulates of French feminists represent only a particular aspect of feminist theory, they are revealing when fitted to Pound's attitudes, in which an idealized, sovereign "man" forms the central critical basis of discourse about modernist history and in which women appear as foolish or misguided figures in need of direction. Pound's language certainly proposes male power and privilege; in his assessments of modernism, he paid little attention to, or actively disparaged, women's activities and focused largely on male writers and artists. As a result of Pound's influence, it is not surprising that women have not been fitted into standard literary histories. In the patriarchal scheme Luce Irigaray describes, woman "resists all adequate definition" (26): "'She' is indefinitely other in herself. This is doubtless why she is said to be whimsical, incomprehensible, agitated, capricious[,] . . . not to mention her language, in which 'she' sets off in all directions leaving 'him' unable to discern the coherence of any meaning. Hers are contradictory words, somewhat mad from the standpoint of reason, inaudible for whoever listens to them with ready-made grids, with a fully elaborated code in hand" (28-29). In these terms, patriarchal culture cannot comprehend what women say and do; women's *différence* can only be seen "as shards, scattered remnants of a violated sexuality[, a] sexuality denied" (30). Irigaray notes that the "rejection, the exclusion of a female imaginary certainly puts woman in the position of experiencing herself only fragmentarily, in the little-structured margins of a dominant ideology, as waste, or excess, what is left of a mirror invested by the (masculine) 'subject' to reflect himself, to copy himself" (30). Pound's language about and treatment of women editors, in which his (male) authority is presumed to be paramount and in which women's work, if not actively denigrated, is not credited, stands as a paradigm for this sort of misunderstanding.

Since the critical and creative work on which modernism is based has been distorted in this way, it is therefore insufficient—although it is necessary—to continue to recover women's work and to reexamine Pound's (and other critics') assertions about it. Obviously a critical assessment of Pound's contributions to literary magazines, and to modernist literature on the whole, must include negative as well as positive aspects, and must take misogyny into account as a pertinent factor in the political machinations behind the written history. On a larger scale, the very foundations of modernism and the nature of critical inquiry must be questioned, dismantled, and reconstructed if necessary in order to reproduce the multiplicity of women's writings, experiences, accomplishments, and meanings in literary history. Once this has been done, historians will have a far stronger and more accurate basis from which to discuss and evaluate modernism in all its engrossing and challenging forms.

AFTERWORD

Further
Speculations

The magazines that women edited created new opportunities for their voices to engage in conversation with the modernist world at large. In contributing to ongoing debates about literature, film, art, aesthetics, psychology, politics, and war, these women also characterized and discussed themselves and each other. As well, these editors' and critics' consciousness about being women in their particular culture charged their work in a number of ways. Gender affected both the contemporary and the historical reception of women's editorial dealings, notably in the cases of Harriet Monroe, Jane Heap, and Margaret Anderson. Gender was part of the nexus of issues that led such women as Bryher, H.D., and Marianne Moore to use their publications as means to create and preserve a sense of artistic community in the face of varying kinds of disruptive masculine authority. Gender has been part of the subtext of women's literary works that, by depressing the value assigned to these activities, has affected their placement in the structure of modernism, leaving many women in the near-invisibility that has obscured Alice Corbin Henderson even after her lifetime of significant literary associations.

It is clear, from the range of women's work surveyed in this study, that one cannot conclude women merely reacted against men's works or against "traditional expectations" in helping to create modernist literature. The inherent dualism of seeing women's work as "other" not only distorts that work through oversimplification but also implies that it somehow is not the norm, somehow must account for itself, which is not at all the same thing as the bold or ironic self-assertions this study has discovered in the productions of women editors. Perhaps one reason critics have approached issues of gender dualistically is that in our culture, as Bonnie Kime Scott notes, "gender is more imposed upon [women], more disqualifying, or more intriguing and stimulating to their creativity" (3), or that, as Virginia Woolf proposed, "narrative emphasis changes when one focuses on gender."[1] Gender was, and is, more of an issue for women than for men, who do not have to prove themselves so persistently against social constraints, and although this situation is changing, women will probably still feel impelled to define themselves *as women* in distinctive ways.

Many feminist scholars have responded to masculinist histories by trying to establish a tradition of counterhegemony, through rediscovering women's works and placing them in a line of female influence. This attempt can result in the urge to reinscribe both hierarchy and selectivity and to gloss over the unevenness of the particular influences of gender, its manifestations, social constructions, and personal formulations; Cheryl Walker warns against the "tendency in some recent feminist criticism to focus on only those aspects of a [woman] poet's work which seem to suggest conflict with patriarchy" (8). Even the many anthologies of women's writings that have appeared in the past decade have often surreptitiously promoted the image of embattled women writers producing mostly texts that depicted heroic struggle against an oppressive masculinist world.[2] At the very least, this study has meant to offer a glimpse into the complexities of contributions that are not easily characterized, since they are collaborative, interactive, international, private, long-term, transitory, and grandiose all at once, but certainly not all premised on the exigencies of gender.

Still, theories about modernism that see gender in terms of oppositions are more useful to feminist historians than theories that ignore gender differences altogether. Many books employ the same few, familiar names and traverse a hard-packed terrain in approaching the subject of modernist literature, for despite the compelling conjunction of women's suffrage movements and World War I (to say nothing of sex-role upheavals in general in twentieth-century life), there are still a number of critics who do not consider gender to be a significant factor in the development of modernist frames of mind. As Scott reminds us, however, gender is a category that is necessary to any consideration of literary history: "Gender, layered with other revised conceptual categories such as race and class, challenges our former sense of the power structures of literary production. We suspect that modernism is not the aesthetic, directed, monological sort of phenomenon sought in their own ways by authors of now-famous manifestos. . . . Modernism as caught in the mesh of gender is polyphonic, mobile, interactive, sexually charged; it has wide appeal, constituting a historic shift in parameters" (4).

The overall sense of flux, anxiety, and dissociation that the early twentieth century generated can certainly be related to stresses between women and men. To attach the metaphor of "sex war" to the modernist sense of cultural turbulence, however, skews the reading of modernist works by presupposing a serious, even deadly, contest between the sexes that many people may not have felt to be the case. The limitations of women's roles in that culture, while acknowledged and depicted by many writers, formed only one aspect of the issues that writers addressed. As found for instance in the writings of women editors studied here, women's perceptions of themselves as inhabitants of patriarchal culture often aligned issues of gender with other matters crucial to their artistic agendas: war was such an issue, as were racial injustice, attention to ethnic literatures, the effects of propaganda and mob psychology, the intellectual bases of anarchy, public education, artistic responsibilities to one's audience, thoughtful use of cultural heritage, psychoanalysis, and the interactions between America and Europe in the development of modern poetry, to name a few of the areas women editors examined closely in their editorials and in the contributions they printed. It is clear that women editors spoke for many persons and issues not accurately represented by hierarchical interpretations of twentieth-century culture when viewed in terms of "sex war," or even of dualistic divisions in general.

One should not presume that gender is simply, or is always, a marker of dualism. To conclude women felt like "outsiders" from modernism assumes that their lives were entirely bordered by social and psychological manifestations of male-oriented traditions, an assumption that enervates their innovations and blinds us to certain observations. Clearly, traditional social expectations did not keep women from helping to create the new century. More accurately, one might say that traditional expectations prevented, and even now prevent, some readers and critics from perceiving the true diversity, range, and radicalism of women's lives and creations. It is far more helpful to note that critical parameters have been too limited to take accurate account of these types and varieties of art by women and men who have been neglected in the foreshortened terms of conventional histories. The most useful scholarly responses to the information presented in this study will be those that continue to investigate how the work of literary editing, and women's contributions to it, can help produce new readings and definitions of modernism itself.

Cooperation and mutuality informed the work of the women studied here.[3] Editorial teams were common, and while this fact provides further complication of the nexus of multiple texts, authorial intentions, and the passage of time that affects critical interpretations, it also underlines the problem critics face when relying on the notion of a unitary, ideal text as the basis for their formulations. Considerable historical data attests to the interactions between editors, authors, and even audiences that has influenced publication of crucial texts. In George Bornstein's words, scholars need to "ponder the deeper implications" of the dynamics of such interactive shaping: "the arbitrariness of excluding all but the final published form of a work, the dissolution of the notion of a single author, and the role of social forces in the literal constitution of a text" (3). Although Bornstein's comment is tied to the critical reception of the restored *Ulysses* (1984) and of Valerie Eliot's edition of *The Waste Land* (1971), it is equally useful when one reconsiders the ways in which historical assessments of modernism are written.

At the same time, the editor's job per se has rarely merited serious discussion in modernist aesthetic history, although it is a gate through which works of art must almost always pass on their way to the public. The power and discernment of editors and the pragmatic exigencies of publication often notably affected the materials in question. Modern little magazines themselves arose as a result of the resistance of established editors and publishers to the radically different productions of twentieth-century writers. Given this situation, it is surprising that much literary criticism of the modernist era has paid only selective attention to textual editing. Generally, critics' response to editorial prerogative has assumed censorship and has expressed dismay, as if the productions of the (often male) artist were necessarily impeded by (often female) editors' responses and suggestions for change. Familiar examples include critics' responses to Monroe's objections to and editing of poems by Yeats, Eliot, and Pound, and Moore's suggestions for altering work by Hart Crane, Pound, and Stein; Joyce's writing offers a case in point particularly with reference to *Finnegans Wake*, for instance in Harriet Shaw Weaver's dislike of the manuscript and in Moore's refusal of portions of "Anna Livia Plurabelle" for the *Dial*.[4] Critics' objections to these women's opinions display the same sort of authoritarianism that has dismissed women's works on the whole under the assumption that women lacked the intellectual capacities to engage or express the profound ideas men expected to find in their own art. Women faced such resistance and continued their work in spite of it, sometimes (like Anderson and Heap) audaciously flaunting their rebelliousness by playing with gendered stereotypes, sometimes (like Moore and Monroe) keeping a lower, more "feminine" profile while continuing to do what they wanted, and sometimes (like H.D. and Bryher) creating international communities of discussion in which issues of gender accompanied other issues related to integrity and individual and public responsibility.

The lack of attention to women editors' work points to a broader issue in contemporary criticism. As Bornstein remarks, "Critics of modernist literature have been slow to see the importance of editing both to the literature they study and to its transmission and reception. Perhaps fewer students of modernism than of any other period (except, of course, the postmodern) have even been aware of such questions."[5] Bornstein's wry comment suggests the extent to which neglect of editing as a factor in literary meaning has pervaded the critical landscape. It may, in fact, relate to the development and legacy of New Critical theory. New Criticism, despite its rejection of the "intentional fallacy," nevertheless posits an "ideal text," which follows traditional ideas about literary editing that presuppose "the principle of 'author's final intention,' whereby the editor (or critic) seeks first to understand and then to implement the final intention of the author regarding the reading of his or her text" (Bornstein 5). Bornstein reminds us that textual scholarship, unlike certain theoretical approaches, has always relied on "historical grounding," attesting to the cultural nexus within which a text appeared; at the same time he agrees with Jerome McGann that "final authorial intention is a deeply problematic concept" (8, 5). One of the problems of studying editorial work is that layers of "intentionality" are difficult enough to deal with on the part of authors who revised and republished certain pieces over the course of years; adding one or more editors into the equation complicates matters exponentially. It is no wonder that some critics find it far easier to base their analyses on a single text, however limited that text may be regarding the multitude of influences passing into and out of it over time. This preference has even occurred among poststructuralist critics who utilize techniques and concepts that attest to the fluidity of textual meanings.

As one solution to the paradox, Bornstein points to the idea of variorum editions, or of "replacing the single text with a series of texts": "Such speculations offer an interesting middle ground between stable, unitary notions of the text on the one hand and poststructuralist freeplay of endless deferral on the other. They clearly dislodge the notion of one privileged form for a text exercising authority over all other forms and, indeed, constituting their teleological ground. Yet they provide a limit to *différance* by limiting the deferral to a finite sequence of versions constituting the bound of that particular text (though not, of course, of intertextuality)" (7).

Intertextuality, of course, is implicated in the kinds of authorial and editorial exchanges discussed in this study. In this case the term encompasses more than stylistic or symbolic comparisons between literary works; it might be said to include the ephemera of the processes of review and publication. Scholars using the methods of new historicism can obviously benefit from the lessons of intertextual reading as from other post-structuralist techniques. Acknowledging the possibilities of yet another layer of meanings, however, is not meant to be the last straw that causes critics finally to despair (if they have not already done so). The complexities of

layered readings of sequential texts, created by writers' and editors' interactions over time, may be considered an example of the kinds of multiplicity some feminist theorists have been seeking in order to include as
many aspects of women's experiences as possible. The fruitful juncture of
feminist and poststructuralist thought offers some new theoretical and
methodological approaches for scholars who want to weave together multiple skeins of textual and historical meanings. Laurie Finke discusses one
of many such possibilities in *Feminist Theory, Women's Writing*, depicting
a "dialogical materialism" that rejects dualism in favor of a new theory of
complexity based on technological models. Finke believes that "feminist
criticism can neither ignore theory nor simply celebrate an untheorized
'difference'; it must engage—and challenge—many aspects of the com-
peting languages that constitute contemporary theoretical discourse" (5).
The "feminist theory of complexity" Finke proposes draws from "nonlin-
ear dynamics, information theory, and fluid mechanics" to discover new
possibilities for seeing order in disorder, and vice versa, avoiding the negative cultural connotations that have been assigned to disorder: "One of
the insights of chaos theory . . . is that disorder is perhaps more produc-
tively conceived of as the presence of information. . . . Although the sci-
ences of chaos are primarily quantitative, their implications for theory
are far more suggestive than the 'application' of a few odd principles to
feminist theories [might indicate]. . . . The concept of complexity enables
us more completely to articulate what we mean when we say that culture
is the collective means by which societies represent themselves to themselves" (8).

Recovering the value of what was previously dismissed as "disorder"
is a meaningful project for scholars concerned about the dismissal of
women—of "the other" who represents the chaos Irigaray describes—
which has for too long characterized literary history. Such approaches offer fresh ways to energize critical theory and textual studies together.[6] Feminist criticism of women writers has been a crucial factor in generating as
well as utilizing poststructuralist innovations in theory and practice. In a
sense, the varieties in current approaches to studying literary women reflect the exuberant creativity of modernists—and may well, in fact, have
developed from those long and tangled feeder-roots of experimentation.

Women editors supported their contributors through publication and payments, and shaped their magazines so as to demonstrate their thinking and promote critical exchange about the most interesting aspects of contemporary work. In effect, they expressed their responses to the modern world in a form that was continually modified and renewed. The connections between editors, writers, and artists embody the cooperation—or at least the critical interaction—that was fundamental to the flux of modernist creation. Therefore, taking notice of the very connections that women supported, and that supported them, precludes drawing reductive conclusions about what women were doing and demands more flexible categories for discussion of genres, influences and affinities, historical milieus, and dynamics of form, format, and content.

The very activity of creating, editing, soliciting for, producing, and sustaining small magazines has been an essential way for women to engage in the development of literature and the aesthetic pondering of their times. Writing critiques, reviews, and letters in response to the work they received, these editors gave artists and writers an immediate, discriminating audience, one that helped to break artistic isolation and that necessarily charged the relationship between artist and public which was a crucial issue for the avant garde. The fact that so many modernist women editors broke new ground makes imperative further serious inquiries into the significance of editing and editorial roles. As well, much women's work was created in disregard of male resistance, and therefore it would be fruitful to "see through" rather than simply "look around" critical expectations predicated upon male resistance, so that we might more accurately see the fullness of women's oeuvres. Learning to read the ways in which women chose to express their own opinions demands critical skill, patience, and flexibility. What Rachel Blau DuPlessis characterizes as the "illusion of stasis" in fiction applies equally well to criticism, and this study of women's methods for accomplishing editorial goals through literary editing may well borrow DuPlessis's main argument in *Writing Beyond the Ending*: "[Woman] is neither wholly 'subcultural' nor, certainly, wholly main-cultural, but negotiates difference and sameness, marginality and inclusion in a constant dialogue, which takes shape variously in the various authors" (178, 43). Although it is not necessarily true that editors share with the writers DuPlessis studies "one end—a rewriting of gender in dominant fiction," it is apparent that they do share "one end" in promoting and influencing modern literature according to their distinctive individual aesthetics.

Obviously, radical reassessments of the modernist canon, and of canon formation itself, must be made when one takes into account the range and variety of women's work. These women were highly literate and eloquent individuals who had the fortitude to speak their minds, debate intellectual and social issues, develop their work along the lines they chose, and (often) live in foreign cultures for decades. In great part, the particular sensibilities expressed in the literary productions and promotions of such women as H.D., Bryher, Marianne Moore, Alice Corbin Henderson, Harriet Monroe, Margaret Anderson, and Jane Heap had a substantial impact on the development of modernist literature on their own terms.

It is inspiring to imagine the profound insights that will be gained from ongoing recovery and reassessment of women's work in modernist writing, criticism, and publishing. Feminist critical approaches have helped to expand the types of questions and the range of tools scholars bring to investigations of literary history. As a result, we are much enriched. We are learning to discard assumptions that have excluded certain writers or works from standard histories and to include complex analyses not only of gender but also of race and class in our discussions of literature and its meanings. Having found much more than was previously seen in women's writings, we also are discovering worlds in the writings of other groups unrepresented or misrepresented by literary tradition. In fact, there is no reason to assume that twentieth-century literary history must include a "modernism" necessarily attached to the productions of certain men. A truly new vision of modern literature would derive, and question, its principles from a vast territory of materials and a number of critical approaches, including but not limited to those that have formed the tradition thus far. Our own literary history will in part be written by the history that we rediscover.

Any movement toward admitting the immense variety of writing by women and other marginalized persons into discussions of literary aesthetics may result in certain difficulties. One of these could be the tendency to reinscribe an authoritarian voice by which selected women as well as men became those who pronounce upon the delineations of "the best" literature. This change does nothing to remove the constrictions of critical authority but merely shifts its parameters—and it is, as Nancy Gray notes, "the business of feminist literary theory to break silence by breaking into and through the cultural codes that produce gender as access or obstacle to language," both as a means of paying attention to what is actually happening and as a way to resist reinscribing patriarchy (2). At the same time, discovering vast resources of literature and art displaying enormous range in theme, subject, and execution seems to threaten a chaotic loss of "standards"—a situation that reiterates the sense of flux from which modernism arose and that many of its "masterpieces" express. Fearing a loss of "standards" in itself betrays a preference for authoritarian pronouncement, whereas an informed tolerance would allow a freer play of production and response in which "the best" works (an arbitrary designation at all times) could arise from and depict their cultural contexts. One can hardly hope to dispense with the effects of patronage and influence, which surely will continue to operate; yet a sort of aesthetic Darwinism may offer the most appropriate means by which contemporary art, and our understanding of it, may develop.[7]

Such a vision of finding our way across the ever-changing terrain of literary study appears in Irigaray's words: "Our horizon will never stop expanding; we are always open. Stretching out, never ceasing to unfold ourselves, we have so many voices to invent in order to express all of us everywhere, even in our gaps, that all the time there is will not be enough" (213). If women's contributions must be categorized under the rubric of women's studies at this point, perhaps in the future such classification will be unnecessary, in part through our taking a lesson from the distinctive and diverse accomplishments that we have found here, a signal of the richness still to be discovered in modernist—indeed, in all—literature.

NOTES

1. MAKING THEIR WAYS

Epigraphs: Robert McAlmon, *Being Geniuses Together, 1920-1930*, rev. ed. by Kay Boyle (San Francisco: North Point Press, 1984) 74; Margaret Anderson, *My Thirty Years' War* (New York: Covici, Friede, 1930) 123.

1. George Bornstein, "Introduction: Why Editing Matters," *Representing Modernist Texts: Editing as Interpretation* (Ann Arbor: U of Michigan P, 1991) 1-2.

2. See Frederick J. Hoffman, Charles Allen, and Carolyn F. Ulrich, *The Little Magazine: A History and a Bibliography* (Princeton: Princeton UP, 1947); Edward E. Chielens, ed., *The Literary Journal in America, 1900-1950*, American Literature, English Literature, and World Literature in English Information Guide Series 16 (Detroit: Gale, 1977); and Shari Benstock and Bernard Benstock, "The Role of Little Magazines in the Emergence of Modernism," *The Library Chronicle of the University of Texas at Austin* 20.4 (1991): 69-87.

3. Gillian Hanscombe and Virginia L. Smyers, in *Writing for Their Lives: The Modernist Women, 1910-1940* (Boston: Northeastern UP, 1987), point out the fallacy in this belief: "This 'universality' is an assumption implicit in men's creative writing and is explicit in their aesthetics. . . . Since a man's viewpoint has primacy and a woman's does not, it has traditionally passed unremarked that male writers have subsumed the female half of 'human' experience and that they have done so without qualification" (5).

4. Two books that have been particularly influential in proposing such differences in women's writings are Sandra M. Gilbert and Susan Gubar, *The Madwoman in the Attic: The Woman Writer and the Nineteenth-Century Literary Imagination* (New Haven: Yale UP, 1979), and Rachel Blau DuPlessis, *Writing Beyond the Ending: Narrative Strategies of Twentieth-Century Women Writers* (Bloomington: Indiana UP, 1984).

5. Malcolm Bradbury and James McFarlane, eds., *Modernism: 1890-1930* (Harmondsworth: Penguin, 1976) 27.

6. *A Coherent Splendor: The American Poetic Renaissance, 1910-1950* (Cambridge: Cambridge UP, 1987) 3. Albert Gelpi's book includes only one woman, Hilda Doolittle, as a major figure. While Gelpi claims he will "call

attention, from time to time, to the ways in which elitist, individualist assumptions about gender, race, and class limit and even distort the work under discussion," his discussion is still predicated upon "what the poetry *does* rather than what it does not do" (6)—which means that the book necessarily privileges the white male purview underlying the bulk of the writing examined, responds to men's works in great part, and marginalizes "gender, race, and class" in a convenient phrase that gives just a nod to three factors that in actual life enormously shape writers' experiences and expressions.

7. This is attested to in the first of Bryher's autobiographical books, *The Heart to Artemis: A Writer's Memoirs* (New York: Harcourt, Brace, 1962) 201.

8. Nicholas Joost, *Ernest Hemingway and the Little Magazines: The Paris Years* (Barre: Barre, 1968) 19-33, 41-42.

9. Hanscombe and Smyers 169-70. See also Jane Lidderdale and Mary Nicholson, *Dear Miss Weaver: Harriet Shaw Weaver, 1876-1961* (New York: Viking, 1970), and Les Garner, *A Brave and Beautiful Spirit: Dora Marsden, 1882-1960* (Aldershot: Avebury/Gower, 1990) 114-16. Marsden and West were not particularly happy about the direction Pound seemed to want to take, but both wanted the paper to increase its literary aspects.

10. Hanscombe and Smyers quote a letter written in 1914 by Aldington to Amy Lowell in which he states, "Hilda is taking over the Egoist. I seem to be a little 'out' with Miss Weaver just now" (176). This piece of evidence suggests that, although Aldington and H.D. worked closely together on a number of literary projects through World War I, H.D. had more influence on the *Egoist* than the "official" date of her literary editorship (1916) would credit. See Cyrena N. Pondrom, ed., "Selected Letters from H.D. to F. S. Flint: A Commentary on the Imagist Period," *Contemporary Literature* 10.4 (1969): 557-86, and my discussion in chapter 4.

11. Lidderdale and Nicholson 459-65.

12. For a discussion of Moore's work for the *Dial*, see chapter 5. I rely heavily on unpublished correspondence in the American literature collection, Beinecke Rare Book and Manuscript Library, Yale University. See also Grace Schulman, *Marianne Moore: The Poetry of Engagement* (Urbana: U of Illinois P, 1986) 9-25, and Taffy Martin, *Marianne Moore: Subversive Modernist* (Austin: U of Texas P, 1986) 48.

13. Of scholarly books, the most useful are Sandra M. Gilbert and Susan Gubar's *No Man's Land: The Place of the Woman Writer in the Twentieth Century*, in three volumes: *The War of the Words* (New Haven: Yale UP, 1988), *Sexchanges* (New Haven: Yale UP, 1989), and *Letters from the Front* (New Haven: Yale UP, 1994); Hanscombe and Smyers's *Writing for Their Lives*; *The Gender of Modernism* (Bloomington: Indiana UP, 1990), edited by Bonnie Kime Scott; Marianne DeKoven's *Rich and Strange: Gender, History, Modernism* (Princeton: Princeton UP, 1991); and Shari Benstock's *Women of the Left Bank: Paris, 1900-1940* (Austin: U of Texas P, 1986).

Among other books, Morrill Cody and Hugh Ford's brief *The Women of Montparnasse* (New York: Cornwall, 1984) examines the lives and contributions of certain of these women; however, the book's approach is neither scholarly nor exhaustive. The same problems arise with Hugh Ford's *Four Lives in Paris* (San Francisco: North Point, 1987), which includes biographical essays on Margaret Anderson and Kay Boyle, and *Published in Paris: American and British Writers,*

Printers, and Publishers in Paris, 1920-1939 (New York: Macmillan, 1975), which presents much fascinating background information without giving citations. Noel Riley Fitch's *Sylvia Beach and the Lost Generation: A History of Literary Paris in the Twenties and Thirties* (New York: Norton, 1983) provides a coherent view of this literary era by focusing on a central figure. Dale Spender's *The Writing or the Sex? Or Why You Don't Have to Read Women's Writing to Know It's No Good* (New York: Pergamon, 1989) provides a slightly different but very provocative angle on the (mis)uses made of women's literary work.

14. Gilbert and Gubar, *War of the Words* 147-56.

15. Benstock x; Gilbert and Gubar, *War of the Words* xii, 66, and *Letters from the Front*, chapter 2.

16. Hanscombe and Smyers 185.

17. See, for example, discussions about privilege and distortions in theorizing in Barbara Christian, "The Race for Theory," *Making Face, Making Soul: Haciendo Caras*, ed. Gloria Anzaldúa (San Francisco: Aunt Lute, 1990): 335-45, and in Susan Stanford Friedman, "Post/Poststructuralist Feminist Criticism: The Politics of Recuperation and Negotiation," *New Literary History* 22.2 (1991): 465-90.

18. Ann Rosalind Jones, "Inscribing Femininity: French Theories of the Feminine," *Making a Difference: Feminist Literary Criticism*, ed. Gayle Greene and Coppélia Kahn (London: Methuen, 1985) 81.

19. See, for example, Elaine Marks and Isabelle de Courtivron, eds., *New French Feminisms* (New York: Schocken, 1981); and Luce Irigaray, *This Sex Which Is Not One*, trans. Catherine Porter (1977; Ithaca: Cornell UP, 1985).

20. See, for example, Nancy J. Chodorow, *Feminism and Psychoanalytic Theory* (New Haven: Yale UP, 1989); Mary Field Belenky, Blythe McVicker Clinchy, Nancy Rule Goldberger, and Jill Mattuck Tarule, *Women's Ways of Knowing: The Development of Self, Voice, and Mind* (New York: Basic, 1986); and Carol Gilligan, *In a Different Voice: Psychological Theory and Women's Development* (Cambridge: Harvard UP, 1982).

21. DuPlessis's *Writing Beyond the Ending*, for instance, offers an approach that mediates between positing an "otherness" on the part of women's experiences and providing space for discussion of the many differing strategies of individual writers.

22. See, for instance, her letters to Pound's mother, quoted in Hanscombe and Smyers 25-27, and her correspondence with Amy Lowell, as discussed in chapter 4.

23. Mina Loy, "Feminist Manifesto," *The Last Lunar Baedeker*, ed. Roger L. Conover (Highlands: Jargon Society, 1982) 269.

24. Laurie A. Finke, in *Feminist Theory, Women's Writing* (Ithaca: Cornell UP, 1992), proposes a technological paradigm based on chaos theory that would allow for polyvocality and greater inclusiveness in theoretical formulations.

2. Beginning in Chicago

1. See, for example, discussions in Hoffman, Allen, and Ulrich; Ellen Williams, *Harriet Monroe and the Poetry Renaissance: The First Ten Years of Poetry, 1912-22* (Urbana: U of Illinois P, 1977); Marilyn J. Atlas, "Harriet Monroe, Margaret

Anderson, and the Spirit of the Chicago Renaissance," *Midwestern Miscellany* 9 (1981): 43-53; and Chielens.

2. Ezra Pound, *The Letters of Ezra Pound, 1907-1941*, ed. D. D. Paige (New York: Harcourt, Brace, 1950). Harriet Monroe's autobiography, published posthumously, is *A Poet's Life* (New York: Macmillan, 1938).

3. One reason for literary historians' consistent emphasis on Pound lies in Monroe's own generous treatment of him in her autobiography; she quotes a number of his letters and writes that it was his intellectual and critical taste that appealed to her and that helped her to overlook some of his more obstreperous moments. *A Poet's Life* helped direct attention to Pound's contributions to modern letters. Subsequently, many of Pound's letters have been published and quoted, while only a few of Monroe's letters to Pound survive in the Ezra Pound archives at Yale University. In her study of *Poetry* and its founder, Ellen Williams relies on copies of Monroe's letters kept in the *Poetry* archives at the University of Chicago. The vicissitudes of scholarly emphases and the relative availability of materials have helped foster a disproportionate reliance on Pound's opinions and actions. Largely due to his influence, perceptions of Monroe have been colored with a condescension that usually ignores or belittles Monroe's point of view.

4. Harriet Monroe, letter to Alice Corbin Henderson, 3 April 1917, Alice Corbin Henderson Papers, Harry Ransom Humanities Research Center, U of Texas at Austin.

5. Craig S. Abbott mentions that the inclusion of seventeen of Stevens's poems in the 1917 volume was particularly notable because Stevens still had not published a book ("Publishing the New Poetry: Harriet Monroe's Anthology," *Journal of Modern Literature* 11 [1984]: 104).

6. Harriet Monroe, letter to Alice Corbin Henderson, 21 November 1918, Alice Corbin Henderson Papers.

7. Alice Corbin Henderson, "Our Friend the Enemy," *Poetry* 6.5 (1915): 259-61; Harriet Monroe, "A Nation-Wide Art," *Poetry* 7.2 (1915): 84-88; Harriet Monroe, "James Whitcomb Riley," *Poetry* 8.6 (1916): 305-7.

8. Scores of letters between Monroe and Henderson are preserved in the *Poetry* archives and in the large, recently augmented collection of Henderson's papers at the Harry Ransom Humanities Research Center, the University of Texas at Austin.

9. Alice Corbin Henderson, "The Rejection Slip," *Poetry* 8.4 (1916): 198.

10. Facts about Henderson's life are taken in large part from T. M. Pearce, *Alice Corbin Henderson*, Southwest Writers Series (Austin: Steck-Vaughn, 1969).

11. Alice Corbin Henderson, letter to Harriet Monroe, attributed to 23 August 1912, *Poetry* Papers, Joseph Regenstein Library, U of Chicago.

12. Harriet Monroe, letter to Alice Corbin Henderson, 3 July 1917, Alice Corbin Henderson Papers.

13. Subsequent to Henderson, Monroe's associate editors were Eunice Tietjens, Helen Hoyt, Emanuel Carnevali, Marion Strobel, George Dillon, Jessica Nelson North, and Morton Dauwen Zabel.

14. Alice Corbin Henderson, letter to Harriet Monroe, attributed to June 1915, *Poetry* Papers.

15. One of Monroe's letters reveals both women's tendencies. She chides Henderson for showing "a trace of temper, thus weakening your effect," and

comments, "[Well,] when you have to come down, it's much better to come down gracefully." Letter to Alice Corbin Henderson, 7 September 1918, Alice Corbin Henderson Papers.

16. Alice Corbin Henderson, letter to Harriet Monroe, 7 June 1916, *Poetry* Papers.

17. Alice Corbin Henderson, letter to Harriet Monroe, 8 August 1916, *Poetry* Papers.

18. Alice Corbin Henderson, "Our Contemporaries," *Poetry* 3.5 (1914): 187.

19. Autograph correspondence and carbon typescripts in the Alice Corbin Henderson papers at the Harry Ransom Humanities Research Center dated 28 November, 1 December, and 8 December 1916 cover their discussion.

20. Alice Corbin Henderson, "A Perfect Return," *Poetry* 1.3 (1912): 90-91.

21. Alice Corbin Henderson, "Too Far from Paris," *Poetry* 4.3 (1914): 107.

22. Alice Corbin Henderson, "Poetic Prose and Vers Libre," *Poetry* 2.2 (1913): 70.

23. Alice Corbin Henderson, "Lazy Criticism," *Poetry* 9.3 (1916): 144-45.

24. Alice Corbin Henderson, letter to Harriet Monroe, 7 June 1916, *Poetry* Papers.

25. Alice Corbin Henderson, "Our Contemporaries [A New School of Poetry]," *Poetry* 8.2 (1916): 103.

26. Alice Corbin Henderson, letter to Harriet Monroe, June 1916, *Poetry* Papers.

27. Harriet Monroe, rev. of *The Adventures of Young Maverick*, by Hervey White, *Poetry* 1.3 (1912): 95-96; "Lindsay's Poems," *Poetry* 3.5 (1914): 182-83; Alice Corbin Henderson, rev. of *Spoon River Anthology*, by Edgar Lee Masters, *Poetry* 6.3 (1915): 145-49; "Cowboy Songs and Ballads," *Poetry* 10.5 (1917): 255-59; "Our Cowboy Poet," *Poetry* 10.6 (1917): 319-20; "Poetry of the North-American Indian," *Poetry* 14.1 (1919): 41-47.

28. Harriet Monroe, "Its Inner Meaning," *Poetry* 6.6 (1915): 302-5.

29. Alice Corbin Henderson, rev. of *Des Imagistes: An Anthology*, *Poetry* 5.1 (1914): 38-40; "Poetic Drama," *Poetry* 7.1 (1915): 31-35; "Our Contemporaries [A New School of Poetry],"; "Imagism: Secular and Esoteric," *Poetry* 11.6 (1918): 339-43.

30. Harriet Monroe, "As It Was," *Poetry* 1.1 (1912): 22.

31. Harriet Monroe, "Moody's Poems," *Poetry* 1.2 (1912): 57; Harriet Monroe, rev. of *The Lyric Year*, by Mitchell Kennerley, *Poetry* 1.4 (1912): 130.

32. Monroe, rev. of *Lyric Year* 131.

33. Harriet Monroe, "The Open Door," *Poetry* 1.2 (1912): 62-64.

34. Harriet Monroe, "The New Beauty," *Poetry* 2.1 (1913): 22.

35. Harriet Monroe, "Rhythms of English Verse II," *Poetry* 3.3 (1913): 110.

36. Harriet Monroe, "Tradition," *Poetry* 2.2 (1913): 67-68.

37. "The tradition is a beauty that we preserve and not a set of fetters to bind us." Ezra Pound, "The Tradition," *Poetry* 3.4 (1914): 137.

38. Harriet Monroe, "'That Mass of Dolts,'" *Poetry* 1.5 (1913): 168-70.

39. At one point, for instance, Monroe wrote to Henderson, "I tremble frequently to think how Ezra must condole with you over the way *Poetry* has slumped since you left it. Is his language very strong?" Letter to Alice Corbin Henderson, 9 April 1917, Alice Corbin Henderson Papers.

40. Henderson wrote to Monroe several times about her own disgust with Pound's actions in this regard. A letter of 9 June 1917 states: "What I indicated in my last letter as having on my chest, was Ezra Pound in the last Little Review. I am utterly disgusted, and am writing him to say so. . . . I wrote and told him when I read the announcement of his connection with that journal that I thought he was a fool, but I wasn't prepared for this indication of it! As far as POETRY is concerned I should make not the least mention of E.P. and the L.R. . . . I have always been a staunch advocate of E.P. and I would hate now to do anything to cut off his income or anything of that sort. But obviously we have different ideals of conduct. I can not understand why he should so calmly [assume] that he was at liberty to be foreign correspondent of The Little Review *and* Poetry, unless he had made arrangements with you in advance? . . . I suppose the real trouble is that Ezra *has no sense of values*." Letter to Harriet Monroe, 9 June 1917, *Poetry* papers. See also her letters of 15 June 1917 and 12 December 1917.

41. Harriet Monroe, letter to Alice Corbin Henderson, 26 October 1921, Alice Corbin Henderson Papers.

42. Monroe quoted Macmillan in a letter to Alice Corbin Henderson, 5 August 1921, Alice Corbin Henderson Papers. Craig Abbott notes that this edition went through four printings in 1917 alone ("Publishing the New Poetry" 100n).

43. This phrase occurs in a pencil draft, which Monroe sent Henderson. Monroe, letter to Ezra Pound [draft], 3 July 1917, Alice Corbin Henderson Papers.

44. Alice Corbin Henderson, letter to Roberts Walker [carbon], 2 May 1922, Alice Corbin Henderson papers.

45. Alice Corbin Henderson, letter to Harriet Monroe, 2 August 1916, *Poetry* Papers.

46. She wrote on 6 February, "I am truly sorry about the anthology for which I feel much to blame. But I certainly had no idea of the fate in store for me. . . . I told Mr. Marsh some time ago that I would send suggestions for advertising circulars to the colleges, etc. and I will do all I can." A letter much later that year asserted, "I am glad to hear that the book is in its fourth edition. I wonder if anything has been done to circularize the colleges? If not, I think a circular should be got up, and I'll help. . . . Send along the reviews and I'll make up some copy." Henderson, letters to Harriet Monroe, 6 February 1917, 12 December 1917, *Poetry* Papers.

47. Alice Corbin Henderson, letter to Harriet Monroe, 25 February 1917, *Poetry* Papers.

48. Harriet Monroe, letter to Alice Corbin Henderson, 14 June 1921, Alice Corbin Henderson Papers.

49. Harriet Monroe, letter to Alice Corbin Henderson, 4 March 1921, Alice Corbin Henderson Papers.

50. At one point Monroe wrote, "I doubt if I [will] ask Yeats for anything, but if I do I shall pay his price for a few recent things." Letter to Alice Corbin Henderson, 14 June 1921, Alice Corbin Henderson Papers.

51. Alice Corbin Henderson, letter to Harriet Monroe [carbon], 6 June 1921, Alice Corbin Henderson Papers.

52. Harriet Monroe, letter to Alice Corbin Henderson, 14 June 1921, Alice Corbin Henderson Papers.

53. Monroe sent Henderson a draft of a letter she had written to George Platt Brett at Macmillan Publishing Company. Letter to [George Platt] Brett [draft], 14 June 1921, Alice Corbin Henderson Papers.

54. Harriet Monroe, letter to George Brett [carbon], 2 February 1921, Alice Corbin Henderson Papers.

55. Harriet Monroe, letter to Alice Corbin Henderson, 16 October 1921, Alice Corbin Henderson Papers.

56. A letter from Monroe to Henderson of 16 October 1921 relates her meetings with Brett and Latham of Macmillan during which Monroe was strongly encouraged to prepare a single, enlarged volume, a suggestion that she finally decided to accept.

57. Monroe related to Henderson her conferences with Macmillan, during which she got Edward Latham to agree that Macmillan would pay for permissions, and in which George Brett stressed the marketing importance of a one-volume anthology for the colleges, so that Monroe finally agreed that the second edition would omit nothing but add about fifty percent. She wrote parenthetically to Henderson, "This because I simply cannot undertake the problem of omissions—it's too difficult, too disheartening, too discourteous to the poets, too provocative to critics and public" (16 October 1921, Alice Corbin Henderson Papers).

58. Both women found the work of these poets less than enduring; moreover, "Scharmel Iris" proved to be a plagiarizing fraud, and it is no surprise that he was evicted from the anthology. See Craig S. Abbott, "The Case of Scharmel Iris," *Papers of the Bibliographic Society of America* 77.1 (1983): 15-34.

59. Harriet Monroe, letter to Alice Corbin Henderson, 16 October 1921, Alice Corbin Henderson Papers. A letter written the following April includes Monroe's suggestions for Yeats: "To a Child Dancing in the Wind," "The Player Queen," "A Woman Homer Sung," "When Helen Lived," "An Irish Airman," which are not included in the 1923 volume, and "The Wild Swans at Coole," "That the Night Come," "No Second Troy," "To a Friend Whose Work," "The Dawn," and "Ego Dominus Tuus," which are included (Monroe, letter to Henderson attributed to April 1922, Alice Corbin Henderson Papers).

60. Alice Corbin Henderson, letter to Harriet Monroe, 20 October 1921, *Poetry* Papers.

61. Alice Corbin Henderson, letter to Harriet Monroe, 1 November 1921, *Poetry* Papers.

62. Harriet Monroe, letter to Alice Corbin Henderson, 30 December 1921, Alice Corbin Henderson Papers.

63. Harriet Monroe, letter to Alice Corbin Henderson, 3 February 1922, Alice Corbin Henderson Papers.

64. Harriet Monroe, letter to Alice Corbin Henderson, 3 February 1922, Alice Corbin Henderson Papers.

65. Alice Corbin Henderson, letter to Harriet Monroe, 15 April 1922, *Poetry* Papers.

66. Harriet Monroe, letter to Alice Corbin Henderson, 23 May 1922, Alice Corbin Henderson Papers.

67. Harriet Monroe, letter to Alice Corbin Henderson, 5 August 1922, Alice Corbin Henderson Papers.

68. In the first issue, Monroe wrote that "we hope to publish in *Poetry* some of the best work now being done in English verse" (28), including longer, "more intimate and serious" things ("The Motive of the Magazine," *Poetry* 1.1 [1912]: 28).

69. Harriet Monroe, letter to Alice Corbin Henderson, 5 August 1922, Alice Corbin Henderson Papers.

3. READER CRITICS

1. Margaret Anderson described her decision to start a literary magazine in her first memoir, *My Thirty Years' War* (1930; New York: Horizon, 1969) 35-36.

2. Ben Hecht, *A Child of the Century* (New York: Simon and Schuster, 1954) 233-35, and Jackson Robert Bryer, "'A Trial-Track for Racers': Margaret Anderson and the *Little Review*," diss., U of Wisconsin, 1965, 30-31. One must keep in mind both Hecht's admiration for Anderson and her lack of interest in his attentions, as suggested in *My Thirty Years' War* (59, 91, 141). Of Anderson's contemporaries, Ezra Pound and Robert McAlmon offer the most extreme opinions: see *Letters of Ezra Pound, 1907-1941*, and McAlmon, *Being Geniuses Together, 1920-1930*, ed. Kay Boyle, rev. ed. (San Francisco: North Point, 1984). *Pound/The* Little Review: *The Letters of Ezra Pound to Margaret Anderson: The* Little Review *Correspondence*, ed. Thomas L. Scott, Melvin J. Friedman, and Jackson R. Bryer (New York: New Directions, 1988) has also been helpful, although it too demonstrates an interest in Pound that occurs sometimes at Anderson's expense. For other examples of commentators who take Anderson at her words, see chapter 18 of Dale Kramer, *Chicago Renaissance* (New York: Appleton-Century, 1966), and Felix Pollak, "Margaret Anderson's Saga of Perpetual Emotion," *Carleton Miscellany* 11.4 (1971): 85-93.

3. Bryer, "'Trial-Track'" 30-31.

4. Hecht 233.

5. Ellen Williams 206. See also remarks about Heap in McAlmon 31, 37.

6. Holly Ann Baggett, "Aloof from Natural Laws: Margaret C. Anderson and the 'Little Review,' 1914-1929," diss., U of Delaware, 1992, chapter 4.

7. While some pieces were not attributed in the magazine's tables of contents, Anderson identified some of the anonymous works as Heap's in *The* Little Review *Anthology*. See *My Thirty Years' War* for her description of how she wheedled Heap into becoming a writer for the magazine (110). Corroboration of Anderson's statements is difficult because few of the two women's personal papers are available. Scattered papers of Anderson's are contained within the Janet Flanner/Solita Solano collection at the Library of Congress; other letters by Anderson and/or Heap survive in the Amy Lowell collection at Harvard, in the Pound and Stein collections at Yale, in the *Poetry* archives at the University of Chicago, at the Harry Ransom Humanities Research Center of the University of Texas at Austin, in the library of the University of Delaware, and especially in the *Little Review* archives at the University of Wisconsin-Milwaukee. Within this last collection, however, there is nothing in the way of intraoffice memoranda or extended notes between Anderson and Heap. Only a few short notes on manuscripts and occasional markings in two

hands are preserved, and this may be all the evidence that exists in written form. Anderson's surviving letters, however, especially those at the Library of Congress to Flanner and Solano, often display a peculiar format with typed correspondence on the right half of the page and written comments—usually in the recipient's hand—on the left, on the back, and in the margins, and sometimes also Anderson's replies to these marginalia, as if the letter had gone back and forth. It is also clear that Anderson frequently retyped portions of others' letters to her, often as parts of letters of her own, and wrote in comments. Thus Anderson's personal correspondence, as well as her own assertions, indicates a consuming interest in (almost an insistence upon) "conversation" in whatever form. Heap's surviving letters are conventional in format.

8. Baggett 76-99. See also Margaret C. Jones, *Heretics and Hellraisers: Women Contributors to* The Masses, *1911-1917* (Austin: U of Texas P, 1993), and June Sochen, *The New Woman in Greenwich Village, 1910-1920* (New York: Quadrangle/New York Times Book Co., 1972).

9. See Abby Ann Arthur Johnson, "The Personal Magazine: Margaret C. Anderson and the *Little Review*, 1914-1929," *South Atlantic Quarterly* 75.3 (1976): 351-63, and Pollak.

10. I find it pertinent to utilize Adrienne Rich's definition of "lesbian" as woman-centered self-identification that specifically rejects male strictures upon women ("Compulsory Heterosexuality and Lesbian Existence," *Blood, Bread, and Poetry: Selected Prose, 1979-1985* [New York: Norton, 1986] 51). While Anderson's writings are not as radical as Rich's, her insistence on resisting authority and revising women's roles clearly extends her personal lesbian identification into wider social meanings.

11. [Margaret Anderson,] "Announcement," *Little Review* 1.1 (1914): 1.

12. Margaret Anderson, "Conversation," *Prose* 2 (1971): 11, qtd. in Baggett 171.

13. [Margaret Anderson,] "Incense and Splendor," *Little Review* 1.4 (1914): 1-3.

14. Baggett discusses, for instance, Anderson's review of Galsworthy's *The Dark Flower*, 60-61.

15. [Margaret Anderson], "Armageddon," *Little Review* 1.6 (1914): 3.

16. [Margaret Anderson,] "'Don'ts for Critics,'" *Little Review* 3.1 (1916): 24. Anderson's title is taken from the piece by Henderson in that number of the magazine.

17. [Jane Heap,] "And—[*Windy McPherson's Son*]," *Little Review* 3.7 (1916): 6-7; [Jane Heap,] "Ulysses," *Little Review* 9.1 (1922): 34-35.

18. Jane Heap, "And—[Tagore]," *Little Review* 3.6 (1916): 21.

19. Jane Heap, "And—[Paderewski and Tagore]," *Little Review* 3.7 (1916): 7-8.

20. See Susan Noyes Platt, "Mysticism in the Machine Age: Jane Heap and the *Little Review*," *Twenty One/Art and Culture* 1.1 (1989): 18-44.

21. Ezra Pound, "Das Schone Papier Vergeudet," *Little Review* 3.7 (1916): 16-17.

22. D.H., "Infantile Paralysis," *Little Review* 3.6 (1916): 25.

23. Frank Lloyd Wright, "A Word from Real Art," *Little Review* 3.6 (1916): 26.

24. [A Contributor,] "Freudian," *Little Review* 3.6 (1916): 26.

25. Jane Heap, ["Freudian,"] *Little Review* 3.6 (1916): 26.

26. Roy George, "The Reader Critic," *Little Review* 3.7 (1916): 22.

27. Alice Groff, "The Reader Critic," *Little Review* 3.7 (1916): 27.

28. [Anonymous,] "The Reader Critic," *Little Review* 3.7 (1916): 27.

29. Daphne Carr, "The Reader Critic," *Little Review* 3.7 (1916): 27.

30. Jane Heap, "Indiscriminate Illusions," *Little Review* 4.3 (1917): 25.

31. [Margaret Anderson], "The Essential Thing," *Little Review* 3.1 (1916): 23.

32. [Jane Heap,] "And—[John Cowper Powys]," *Little Review* 3.6 (1916): 20. "Q.K." wrote criticism of literature and theater for the *New Republic*; a July 1916 column asserted of Powys, "I imagine him a pretentious, emphatic, talkative man, sincerely loving many good books, a little inclined to suggest that he knows well certain books that he knows slightly[,] . . . an utterer of sensible and stupid things with about the same eagerness[,] . . . half a quack and very much in earnest, with a streak of poetry in him" ("Mr. Powys' Book," *New Republic* 7.88 [1916]: 256).

33. Jane Heap, "And—[A Decadent Art!]," *Little Review* 3.8 (1917): 6-7.

34. Jane Heap, "Mary Garden," *Little Review* 3.9 (1917): 5-9.

35. Margaret Anderson, "Isadora Duncan's Misfortune," *Little Review* 3.10 (1917): 5-7.

36. Anderson's choices, arrangements, and particularly alterations in *Anthology* materials deserve further attention. For instance, one of Heap's most radical pieces, "Push-Face," in the *Little Review* in 1917 described a riot that grew out of a rally following the United States' entry into World War I. This piece resulted in some cancellations of subscriptions to the magazine. Anderson's anthology, however, collected a set of Heap's smaller pieces under the same title; her reasons for doing so, in the early 1950s, are worth consideration. So, too, are her alterations of Pound's letters as they appeared in *My Thirty Years' War*.

37. Jane Heap and Jean de Bosschère, "Ezra Pound's Critics," *Little Review* 4.9 (1918): 56-59.

38. Jane Heap, "The Episode Continued," *Little Review* 5.7 (1918): 35.

39. For a discussion of the prosecution of the *Little Review* for publishing portions of *Ulysses*, see Jackson Robert Bryer, "Joyce, *Ulysses* and the *Little Review*," *South Atlantic Quarterly* 66.2 (1967): 148-64.

40. See particularly Jane Heap, "Art and the Law," *Little Review* 7.3 (1920): 5-7; Margaret Anderson, "An Obvious Statement," *Little Review* 7.3 (1920): 8-16, and "'Ulysses' in Court," *Little Review* 7.4 (1921): 22-25.

41. Margaret Anderson, "Dialogue," *Little Review* 9.2 (1922): 24-25.

42. Norine Voss, "'Saying the Unsayable': An Introduction to Women's Autobiography," *Gender Studies: New Directions in Feminist Criticism*, ed. Judith Spector (Bowling Green: Bowling Green SU Popular P, 1986) 230.

43. Baggett notes that as early as July 1917, Heap wrote to her friend Florence Reynolds that Anderson was not much interested in producing the magazine and that Heap was doing most of the production-related work (338). Anderson herself, in *My Thirty Years' War* (230), writes that she wanted to give up the magazine after printing *Ulysses*—not just because the trial was draining but also because the novel was such good art that it seemed to her the *Little Review* would have achieved its aims magnificently and thus had no need to continue.

44. Jane Heap, "Wreaths," *Little Review* 12.2 (1929): 62.

45. As early as spring 1923, the *Little Review* presented four Miró paintings, followed by work by Andre Masson that winter; see Susan Noyes Platt, *Modernism in the 1920s: Interpretations of Modern Art in New York from Expressionism to Constructivism* (Ann Arbor: UMI Research P, 1985) 106. The first Surrealist show is identified in J. P. Hodin, *Modern Art and the Modern Mind* (Cleveland: Case Western Reserve UP, 1972) 341, 342.

46. See Platt, "Mysticism in the Machine Age," above, and also "*The Little Review*: Early Years and Avant-Garde Ideas," in *The Old Guard and the Avant Garde: Modernism in Chicago, 1910-1940*, ed. Sue Ann Prince (Chicago: U of Chicago P, 1990) 139-54.

47. Susan Noyes Platt, "Modernism, Formalism, and Politics: The 'Cubism and Abstract Art' Exhibition of 1936 at The Museum of Modern Art," *Art Journal* 47.4 (1988): 289.

48. Platt, "Modernism, Formalism" 288. Barr did use Pound's article on Brancusi, which appeared in the *Little Review* in autumn 1921, in his catalog's bibliography.

49. Ford, *Published in Paris* 56.

50. See, for example, James R. Mellow, *Charmed Circle: Gertrude Stein and Company* (New York: Avon, 1974) 378-84.

51. While Stein averred that she "graciously allowed" McAlmon to publish her book, McAlmon wrote that Stein had asked him to tea and suggested that he publish the book in several installments over a period of two years (Ford, *Published in Paris* 56, 233; McAlmon 206). Ford points out that Carl Van Vechten, as well as Heap, had been trying to place portions of *Americans* even before McAlmon's first meeting with Stein. McAlmon did initiate contact with Stein in a letter of August 1924, asking whether she would like to be one of the group published in the *Contact Collection*, for which she submitted "Two Women" (Ford, *Published in Paris* 59). McAlmon and Stein then met in January 1925 to discuss publishing *Americans* in several volumes, although Ford points out McAlmon's haste in agreeing to this plan without fully realizing the extent of the project (*Published in Paris* 58-59).

James R. Mellow asserts that Stein used "considerable charm" in persuading McAlmon to take on the task, projecting sales of at least fifty copies—a dubious point in favor of putting out a thousand-page book. He goes on to note that "while Gertrude was negotiating her contract with McAlmon, who seems to have wanted to keep it on a gentlemen's-agreement basis, Jane Heap was trying to interest New York publishers in publishing an edition from the sheets of McAlmon's printing" (378-79).

52. It seems that Stein's appearances in the *Little Review* occurred as a result of Heap's advocacy, for Anderson wrote later, "I have never had any art enthusiasm for Gertrude Stein. . . . If she had only achieved what her interpreters credit her with, I would have been interested in her own writing" (*The* Little Review *Anthology* [New York: Horizon, 1953] 317).

53. Mellow (344) mentions this situation but does not quote the letter on which his comment is based: Jane Heap, letter to Gertrude Stein, n.d. [attributed to 1924], Gertrude Stein Papers, Beinecke Rare Book and Manuscript Library, Yale University.

54. Mellow 379. Boni and Liveright had advertised for years in the *Little Review*, and in one of her "Notes" in 1922, Heap commented that "Boni and Liveright seem to have an ambition to publish books of permanent literary value. They would do well to take more pride in the making of the books themselves." [Jane Heap], "Notes," *Little Review* 9.1 (1922): 36. This acknowledgment of Boni and Liveright, although equivocal, may have set the stage for Heap's later approach to the reorganized firm with reference to Stein's book.

55. Jane Heap, letter to Gertrude Stein, n.d. [1925], Gertrude Stein Papers.

56. Jane Heap, letter to Gertrude Stein, n.d. [attributed to 1926], Gertrude Stein Papers. This letter asks whether Darantière, the printer, had made plates or had distributed the type, so it must have been written in 1926.

57. Jane Heap, letter to Gertrude Stein, 18 May 1926, Gertrude Stein Papers.

58. Ford writes, "In England [McAlmon] had met a representative of the newly formed firm of Albert and Charles Boni, who, having been alerted to the forthcoming publication of Miss Stein's book by the hard-working Miss Heap, had proposed that McAlmon instruct Darantière to print a thousand instead of five hundred sets of sheets, which the Bonis would bind and distribute in America" (*Published in Paris* 66).

59. Jane Heap, letter to Gertrude Stein, 18 July 1926, Gertrude Stein Papers.

60. Jane Heap, letter to Gertrude Stein, n.d. [attributed to 1926], Gertrude Stein Papers.

61. See Baggett, chapter 7, for an in-depth discussion of the magazine's promotion of women writers.

4. TOWARD INTERNATIONAL COOPERATION

1. Cyrena Pondrom has pointed out H.D.'s extensive activity in that circle of young English writers, in "Selected Letters" and especially in "H.D. and the Origins of Imagism," *Sagetrieb* 4.1 (1985): 73-97, reprinted in *Signets: Reading H.D.*, ed. Susan Stanford Friedman and Rachel Blau DuPlessis (Madison: U of Wisconsin P, 1990) 85-109.

2. Holly Baggett believes that Lowell had planned to oust Pound during her 1914 trip, based on Lowell's offer to Margaret Anderson to write a "London Letter" for the *Little Review* in May of 1914, and on Fletcher's opinion that Lowell's trip was part of a "campaign"; see his autobiography, *Life Is My Song* (New York: Farrar and Rinehart, 1937) 145. Lowell was certainly capable of such a plan, although Fletcher was equally capable of exaggerating his reading of Lowell; the offer of a "London Letter" was obviously going to be a short-term proposition in any case. See Baggett 128-31.

3. H.D., letter to Amy Lowell, 17 December 1914, MS Lowell 19, Amy Lowell Papers, Houghton Library, Harvard University. This letter is printed in Scott's *The Gender of Modernism* (134-35).

4. Ezra Pound, letter to Amy Lowell, 1 August 1914, Amy Lowell Papers. In a subsequent letter Pound suggests that Lowell use another title for the book, or if she insisted on using "Imagisme" that she add a subtitle such as "'an anthology

devoted to Imagisme, vers libre and modern movements in verse' or something of that sort" (letter to Amy Lowell, 12 August 1914, Amy Lowell Papers).

5. H.D., letter to Amy Lowell, 17 December 1914, Amy Lowell Papers.

6. H.D., letter to Amy Lowell, 14 January 1915, Amy Lowell Papers.

7. H.D., letters to Amy Lowell, 23 November 1914; 27 April 1915; 7 October 1915; 30 August 1916, Amy Lowell Papers.

8. H.D., letter to Amy Lowell, February 1916, Amy Lowell Papers.

9. H.D., letter to Amy Lowell, 24 January 1916, Amy Lowell Papers.

10. Pondrom notes that this card is "postmarked November 23, 1914" ("Selected Letters" 561). Since Weaver and H.D. saw each other frequently, there was not much need for correspondence between them. There is very little material on H.D. among the Harriet Shaw Weaver papers in the British Library.

11. Jane Lidderdale, personal interview, January 1988.

12. In 1913 Pound became literary editor of the *New Freewoman* through the agency of Rebecca West, who had solicited work from him. The issue of 15 August 1913 found West introducing "Imagisme" in an article that briefly recapitulated segments of Flint's essay and Pound's "A Few Don'ts," followed by Pound's "Contemporania." The prose works had previously appeared in America in *Poetry*.

13. F. S. Flint, "The History of Imagism," *Egoist* 2.5 (1915): 70-71; Richard Aldington, "The Poetry of Ezra Pound," *Egoist* 2.5 (1915): 71-72; F. S. Flint, "The Poetry of H.D.," *Egoist* 2.5 (1915): 72-73; Ferris Greenslet, "The Poetry of John Gould Fletcher," *Egoist* 2.5 (1915): 73; Harold Monro, "The Imagists Discussed," *Egoist* 2.5 (1915): 77-80; Richard Aldington, "The Poetry of F. S. Flint," *Egoist* 2.5 (1915): 80-81; O[livia] Shakespear, "The Poetry of D. H. Lawrence," *Egoist* 2.5 (1915): 81; John Gould Fletcher, "The Poetry of Amy Lowell," *Egoist* 2.5 (1915): 81-82.

14. "George Lane" [Amy Lowell and John Gould Fletcher], "Some Imagist Poets," *Little Review* 2.3 (1915): 27-35. This issue included Aldington's article "Remy de Gourmont," Lowell's "The Poetry Bookshop," and Fletcher's prose-poems under the title "America, 1915," as well as Aldington's review.

15. H.D., letter to Amy Lowell, 27 April 1915, Amy Lowell Papers.

16. Monro 78. Although the context set by this article is useful, Monro's comments about H.D. are less so, since he found her work "fragile," "restrained," and too "petty" or "small" to represent the direction in which he saw Imagism developing.

17. Barbara Guest, *Herself Defined: The Poet H.D. and Her World* (New York: Quill, 1984) 69.

18. H.D., letter to Amy Lowell, February 1916, Amy Lowell Papers. This letter is printed in *The Gender of Modernism* (135-36).

19. H.D., letters to Amy Lowell, March 1916; 14 August 1916, Amy Lowell Papers.

20. H.D., letter to Amy Lowell, 10 August 1917, Amy Lowell Papers.

21. H.D., letter to Amy Lowell, 23 November 1914, Amy Lowell Papers.

22. H.D., letters to Amy Lowell, November 1915; 13 October 1916; 12 November 1916; 1 December 1916, Amy Lowell Papers. There is an interesting issue concerned with Aldington's military service and effective absence from literary

life had it not been for H.D.'s role as promoter of her husband's work. Aldington himself noted in his memoirs that, during the war, he was able to write almost nothing. But in the letter to Lowell dated 1 December 1916, H.D. comments, "R. is sending occasional 'notes' which I am trying to work up for publication. He is tremendously fine—we can not admire him too much." It is clear that by saying Aldington was "tremendously fine," H.D. was referring not to his poetry but to his perseverance and character, since during these same years she was making comments to Lowell about aspects of Aldington's poems to which she objected. Her defense of his work, when considered alongside her letters of the war years, shows more concern for encouraging Aldington's aspirations and spirits than satisfaction with his poetry per se. Of the items that may have been assembled by H.D. for publication in the *Egoist* under Aldington's name, one finds his "Notes from France," *Egoist* 4.3 (1917): 38—in which he writes "I have not done any poems. I am having too good a time. Soon I will get miserable and write some more"—and especially "Evil Malady," *Egoist* 4.5 (1917): 70, "The Road," *Egoist* 5.7 (1918): 97-98, and "Dawns," *Egoist* 5.9 (1918): 121, which in their loose, impressionistic structure suggest they were garnered from notes. The likelihood that H.D. actively put Aldington into print during his military service shows her willingness to efface herself in favor of Aldington, and to let him receive credit for work that may have been partially hers, perhaps including literary editing at the *Egoist*. The evidence also suggests that H.D. was at least as involved in assembling the anthologies as was Aldington, particularly considering the time constraints he suffered as a result of military training and service. The disruptions of their lives during these years, as described by Caroline Zilboorg, pulled Aldington away from many direct involvements in publishing and editing and often left him too exhausted to pursue his literary work. The destruction of many of H.D.'s letters to Aldington complicates such interpretations, and some of Aldington's claims— such as that he "discovered" Marianne Moore—add to the confusion. See Caroline Zilboorg, ed., *Richard Aldington and H.D.: The Early Years in Letters* (Bloomington: Indiana UP, 1992), and *Richard Aldington: An Autobiography in Letters*, ed. Norman T. Gates (University Park: Pennsylvania State UP, 1992).

    Postwar evidence also indicates that H.D.'s connections served Aldington well. In his memoir, *Life for Life's Sake* (New York: Viking, 1941), he described his search for a job after demobilization, finding a position at the *Times* (in which Bryher's father owned a controlling interest) after Bryher "had spoken to her father on my behalf" (212).

    23. H.D., letter to Amy Lowell, 5 March 1917, Amy Lowell Papers.

    24. In *Marianne Moore: A Literary Life* (New York: Atheneum, 1990), Charles Molesworth cites Aldington's mention of Moore's work in the context of a piece on Imagism for *Bruno's Weekly* in 1915 (112, 119); the actual reference is "The Imagists," *Bruno Chap Books*, special ser. 5, 1915. Aldington mentions Moore in only one sentence: "Two American girls, Miss C. Shanafeldt and Miss Marianne Moore show promise" (72).

    25. This has been amply detailed in Cyrena N. Pondrom, "Marianne Moore and H.D.: Female Community and Poetic Achievement," *Marianne Moore: Woman and Poet*, ed. Patricia C. Willis (Orono: National Poetry Foundation, 1990) 371-402, which discusses the long-term relationship between H.D., Moore, and Bryher,

and establishes, at the very least, Moore's knowledge of her friends' efforts on her behalf.

26. H.D., "Marianne Moore," *Egoist* 3.8 (1916): 118.

27. Marianne Moore, "The Accented Syllable," *Egoist* 3.10 (1916): 151-52.

28. H.D., letter to Marianne Moore, 3 September [1916] (V:23:32), Marianne Moore Papers, the Rosenbach Museum and Library, Philadelphia.

29. H.D., letter to Marianne Moore, 3 September [1916] (V:23:32), Marianne Moore Papers.

30. H.D., "The Farmer's Bride," *Egoist* 3.9 (1916): 135.

31. H.D., "Goblins and Pagodas," *Egoist* 3.12 (1916): 183. At nearly the same time, Fletcher reviewed H.D.'s *Sea-Garden* appreciatively, calling her artistic vision that of a "mystic," although he did comment that as he reread the book, he "cease[d] to care whether this is or is not what the academic critics choose to label Poetry, or whether it is or is not Imagism," noting the perfection and fusion of the book's form and substance ("H.D.'s Vision," *Poetry* 9.5 [1917]: 268).

32. Rachel Blau DuPlessis writes that H.D. felt constricted by a "romantic thralldom" in her early work—a powerful love for figures of male power to whom she felt unequal (*Writing Beyond the Ending*, chapter 5). William Carlos Williams claimed at about this time in the *Little Review* that H.D. always asked him about her early writing: "'You're not satisfied with me, are you Billy? There's something lacking, isn't there?'" He follows this passage, however, with a letter from H.D. as assistant editor of the *Egoist* in which she clearly shows artistic self-assurance: "I trust you will not hate me for wanting to delete from your poem all its flippancies. . . . I consider this business of writing a very sacred thing! . . . I think you have the 'spark,' am sure of it, and when you speak *direct* are a poet. I feel in the hey-ding-ding touch running through your poem a derivative tendency which, to me, is not *you*. . . . It's very well to *mock* at yourself—it is a spiritual sin to mock at your inspiration" ("Prologue: The Return of the Sun," *Little Review* 5.11 [1919]: 7).

33. Guest credits Aldington with deciding that Bryher, as a possible patron, should be included in the series; in the same paragraph, however, she notes that the sea poems were suggested to Bryher by H.D., and since H.D. was much closer to Bryher than was Aldington, one may suppose that the person who really brought Bryher to the Egoist Press was H.D. (107). Lidderdale and Nicholson note that, subsequently, Weaver and Bryher became genuine friends (177). It is unclear whether the "Six Sea Poems" actually appeared.

34. Receipts made out by Harriet Shaw Weaver include "£31 for Marianne Moore's *Poems*, from Bryher" and "£30 for *Hymen*, from Bryher" (Lidderdale and Nicholson 461). These writers also state that the Egoist Press's edition of Jean Cocteau's *Cock and Harlequin* (Winter 1920/21) was "the last of the books paid for by Egoist Press funds," but that Weaver "was very willing to publish subsidized books. It was not long before several others were added to her list, financed by her new friend Bryher" (177).

35. In her memoir, Bryher notes that her money subsidized McAlmon's publishing (*Heart to Artemis* 201).

36. Lidderdale and Nicholson 177, 464. Bearing in mind H.D. and Bryher's involvement with Egoist Press books, it seems that Weaver's acceptance of

McAlmon's book was likely a generous gesture of friendship rather than a strong endorsement of his prose. McAlmon's previous experience with publishing *Contact* seems not to have been demanding, involving mimeographed copies of two sheets each.

37. Robert E. Knoll, "Robert McAlmon: Expatriate Writer and Publisher," *University of Nebraska Studies* n.s. 18 (1957): 16, 81-84. If Contact Editions was what Knoll calls "a kind of pump-primer" or a "showcase for the talents of the expatriates" that eventually "got American publishers for [its] authors," then Bryher's importance as a backer should not be overlooked, good intentions being one thing and actual productivity another. Knoll persistently refers to McAlmon's impatience, his inability to persevere in detail work, and his migratory tendencies (not to mention his "errors of convenience" in retyping the "Penelope" chapter of Joyce's *Ulysses*), all of which would seem to mitigate against finding McAlmon an effective businessman.

Sanford J. Smoller notes in *Adrift Among Geniuses: Robert McAlmon, Writer and Publisher of the Twenties* (University Park: Pennsylvania State UP, 1975) that when McAlmon left London in 1921 a few months after his marriage, he went to Paris "with only letters of introduction and the names of people to look up" (56), but he does not emphasize the importance of having those names and letters of introduction. The story of *The Making of Americans* is discussed in chapter 3.

38. Knoll mentions that, in later years as McAlmon's literary work waned, one of his (reworked) stories appeared in "*Life and Letters*, the distinguished British publication, in 1934," without noting Bryher's connection to the magazine, which probably accounted for the publication (56, 72). Bryher's review was "The Biography of Continents," *Poetry* 28.5 (1926): 280-82.

39. See Pondrom, "Marianne Moore and H.D.," and John M. Slatin, who writes, "Moore's *Poems* was compiled by H.D. and Winifred Ellerman (Bryher). It is usually said that they worked without Moore's knowledge; but the most that can be said is that while Moore did not actively collaborate in producing the volume, she probably gave tacit consent. Laurence Stapleton quotes a letter from Moore to H.D. which shows no surprise at the fact of the book's publication; on the contrary, Moore is surprised only by how well she comes off. See Stapleton, 28" (*The Savage's Romance: The Poetry of Marianne Moore* [University Park: Pennsylvania State UP, 1986] 266).

40. Marianne Moore, letter to Bryher, 13 December 1920, Bryher Papers, Beinecke Rare Book and Manuscript Library, Yale University.

41. H.D.'s contributions to *Close Up* include some editorial work as well as a number of articles in which her associative and cinematographic style enacts her aesthetic and technical concerns of the time, as discussed in this chapter. Pool Publishing House was an enterprise related to *Close Up*. Some time after *Close Up* ended, Bryher renewed her ties to publishing through her association with the magazine *Life and Letters To-Day*.

42. Bryher, "G. W. Pabst: A Survey," *Close Up* 1.6 (1927): 58, 59.

43. Anne Friedberg has noted that "*Close Up* . . . was responsible for the publication of many of the first English translations of Eisenstein's theory" ("Approaching *Borderline*," *H.D.: Woman and Poet*, ed. Michael King [Orono: National Poetry Foundation, 1986] 378).

44. Rachael Low, *The History of the British Film: 1918-1929* (London: Allen & Unwin, 1971) 22.

45. Kenneth Macpherson, letter to Bryher, n.d. (attributed to January 1931), Bryher Papers. This point is significant when one notes the changes in the magazine's pictorial design over the years, as the interspersed sets of stills that early issues contained gave way to a more complex visual design, particularly in the intricate coordination of text and photographs, in volumes eight through ten. While the change in format seems to have been a collaborative decision, Bryher handled the production.

46. Macpherson, letter to Bryher, n.d. (attributed to June 1931), Bryher Papers.

47. Bryher, letter to H.D., 15 September 1932, H.D. Papers, Beinecke Rare Book and Manuscript Library, Yale University.

48. Walter Laqueur, *Weimar: A Cultural History, 1918-1933* (New York: Putnam, 1974) 231.

49. Hugh Ridley, "Tretjakov in Berlin," *Culture and Society in the Weimar Republic*, ed. Keith Bullivant (Manchester: Manchester UP, 1977) 158. I am indebted to Nancy Romalov for first mentioning to me the "pan-European" interests of Weimar intellectuals.

50. Bryher, "The War from Three Angles," *Close Up* 1.1 (1927): 17.

51. Bryher, "The War from More Angles," *Close Up* 1.4 (1927): 45.

52. See, for example, Bryher's discussions in "Defence of Hollywood," *Close Up* 2.2 (1928): 44-51; "West and East of the Atlantic," *Close Up* 9.2 (1932): 131-33; and "Notes on Some Films," *Close Up* 9.3 (1932): 196-99.

53. See discussions of the international appeal and relative political "neutrality" of cinema in Laqueur, chapter 7, and John Willett, *Art and Politics in the Weimar Period: The New Sobriety, 1917-1933* (New York: Pantheon, 1978) 139-49.

54. Bryher, "Films in Education: The Complex of the Machine," *Close Up* 1.2 (1927): 49, 51.

55. Bryher, "How I Would Start a Film Club," *Close Up* 2.6 (1928): 34.

56. Bryher, "Films for Children," *Close Up* 3.2 (1928): 18-19.

57. Bryher, "What Can I Do," *Close Up* 2.3 (1928): 21-25; "What Can I Do!" *Close Up* 2.5 (1928): 32-37; "How I Would Start a Film Club"; "How to Rent a Film," *Close Up* 3.6 (1928): 45-51.

58. Bryher, "How to Rent a Film"; "A New Commission," *Close Up* 6.3 (1930): 223-24.

59. Bryher, "What Shall You Do in the War?" *Close Up* 10.2 (1933): 188-92.

60. See especially Susan Stanford Friedman, *Psyche Reborn: The Emergence of H.D.* (Bloomington: Indiana UP, 1981).

61. Jackson Robert Bryer and Pamela Roblyer, "H.D.: A Preliminary Checklist," *Contemporary Literature* 10.4 (1969): 654-55. H.D. also published two poems in the *Adelphi*, "At Athens" in December 1924 and "Antipater of Sidon" in June 1925.

62. H.D., letter to Viola Jordan, 6 June 1927, Viola Jordan Papers, Beinecke Rare Book and Manuscript Library, Yale University.

63. Some critics who have begun to examine the interrelationships between H.D.'s writings and film include Charlotte Mandel, "Magical Lenses," *H.D.:*

Woman and Poet, ed. Michael King (Orono: National Poetry Foundation, 1986): 301-17; "Garbo/Helen: The Self-Projection of Beauty by H.D.," *Women's Studies* 7.1/2 (1980): 127-35; "The Redirected Image: Cinematic Dynamics in the Style of H.D. (Hilda Doolittle)," *Literature/Film Quarterly* 9.1 (1983): 36-45; and "H.D.'s 'Projector II' and *Chang*, a Film of the Jungle," *H.D. Newsletter* 1.2 (1987): 42-45. See also Anne Friedberg, "Approaching *Borderline*"; "On H.D., Woman, History, Recognition," *Wide Angle* 5.2 (1982): 26-31; "The POOL Films," *H.D. Newsletter* 1.1 (1987): 10-11; and Chris Brown, "A Filmography for H.D.," *H.D. Newsletter* 2.1 (1988): 19-24.

64. H.D., "The Cinema and the Classics. I: Beauty," *Close Up* 1.1 (1927): 27-28, 30-32; "The Cinema and the Classics. II: Restraint," *Close Up* 1.2 (1927): 30.

65. H.D., "Conrad Veidt. The Student of Prague," *Close Up* 1.3 (1927): 34-44.

66. H.D., "The Cinema and the Classics. III: The Mask and the Movietone," *Close Up* 1.5 (1927): 18-31.

67. At one point, H.D. wrote, "Is Art religion? Is religion art? That is where the point comes. But all discussions of Art, Religion and Life are febrile and old-fashioned really. All I can know is that I, personally, am attuned to certain vibration[s], that there comes a moment when I can 'witness' almost fanatically the 'truth'" ("Expiation," *Close Up* 2.5 [1928]: 43).

5. THE IRONIC "EDITORIAL WE"

1. See Moore's two-part comment "*The Dial*: A Retrospect" in *Life and Letters To-Day* 27.3 (1940): 175-83, and *Life and Letters To-Day* 28.1 (1941): 3-9. This reminiscence was reprinted in the *Partisan Review* 9.1 (1942): 52-58, and, with some alterations in wording and punctuation, in *Predilections* (New York: Viking, 1955) 103-14. This later version is the one reprinted in *The Complete Prose of Marianne Moore*, ed. Patricia C. Willis (New York: Viking, 1986) 357-64. Willis does not comment on the changes Moore has made; thus, when there are substantive differences between versions which affect my argument, I will discuss them. Moore also made some remarks about the *Dial* in her "Interview with Donald Hall," *A Marianne Moore Reader* (1961; New York: Viking, 1965) 253-73.

2. An early acknowledgment of Thayer's illness was made by Mary Colum in *Life and the Dream* (Garden City: Doubleday, 1947) 259, as William Wasserstrom notes in *The Time of* The Dial (Syracuse: Syracuse UP, 1963) 109, 112. See also Helen Vendler, "Marianne Moore," *Marianne Moore*, ed. Harold Bloom (New York: Chelsea House, 1987) 74, and Patricia Willis, "William Carlos Williams, Marianne Moore, and *The Dial*," *Sagetrieb* 3.2 (1984): 51. Charles Molesworth also discusses the relationship of Thayer and Moore (213-14).

3. See, for example, Marianne Moore, letters to Bryher, 29 November 1920; 28 March 1921; 3 May 1921, Bryher Papers. See also *Predilections* 104.

4. *Predilections* 103. The earlier version uses different wording in two places: "As growth-rings in the cross section of a tree present a contrastingly differentiated record of experience," and "It is that *Dial* which I know best, and when I think of it, recollections spring up, of manuscripts; of letters; of people" (*Partisan Review*

9.1 [1942]: 52). The more personal tone and the suggestion of "contrasting" procedures in the earlier version hint at the personal nature of Moore's involvement and at her perception of editorial distinctions, aspects that are less evident in the 1955 piece.

5. *Predilections* 107; in the *Partisan Review*, this passage reads, "Rivalling manuscript in its significance, were the letters; those from certain contributors, indivisible as art from their more impersonal writings" (54). The tone of the earlier version suggests explicit selectivity, which for the later version has been recast into a more general assertion.

6. *Predilections* 110, 114. The earlier version of the final paragraph differs in a few points from the later one, shifting emphasis through punctuation and again altering the earlier sense of close personal involvement: "Those of us employed at *The Dial*, felt that the devisers of the organization we represented could do better than we, what we were trying to do, and we always will feel, *The Dial*'s strength of purpose toward straightness, crispness, and usefulness. 'If,' as has been said, 'it had rough seas to navigate because it chose to sail uncharted zones, the structure was the better tested'; and we think back with gladness to the days when we were part of it" (*Partisan Review* 9.1 [1942]: 58).

7. Celeste Goodridge, *Hints and Disguises: Marianne Moore and Her Contemporaries* (Iowa City: U of Iowa P, 1990) 14.

8. While Martin is correct in stating that Moore's *Dial* accomplishments should be understood on their own, rather than as a footnote to the poetry, her main concern lies in rereading the "Comments" to detect the components of Moore's aesthetic position.

9. Marianne Moore, letter to Bryher, 29 November 1920, Bryher Papers.

10. Marianne Moore, letter to H.D., 17 April 1924, H.D. Papers.

11. Marianne Moore, letter to H.D., 26 October 1924, H.D. Papers.

12. Alyse Gregory, letter to Marianne Moore [carbon], 26 February 1924, *Dial* Papers, Beinecke Rare Book and Manuscript Library, Yale University.

13. Alyse Gregory, letter to Marianne Moore [carbon], 28 February 1924, *Dial* Papers.

14. Marianne Moore, letter to Alyse Gregory, 13 May 1924, *Dial* Papers.

15. The offer was initially extended to Van Wyck Brooks, who was unable to accept. Others whom Thayer and Watson had considered were *Dial* staffers Gilbert Seldes, Alyse Gregory, Raymond Mortimer, and Kenneth Burke (J. Sibley Watson, letter to Scofield Thayer, 15 March 1923, *Dial* Papers).

16. Marianne Moore, letter to Scofield Thayer, 2 March 1925, *Dial* Papers. Watson and Thayer were already well aware of Moore's hestitation in such matters, having had to persuade her to accept the *Dial* award earlier that year (J. Sibley Watson, letter to Scofield Thayer, 14 August 1924, *Dial* Papers).

17. A letter from Moore to Alyse Gregory expresses Moore's great disappointment (14 March 1925, *Dial* Papers).

18. Dorothy Elise De Pollier, letter to Marianne Moore, 6 March 1925 [carbon], *Dial* Papers, Beinecke Rare Book and Manuscript Library, Yale University. Moore's reply reads, "I have read Mr. Hemingway's story with great interest. As it stands, I would say no" (Letter to Dorothy Elise De Pollier, 7 March 1925, *Dial* Papers).

19. Marianne Moore, letter to Scofield Thayer, 15 May 1925, *Dial* Papers.
20. Marianne Moore, letter to Scofield Thayer, 10 December 1925, *Dial* Papers.
21. Marianne Moore, letter to Scofield Thayer, 23 April 1926, *Dial* Papers.
22. Letters from Moore to Scofield Thayer in the Beinecke Library refer to Thayer's accusations about staff members (15 May 1925; 29 June 1925, *Dial* Papers). Letters from Moore to Watson in the Rosenbach Museum and Library refer to the situation more specifically. A carbon of a letter from Moore to Watson mentions that Moore had thought of resigning (Letter to J. Sibley Watson [draft], n.d., written on verso of J. Sibley Watson, letter to Marianne Moore, n.d. [attributed to 30 November 1925] [V:75:02], Marianne Moore Papers).
23. Marianne Moore, letter to Scofield Thayer, 7 September 1925, *Dial* Papers.
24. In a letter of September 1925 Moore told Scofield Thayer that Max Robin, visiting the office, spoke "musingly and regretfully of [your absence] and keeps asking what you will think of his writing. . . . Upon the occasion of his last visit he said, 'Is Mr Thayer a person of some years? And why did he go to Germany? To study?['] I said, 'Yes, to study and to do some writing; and he likes the climate.' Mr Robin looked at me apprehensively and exclaimed, 'He'll freeze'" (11 September 1925, *Dial* Papers). By treating the situation with humor, Moore seems to be comforting Thayer with the thought that he was respected and missed; at the same time, her excuse to Robin underlines Moore's determination to protect Thayer's name publicly.
25. Marianne Moore, letter to Scofield Thayer, 12 March 1926, *Dial* Papers.
26. Marianne Moore, letter to J. Sibley Watson [draft], n.d., written on verso of J. Sibley Watson, letter to Marianne Moore, n.d. (attributed to 30 November 1925) (V:75:02), Marianne Moore Papers.
27. Marianne Moore, letter to J. Sibley Watson [carbon], 29 April 1926 (V:75:03), Marianne Moore Papers. Ellen Thayer was office assistant and Scofield Thayer's cousin.
28. Marianne Moore, letter to J. Sibley Watson [carbon], 29 April 1926 (V:75:03), Marianne Moore Papers.
29. Nicholas Joost and Alvin Sullivan, The Dial: *Two Author Indexes* (Carbondale: Southern Illinois Univ. Libraries, 1971) vii. Late in 1925, Moore told Watson she regretted asking him to do "press-work" such as checking proof (Letter to J. Sibley Watson [carbon], 21 December 1925 [V:75:02], Marianne Moore Papers).
30. Moore mentioned Watson's absence in letters to Scofield Thayer: "Dr Watson has been away since you left but responds quickly and with patience to my pertinacities" (7 September 1925, *Dial* Papers). A few months later, Moore noted, "Dr Watson made us a visit last week of a half hour or more. His cheer and humorous nonchalance despite the select corps of our few pestilential contributors, was most reassuring. Also, feeling as we do the loss of Mr Burke's experience and efficiency, it was no small support to have him inspect our procedure" (Letter to Scofield Thayer, 28 December 1925, *Dial* Papers).
31. J. Sibley Watson, letter to Marianne Moore, n.d. (attributed to May 1926) (V:75:03), Marianne Moore Papers.
32. Marianne Moore, letter to Bryher, 28 June 1929, Bryher Papers.

33. J. Sibley Watson, letter to Marianne Moore, n.d. (attributed to 1 June 1926) (V:75:03), Marianne Moore Papers.

34. Marianne Moore, letter to J. Sibley Watson [carbon], 12 April 1926 (V:75:03), Marianne Moore Papers.

35. J. Sibley Watson, letter to Marianne Moore, 29 January 1927 (V:75:03), Marianne Moore Papers.

36. Marianne Moore, letter to Ezra Pound, 28 August 1928, Ezra Pound Papers, Beinecke Rare Book and Manuscript Library, Yale University.

37. J. Sibley Watson, letter to Marianne Moore, n.d. (attributed to 29 August 1925) (V:75:02), Marianne Moore Papers. See also Walter Sutton, ed., *Pound, Thayer, Watson and* The Dial: *A Story in Letters* (Gainesville: UP of Florida, 1994) 308.

38. A letter from Thayer to Watson reads in part, "I am allowing Gilbert to try to get some *Parisian* correspondent to take the place of our Idaho Barker. I have written Gilbert to do this now rather than wait until I reach Paris because Pound is now living in Italy and we then have a particularly good excuse with what was after all expressly stated by me upon his appointment, to be merely a stop gap until we could find the ideal *Parisian* correspondent" (20 March 1923, *Dial* Papers). Subsequently, Thayer asked to have any further contributions from Pound forwarded to him to read; Watson did not like this arrangement but acceded (Scofield Thayer, letter to J. Sibley Watson, 27 March 1923, *Dial* Papers; J. Sibley Watson, letter to Scofield Thayer, 10 May 1923, *Dial* Papers).

39. J. Sibley Watson, letter to Marianne Moore, n.d. (attributed to 10 October 1925) (V:75:02), Marianne Moore Papers.

40. Marianne Moore, letter to Scofield Thayer, 8 June 1921, *Dial* Papers.

41. J. Sibley Watson, letter to Marianne Moore, n.d. (attributed to 10 October 1925) (V:75:02), Marianne Moore Papers. Wasserstrom notes that Watson's appreciation for Pound's work extended to accepting some of it in November 1927 without consulting Moore (*Time of* The Dial 115-16, 175n); this occurrence, however, came some years after Moore's initial decision to make overtures to Pound.

42. Watson suggested that Moore review Cummings's book *XLI Poems* rather than asking Pound to do it because Pound would be hurt (Letter to Marianne Moore, 7 October 1925 [V:75:02], Marianne Moore Papers). While Watson did not detail the reason why, his implication was that Pound would resent the *Dial*'s attention to Cummings when his own work had been refused. A few days later, Moore agreed to do the review (Marianne Moore, letter to J. Sibley Watson [carbon], 13 October 1925 [V:75:02], Marianne Moore Papers). In a letter to Pound, Moore referred to herself and Watson having asked Pound to review Stendhal (8 December 1925, Ezra Pound Papers). Watson's letter to Moore of August 1925 suggests, "How about Ezra Pound for the Stendhal complete works— or wouldn't Scofield approve?" (Sutton 308). Watson at this time was not in contact with Pound, according to Sutton's book.

43. Marianne Moore, letter to Scofield Thayer, 15 October 1925, *Dial* Papers.

44. Scofield Thayer, letter to J. Sibley Watson, 27 March 1923, *Dial* Papers. The holdings of the Rosenbach Museum and Library and the Beinecke Library do not seem to include a letter from Thayer to Moore or to Watson suggesting that Pound contribute. A letter from Watson to Thayer of 10 May 1923 reads in part, "I am having the revised Cantos sent to you. Are you not grateful to me for giving

you a chance to stop 'these little ones' when I might easily have said they had been already accepted and closed the matter for 6 months? . . . Why not cable if you want us to run the Cantos?" This comment throws interesting light on the laissez-faire editorial dynamics between the two men as well as on their difference of opinion about Pound. At any rate, even if Thayer had "veto power" in 1923, by 1925 when Moore decided to retrieve Pound, Thayer's arrangement had in effect been nullified; no letters at that time refer to this arrangement (10 May 1923, *Dial* Papers).

45. Marianne Moore, letter to Ezra Pound, 8 December 1925, Ezra Pound Papers.

46. Marianne Moore, letter to Ezra Pound, 26 April 1927, Ezra Pound Papers.

47. Marianne Moore, letter to Ezra Pound [damaged], 9 February 1928, Ezra Pound Papers.

48. Marianne Moore, letter to Ezra Pound [damaged], n.d. (attributed to February or March 1928), Ezra Pound Papers.

49. James R. Mellow writes that one night Pound brought Thayer to Stein's home, and all participated in an argument that ended when Pound broke one of Stein's chairs; "nobody [was] too well pleased" with the evening (305).

50. A letter from Moore to Alyse Gregory reads in part, "Thank you again for bidding me to name books which I should enjoy reviewing. . . . [One] book the appearing of which I anticipate with pleasure, is Gertrude Stein: The Making of an American Family" (11 July 1924, *Dial* Papers).

51. Marianne Moore, letter to Gertrude Stein, 13 July 1926, Gertrude Stein Papers, Beinecke Rare Book and Manuscript Library, Yale University.

52. Marianne Moore, letter to Gertrude Stein, 4 March 1927, Gertrude Stein Papers.

53. Marianne Moore, letter to Gertrude Stein, 5 April 1927, Gertrude Stein Papers.

54. Marianne Moore, letter to Gertrude Stein, 24 February 1928, Gertrude Stein Papers.

55. Scofield Thayer, letter to Marianne Moore, 6 December 1925 (V:65:04), Marianne Moore Papers.

56. Marianne Moore, letter to Bryher, 27 March 1926, Bryher Papers.

57. Marianne Moore, letter to J. Sibley Watson [carbon], 14 January 1926 (V:75:02), Marianne Moore Papers. In a letter from Watson to Moore later in January he wrote that he was glad she had "noticed" *In the American Grain* (24 January 1926 [V:75:02], Marianne Moore Papers).

58. Marianne Moore, letter to Ezra Pound, 19 December 1932, Ezra Pound Papers.

59. Marianne Moore, letter to Ezra Pound, 2 March 1933, Ezra Pound Papers.

60. See Pondrom, "Marianne Moore and H.D." 371-402.

6. A Distorting Lens

1. Ezra Pound, "Date Line," *Make It New. Essays by Ezra Pound* (New Haven: Yale UP, 1935), 12; quoted with commentary in Ezra Pound and James Joyce, *Pound/Joyce*, ed. Forrest Read (New York: New Directions, 1970) 9. Pound also

made notes about his own background as if it were a history of Imagism, in a letter to F. S. Flint, 30 January 1921, F. S. Flint Papers, Harry Ransom Humanities Research Center, U of Texas at Austin.

2. There is no date given for this letter, quoted in Edward Larrissy, *Reading Twentieth-Century Poetry: The Language of Gender and Objects* (Oxford: Basil Blackwell, 1990) 36.

3. Ezra Pound and Ford Madox Ford, *Pound/Ford: The Story of a Literary Friendship*, ed. Brita Lindberg-Seyersted (New York: New Directions, 1982) vii, 5.

4. Arthur Mizener, *The Saddest Story: A Biography of Ford Madox Ford* (New York: World Publishing, 1971) 329. See also Bernard J. Poli, *Ford Madox Ford and* The Transatlantic Review (Syracuse: Syracuse UP, 1967) 26-29.

5. James Laughlin, *Pound as Wuz: Essays and Lectures on Ezra Pound* (St. Paul: Greywolf, 1987).

6. Richard Aldington, letter to Harriet Monroe, 28 November 1913, quoted in Ellen Williams 82.

7. *Pound/Joyce* 184. Anderson's published accounts of this period do not give a full account; see *My Thirty Years' War*. For an account of the problems attending this serial publication, see Bryer, "Joyce, *Ulysses* and the *Little Review*."

8. *Letters of Ezra Pound, 1907-1941* 107. H.D.'s piece on Marianne Moore appeared in 1916 in the *Egoist*; Pound's appeared in 1918 in *Future*.

9. Ezra Pound and Wyndham Lewis, *Pound/Lewis*, ed. Timothy Materer (New York: New Directions, 1985).

10. See, for example, Garner 132-33, 138-39. I would also like to thank Bonnie Kime Scott for information about letters from Rebecca West to Jane Lidderdale in early 1967, held by the McFarlin Library of the University of Tulsa, describing Pound's apparent intention to take over the paper.

11. Ezra Pound, letter to Alice Corbin Henderson, n.d., letter 3 in *The Letters of Ezra Pound to Alice Corbin Henderson*, ed. Ira B. Nadel (Austin: U of Texas P, 1993) 8. Nadel dates this December 1912 or January 1913. I have followed his orthography and transcriptions, although my notes differ from his in some respects.

12. Ezra Pound, letter to Alice Corbin Henderson, 24 January 1916, letter 44 in *Letters of Pound to Henderson* 128.

13. Ezra Pound, letter to Harriet Monroe, 26 October 1912, enclosed with letter 23 in *Letters of Pound to Henderson* 68.

14. Ezra Pound, letter to Alice Corbin Henderson, 22 May 1915, letter 37 in *Letters of Pound to Henderson* 101.

15. Ezra Pound, letter to Alice Corbin Henderson, December 1913, letter 22 in *Letters of Pound to Henderson* 64.

16. Ezra Pound, letter to Alice Corbin Henderson, 20 January 1913, letter 7 in *Letters of Pound to Henderson* 18-19.

17. Ezra Pound, letter to Alice Corbin Henderson, n.d., letter 2; July/August 1913, letter 18; and 27 January 1914, letter 23 in *Letters of Pound to Henderson* 2, 50, 65-66.

18. See *Pound/*The Little Review 29-41, 43, 49, 52.

19. Ezra Pound, letter to Alice Corbin Henderson, January 1913, letter 8 in *Letters of Pound to Henderson* 26.

20. Ezra Pound, letter to Margaret Anderson, 17 May 1917, letter 20 in *Pound/*The Little Review 52.

21. Ezra Pound, letter to Margaret Anderson, 26 January 1917, letter 4 in *Pound*/The Little Review 8.

22. Ezra Pound, letter to Alice Corbin Henderson, 14 October 1913, letter 20 in *Letters of Pound to Henderson* 55.

23. Ezra Pound, letter to Alice Corbin Henderson, 8/9 August 1913, letter 19 in *Letters of Pound to Henderson* 52.

24. Ezra Pound, letter to Alice Corbin Henderson, May 1913, letter 14 in *Letters of Pound to Henderson* 41.

25. Ellen Williams 253-54, 242-44.

26. Schulman 2; Patricia Willis, in Moore, *The Complete Prose of Marianne Moore* v-vi. Ellen Williams gives credit to T. S. Eliot, who also wrote about Moore in 1918 (286n).

27. Pondrom, "H.D. and the Origins of Imagism."

AFTERWORD

1. Discussed in DuPlessis, *Writing Beyond the Ending* 152.

2. See the cogent discussion of this problem in Margaret J. M. Ezell, *Writing Women's Literary History* (Baltimore: Johns Hopkins UP, 1993).

3. See also the discussion of editorial group activity in Pauline Butling, "'Hall of Fame Blocks Women'—Re/Righting Literary History: Women and B.C. Little Magazines," *Women's Writing and the Literary Institution/L'Écriture au Féminin et l'Institution Littéraire*, ed. C. Potvin and J. Williamson (Edmonton: Research Institute for Comparative Literature, U of Alberta, 1992), 53-68.

4. Lidderdale and Nicholson 231, 238; William Wasserstrom, "Marianne Moore, *The Dial*, and Kenneth Burke," *Western Humanities Review* 17.3 (1963): 254-56.

5. Bornstein 2.

6. One is reminded of DuPlessis's earlier experiment in taking a multifaceted critical approach to literary scholarship in "For the Etruscans: Sexual Difference and Artistic Production—The Debate over a Female Aesthetic," *The Future of Difference*, ed. Alice Jardine and Hester Eisenstein (Boston: G. K. Hall, 1981) 128-56, and of the recent volume *The Intimate Critique: Autobiographical Literary Criticism*, ed. Diane P. Freedman, Olivia Frey, and Frances Murphy Zauhar (Durham: Duke UP, 1993).

7. Robert Johnstone notes that "the value of given [literary] histories as designs, their gain in conversational meaning at the expense of the illusion of truth, depends on their being read together. . . . Taken together . . . the designs constitute a debate about the image and ideals of the culture; taken in succession, they form a series of differentiations that also points to the future." This observation offers a way to theorize how even traditional literary histories may fit with poststructuralist or revisionist views of histories in flux ("The Impossible Genre: Reading Comprehensive Literary History," *Publications of the Modern Language Association of America* 107.1 [1992]: 31).

BIBLIOGRAPHY

Abbott, Craig S. "The Case of Scharmel Iris." *Papers of the Bibliographic Society of America* 77.1 (1983): 15-34.

———. *Marianne Moore: A Bibliography*. Pittsburgh Series in Bibliography. Pittsburgh: U of Pittsburgh P, 1977.

———. "Publishing the New Poetry: Harriet Monroe's Anthology." *Journal of Modern Literature* 11 (1984): 89-108.

Aldington, Richard. "Dawns." *Egoist* 5.9 (1918) 121.

———. "Evil Malady." *Egoist* 4.5 (1917): 70.

———. "The Imagists." *Bruno Chap Books* special ser. 5 (1915).

———. Letter to Amy Lowell. 29 November 1915. Amy Lowell Papers. Houghton Library, Harvard U.

———. *Life for Life's Sake*. New York: Viking, 1941.

———. "Notes from France." *Egoist* 4.3 (1917): 38.

———. "The Poetry of Ezra Pound." *Egoist* 2.5 (1915): 71-72.

———. "The Poetry of F. S. Flint." *Egoist* 2.5 (1915): 80-81.

———. "Remy de Gourmont." *Little Review* 2.3 (1915): 10-13.

———. *Richard Aldington: An Autobiography in Letters*. Ed. Norman T. Gates. University Park: Pennsylvania State UP, 1992.

———. "The Road." *Egoist* 5.7 (1918): 97-98.

Anderson, Margaret. "Announcement." *Little Review* 1.1 (1914): 1-2.

———. "Armageddon." *Little Review* 1.6 (1914): 3-4.

———. "Conversation." *Prose* 2 (1971): 5-21.

———. "Dialogue." *Little Review* 9.2 (1922): 24-25.

———. "'Don'ts for Critics.'" *Little Review* 3.1 (1916): 23-24.

———. "The Essential Thing." *Little Review* 3.1 (1916): 23.

———. "Incense and Splendor." *Little Review* 1.4 (1914): 1-3.

———. "Isadora Duncan's Misfortune." *Little Review* 3.10 (1917): 5-7.

————. *My Thirty Years' War.* 1930. New York: Horizon, 1969.

————. "Notes on Music and the Theatre (and the Critics)." *Little Review* 5.11 (1919): 55-61.

————. "An Obvious Statement." *Little Review* 7.3 (1920): 8-16.

————. "'Ulysses' in Court." *Little Review* 7.4 (1921): 22-25.

————. "What the Public Doesn't Want." *Little Review* 4.4 (1917): 20-22.

————, ed. *The* Little Review *Anthology.* New York: Horizon, 1953.

[Anonymous.] "The Reader Critic." *Little Review* 3.7 (1916): 27.

Atlas, Marilyn J. "Harriet Monroe, Margaret Anderson, and the Spirit of the Chicago Renaissance." *Midwestern Miscellany* 9 (1981): 43-53.

Baggett, Holly Ann. "Aloof from Natural Laws: Margaret C. Anderson and the 'Little Review,' 1914-1929." Diss. U of Delaware, 1992.

Bauer, Dale M., and S. Janet McKinstry, eds. *Feminism, Bakhtin, and the Dialogic.* Albany: State U of New York P, 1991.

Belenky, Mary Field, Blythe McVicker Clinchy, Nancy Rule Goldberger, and Jill Mattuck Tarule. *Women's Ways of Knowing: The Development of Self, Voice, and Mind.* New York: Basic, 1986.

Benstock, Shari. *Women of the Left Bank: Paris, 1900-1940.* Austin: U of Texas P, 1986.

Benstock, Shari, and Bernard Benstock. "The Role of Little Magazines in the Emergence of Modernism." *The Library Chronicle of the University of Texas at Austin* 20.4 (1991): 69-87.

Bornstein, George. "Introduction: Why Editing Matters." *Representing Modernist Texts: Editing as Interpretation.* Ann Arbor: U of Michigan P, 1991. 1-16.

Bradbury, Malcolm, and James McFarlane, eds. *Modernism: 1890-1930.* Harmondsworth: Penguin, 1976.

Brown, Chris. "A Filmography for H.D." *H.D. Newsletter* 2.1 (1988): 19-24.

Brownstein, Marilyn L. "Marianne Moore (1887-1972)." *The Gender of Modernism.* Ed. Bonnie Kime Scott. Bloomington: Indiana UP, 1990. 323-34.

Bryer, Jackson Robert. "Joyce, *Ulysses* and the *Little Review.*" *South Atlantic Quarterly* 66.2 (1967): 148-64.

————. "'A Trial-Track for Racers': Margaret Anderson and the *Little Review.*" Diss. U of Wisconsin, 1965.

Bryer, Jackson Robert, and Pamela Roblyer. "H.D.: A Preliminary Checklist." *Contemporary Literature* 10.4 (1969): 654-55.

Bryher. "The Biography of Continents." *Poetry* 28.5 (1926): 280-82.

————. "Chance Encounter." *Little Review* 10.2 (1924-25): 35-39.

————. "Defence of Hollywood." *Close Up* 2.2 (1928): 44-51.

————. "Films for Children." *Close Up* 3.2 (1928): 16-20.

————. "Films in Education: The Complex of the Machine." *Close Up* 1.2 (1927): 49-54.

————. "G. W. Pabst: A Survey." *Close Up* 1.6 (1927): 56-61.

————. *The Heart to Artemis: A Writer's Memoirs.* New York: Harcourt, Brace, 1962.

————. "How I Would Start a Film Club." *Close Up* 2.6 (1928): 30-36.

————. "How to Rent a Film." *Close Up* 3.6 (1928): 45-51.

————. Letters to Gertrude Stein. 7 July 1927; 8 August 1927. Gertrude Stein Papers. Beinecke Rare Book and Manuscript Library, Yale U.

————. Letter to H.D. 15 September 1932. H.D. Papers. Beinecke Rare Book and Manuscript Library, Yale U.

————. "A New Commission." *Close Up* 6.3 (1930): 223-24.

————. "Notes on Some Films." *Close Up* 9.3 (1932): 196-99.

————. "The War from More Angles." *Close Up* 1.4 (1927): 44-48.

————. "The War from Three Angles." *Close Up* 1.1 (1927): 16-22.

————. "West and East of the Atlantic." *Close Up* 9.2 (1932): 131-33.

————. "What Can I Do." *Close Up* 2.3 (1928): 21-25.

————. "What Can I Do!" *Close Up* 2.5 (1928): 32-37.

————. "What Shall You Do in the War?" *Close Up* 10.2 (1933): 188-92.

Burnett, Gary. *H.D. Between Image and Epic.* Ann Arbor: UMI Research P, 1990.

————. "A Poetics Out of War: H.D.'s Responses to the First World War." *Agenda* 25.3/4 (1987-88): 54-63.

Bush, Ronald. "Ezra Pound (1885-1972)." *The Gender of Modernism.* Ed. Bonnie Kime Scott. Bloomington: Indiana UP, 1990. 353-59.

Butling, Pauline. "'Hall of Fame Blocks Women'—Re/Righting Literary History: Women and B.C. Little Magazines." *Women's Writing and the Literary Institution/L'Écriture au Féminin et l'Institution Littéraire.* Ed. C. Potvin and J. Williamson. Edmonton: Research Institute for Comparative Literature, U of Alberta, 1992. 53-68.

Cane, Melville. "The Ladies of the *Dial.*" *American Scholar* 40.2 (1971): 316-21.

Carpenter, Humphrey. *A Serious Character: The Life of Ezra Pound.* London: Faber, 1988.

Carr, Daphne. "The Reader Critic." *Little Review* 3.7 (1916): 27.

Chielens, Edward E., ed. *The Literary Journal in America, 1900-1950.* American Literature, English Literature, and World Literature in English Information Guide Series 16. Detroit: Gale, 1977.

Chodorow, Nancy J. *Feminism and Psychoanalytic Theory.* New Haven: Yale UP, 1989.

Christian, Barbara. "The Race for Theory." *Making Face, Making Soul: Haciendo Caras*. Ed. Gloria Anzaldúa. San Francisco: Aunt Lute, 1990. 335-45.

Cody, Morrill, and Hugh Ford. *The Women of Montparnasse*. New York: Cornwall, 1984.

Colum, Mary. *Life and the Dream*. Garden City: Doubleday, 1947.

Cone, Eddie Gay. "The Free-Verse Controversy in American Magazines: 1912-1922." Diss. Duke U, 1971.

[A Contributor.] "Freudian." *Little Review* 3.6 (1916): 26.

Cox, Jeffrey N., and Larry J. Reynolds, eds. *New Historical Literary Study: Essays on Reproducing Texts, Representing History*. Princeton: Princeton UP, 1993.

"D.H." "Infantile Paralysis." *Little Review* 3.6 (1916): 25.

D[oolittle], H[ilda]. "The Cinema and the Classics. I: Beauty." *Close Up* 1.1 (1927): 22-33.

———. "The Cinema and the Classics. II: Restraint." *Close Up* 1.2 (1927): 30-39.

———. "The Cinema and the Classics. III: The Mask and the Movietone." *Close Up* 1.5 (1927): 18-31.

———. "Conrad Veidt. The Student of Prague." *Close Up* 1.3 (1927): 34-44.

———. "Expiation." *Close Up* 2.5 (1928): 38-49.

———. "The Farmer's Bride." *Egoist* 3.9 (1916): 135.

———. "Goblins and Pagodas." *Egoist* 3.12 (1916): 183-84.

———. Letters to Amy Lowell. 23 November 1914; 17 December 1914; 14 January 1915; 27 April 1915; 7 October 1915; November 1915; 24 January 1916; February 1916; March 1916; 14 August 1916; 30 August 1916; 13 October 1916; 12 November 1916; 1 December 1916; 5 March 1917; 10 August 1917. MS Lowell 19, Amy Lowell Papers. Houghton Library, Harvard U.

———. Letter to Marianne Moore. 3 September [1916] (V:23:32). Marianne Moore Papers. The Rosenbach Museum and Library, Philadelphia.

———. Letter to Viola Jordan. 6 June 1927. Viola Jordan Papers. Beinecke Rare Book and Manuscript Library, Yale U.

———. "Marianne Moore." *Egoist* 3.8 (1916): 118-19.

Damon, S. Foster. *Amy Lowell. A Chronicle with Extracts from Her Correspondence*. Boston: Houghton Mifflin, 1935.

DeKoven, Marianne. *Rich and Strange: Gender, History, Modernism*. Princeton: Princeton UP, 1991.

De Pollier, Dorothy Elise. Letter to Marianne Moore [carbon]. 6 March

1925. *Dial* Papers. Beinecke Rare Book and Manuscript Library, Yale U.

DuPlessis, Rachel Blau. *Writing Beyond the Ending: Narrative Strategies of Twentieth-Century Women Writers.* Bloomington: Indiana UP, 1984.

DuPlessis, Rachel Blau, and Members of Workshop 9. "For the Etruscans: Sexual Difference and Artistic Production—The Debate over a Female Aesthetic." *The Future of Difference.* Ed. Alice Jardine and Hester Eisenstein. Boston: G. K. Hall, 1981. 128-56.

Ezell, Margaret J. M. *Writing Women's Literary History.* Baltimore: Johns Hopkins UP, 1993.

Filreis, Alan. "Voicing the Desert of Silence: Stevens's Letters to Alice Corbin Henderson." *Wallace Stevens Journal* 12.1 (1988): 3-20.

Finke, Laurie A. *Feminist Theory, Women's Writing.* Ithaca: Cornell UP, 1992.

Fitch, Noel Riley. *Sylvia Beach and the Lost Generation: A History of Literary Paris in the Twenties and Thirties.* New York: Norton, 1983.

Fletcher, John Gould. "America, 1915." *Little Review* 2.3 (1915): 23-25.

———. "H.D.'s Vision." *Poetry* 9.5 (1917): 266-69.

———. *Life Is My Song.* New York: Farrar and Rinehart, 1937.

———. "The Poetry of Amy Lowell." *Egoist* 2.5 (1915): 81-82.

Flint, F. S. "The History of Imagism." *Egoist* 2.5 (1915): 70-71.

———. "The Poetry of H.D." *Egoist* 2.5 (1915): 72-73.

Ford, Hugh. *Four Lives in Paris.* San Francisco: North Point, 1987.

———. *Published in Paris: American and British Writers, Printers, and Publishers in Paris, 1920-1939.* New York: Macmillan, 1975.

Freedman, Diane P., Olivia Frey, and Frances Murphy Zauhar, eds. *The Intimate Critique: Autobiographical Literary Criticism.* Durham: Duke UP, 1993.

Friedberg, Anne. "Approaching *Borderline.*" *H.D.: Woman and Poet.* Ed. Michael King. Orono: National Poetry Foundation, 1986. 369-90.

———. "On H.D., Woman, History, Recognition." *Wide Angle* 5.2 (1982): 26-31.

———. "The POOL Films." *H.D. Newsletter* 1.1 (1987): 10-11.

Friedman, Susan Stanford. "H.D. (1886-1961)." *The Gender of Modernism.* Ed. Bonnie Kime Scott. Bloomington: Indiana UP, 1990. 85-92.

———. "Post/Poststructuralist Feminist Criticism: The Politics of Recuperation and Negotiation." *New Literary History* 22.2 (1991): 465-90.

———. *Psyche Reborn: The Emergence of H.D.* Bloomington: Indiana UP, 1981.

Friedman, Susan Stanford, and Rachel Blau DuPlessis, eds. *Signets: Reading H.D.* Madison: U of Wisconsin P, 1990.

Gallup, Donald. *Ezra Pound: A Bibliography*. Charlottesville: UP of Virginia, 1983.

Garner, Les. *A Brave and Beautiful Spirit: Dora Marsden, 1882-1960*. Aldershot: Avebury/Gower, 1990.

Gelpi, Albert. *A Coherent Splendor: The American Poetic Renaissance, 1910-1950*. Cambridge: Cambridge UP, 1987.

George, Roy. "The Reader Critic." *Little Review* 3.7 (1916): 22-24.

Gilbert, Sandra M., and Susan Gubar. *The Madwoman in the Attic: The Woman Writer and the Nineteenth-Century Literary Imagination*. New Haven: Yale UP, 1979.

———. *No Man's Land: The Place of the Woman Writer in the Twentieth Century. Vol. I: The War of the Words*. New Haven: Yale UP, 1988.

———. *No Man's Land: The Place of the Woman Writer in the Twentieth Century. Vol. II: Sexchanges*. New Haven: Yale UP, 1989.

———. *No Man's Land: The Place of the Woman Writer in the Twentieth Century. Vol. III: Letters from the Front*. New Haven: Yale UP, 1994.

Gilligan, Carol. *In a Different Voice: Psychological Theory and Women's Development*. Cambridge: Harvard UP, 1982.

Goodridge, Celeste. *Hints and Disguises: Marianne Moore and Her Contemporaries*. Iowa City: U of Iowa P, 1990.

Gray, Nancy. *Language Unbound: On Experimental Writing by Women*. Urbana: U of Illinois P, 1992.

Greenslet, Ferris. "The Poetry of John Gould Fletcher." *Egoist* 2.5 (1915): 73.

Gregory, Alyse. Letters to Marianne Moore [carbons]. 26 February 1924; 28 February 1924. *Dial* Papers. Beinecke Rare Book and Manuscript Library, Yale U.

Groff, Alice. "The Reader Critic." *Little Review* 3.7 (1916): 27.

Guest, Barbara. *Herself Defined: The Poet H.D. and Her World*. New York: Quill, 1984.

Hall, Donald. *Marianne Moore: The Cage and the Animal*. New York: Pegasus, 1970.

Hanscombe, Gillian, and Virginia L. Smyers. *Writing for Their Lives: The Modernist Women, 1910-1940*. Boston: Northeastern UP, 1987.

Heap, Jane. "And—[A Decadent Art!]." *Little Review* 3.8 (1917): 6-7.

———. "And—[John Cowper Powys]." *Little Review* 3.6 (1916): 20.

———. "And—[Paderewski and Tagore]." *Little Review* 3.7 (1916): 7-8.

———. "And—[Tagore]." *Little Review* 3.6 (1916): 21.

———. "And—[*Windy McPherson's Son*]." *Little Review* 3.7 (1916): 6-7.

———. "Art and the Law." *Little Review* 7.3 (1920): 5-7.

———. "Dada—." *Little Review* 8.2 (1922): 46.

————. "The Episode Continued." *Little Review* 5.7 (1918): 35-37.

————. ["Freudian."] *Little Review* 3.6 (1916): 26.

————. "I Cannot Sleep." *Little Review* 9.2 (1922): 3-4.

————. "Indiscriminate Illusions." *Little Review* 4.3 (1917): 25.

————. Letters to Gertrude Stein. 1924; 1925; 1926; 18 May 1926; 18 July 1926. Gertrude Stein Papers. Beinecke Rare Book and Manuscript Library, Yale U.

————. "Mary Garden." *Little Review* 3.9 (1917): 5-9.

————. "Notes." *Little Review* 5.2 (1918): 62.

————. "Notes." *Little Review* 9.1 (1922): 36.

————. "Notes from an Article by May Sinclair in the 'English Review.'" *Little Review* 7.2 (1920): 36-37.

————. "Push-Face." *Little Review* 4.2 (1917): 4-7.

————. ["That International Episode."] *Little Review* 5.10 (1919): 64-65.

————. "Ulysses." *Little Review* 9.1 (1922): 34-35.

————. "Wreaths." *Little Review* 12.2 (1929): 60-63.

Heap, Jane, and Jean de Bosschère. "Ezra Pound's Critics." *Little Review* 4.9 (1918): 56-59.

Hecht, Ben. *A Child of the Century*. New York: Simon and Schuster, 1954.

Hemingway, Ernest. "Mr. and Mrs. Elliot." *Little Review* 10.2 (1924-25): 9-12.

Henderson, Alice Corbin. "Cowboy Songs and Ballads." *Poetry* 10.5 (1917): 255-59.

————. "Don'ts for Critics." *Little Review* 3.1 (1916): 12-14.

————. "Imagism: Secular and Esoteric." *Poetry* 11.6 (1918): 339-43.

————. "Lazy Criticism." *Poetry* 9.3 (1916): 144-49.

————. Letters to Harriet Monroe [carbons]. 28 November 1916; 1 December 1916; 8 December 1916; 6 June 1921. Alice Corbin Henderson Papers. Harry Ransom Humanities Research Center, U of Texas at Austin.

————. Letters to Harriet Monroe. 23 August 1912; June 1915; June 1916; 7 June 1916; 2 August 1916; 8 August 1916; 6 February 1917; 25 February 1917; 9 June 1917; 15 June 1917; 12 December 1917; 20 October 1921; 1 November 1921; 15 April 1922. *Poetry* Papers. Joseph Regenstein Library, U of Chicago.

————. Letter to Roberts Walker [carbon]. 2 May 1922. Alice Corbin Henderson Papers. Harry Ransom Humanities Research Center, U of Texas at Austin.

————. "Our Contemporaries." *Poetry* 3.5 (1914): 187-89.

————. "Our Contemporaries [A New School of Poetry]." *Poetry* 8.2 (1916): 103-5.

————. "Our Contemporaries [What Would Walt Think?]" *Poetry* 7.1 (1915): 48-49.

————. "Our Cowboy Poet." *Poetry* 10.6 (1917): 319-20.

————. "Our Friend the Enemy." *Poetry* 6.5 (1915): 259-61.

————. "A Perfect Return." *Poetry* 1.3 (1912): 87-91.

————. "Poetic Drama." *Poetry* 7.1 (1915): 31-35.

————. "Poetic Prose and Vers Libre." *Poetry* 2.2 (1913): 70-72.

————. "Poetry of the North-American Indian." *Poetry* 14.1 (1919): 41-47.

————. "The Rejection Slip." *Poetry* 8.4 (1916): 197-99.

————. Rev. of *Des Imagistes: An Anthology. Poetry* 5.1 (1914): 38-40.

————. Rev. of *Spoon River Anthology*, by Edgar Lee Masters. *Poetry* 6.3 (1915): 145-49.

————. "Too Far from Paris." *Poetry* 4.3 (1914): 105-11.

Hodin, J.P. *Modern Art and the Modern Mind.* Cleveland: Case Western Reserve UP, 1972.

Hoffman, Frederick J. *The Twenties: American Writing in the Postwar Decade.* 1949. Rev. ed. New York: Macmillan, 1965.

Hoffman, Frederick J., Charles Allen, and Carolyn F. Ulrich. *The Little Magazine: A History and a Bibliography.* Princeton: Princeton UP, 1947.

Irigaray, Luce. *This Sex Which Is Not One.* Trans. Catherine Porter. 1977. Ithaca: Cornell UP, 1985.

Johnson, Abby Ann Arthur. "The Personal Magazine: Margaret C. Anderson and the *Little Review*, 1914-1929." *South Atlantic Quarterly* 75.3 (1976): 351-63.

Johnstone, Robert. "The Impossible Genre: Reading Comprehensive Literary History." *Publications of the Modern Language Association of America* 107.1 (1992): 26-37.

Jones, Ann Rosalind. "Inscribing Femininity: French Theories of the Feminine." *Making a Difference: Feminist Literary Criticism.* Ed. Gayle Greene and Coppélia Kahn. London: Methuen, 1985. 80-112.

Jones, Margaret C. *Heretics and Hellraisers: Women Contributors to* The Masses, *1911-1917.* Austin: U of Texas P, 1993.

Joost, Nicholas. *Ernest Hemingway and the Little Magazines: The Paris Years.* Barre: Barre, 1968.

————. *Scofield Thayer and* The Dial. Carbondale: Southern Illinois UP, 1964.

Joost, Nicholas, and Alvin Sullivan. *D. H. Lawrence and* The Dial. Carbondale: Southern Illinois UP, 1970.

————. The Dial, *Two Author Indexes: Anonymous and Pseudonymous Contributors; Contributions in Clipsheets.* Carbondale: Southern Illinois U Libraries, 1971.

Josephson, Matthew. "Letter to My Friends." *Little Review* 12.1 (1926): 17-19.

Kenner, Hugh. *The Pound Era*. Berkeley: U of California P, 1971.

Knoll, Robert E. "Robert McAlmon: Expatriate Writer and Publisher." *University of Nebraska Studies* ns 18 (1957).

Kramer, Dale. *Chicago Renaissance*. New York: Appleton-Century, 1966.

Lane, George [Amy Lowell and John Gould Fletcher]. "Some Imagist Poets." *Little Review* 2.3 (1915): 27-35.

Laqueur, Walter. *Weimar: A Cultural History, 1918-1933*. New York: Putnam, 1974.

Larrissy, Edward. *Reading Twentieth-Century Poetry: The Language of Gender and Objects*. Oxford: Basil Blackwell, 1990.

Laughlin, James. "EP: A Loving Man." *American Poetry* 2.3 (1985): 64-69.

———. *Pound as Wuz: Essays and Lectures on Ezra Pound*. St. Paul: Greywolf, 1987.

Levenson, Michael H. *A Genealogy of Modernism*. Cambridge: Cambridge UP, 1984.

Lidderdale, Jane. Personal interview. January 1988.

Lidderdale, Jane, and Mary Nicholson. *Dear Miss Weaver: Harriet Shaw Weaver, 1876-1961*. New York: Viking, 1970.

Low, Rachael. *The History of the British Film: 1918-1929*. London: Allen & Unwin, 1971.

Lowell, Amy. "The Poetry Bookshop," *Little Review* 2.3 (1915): 19-22.

Loy, Mina. "Feminist Manifesto." *The Last Lunar Baedeker*. Ed. Roger L. Conover. Highlands: Jargon Society, 1982. 269-71.

Macpherson, Kenneth. Letters to Bryher. January 1931; June 1931. Bryher Papers. Beinecke Rare Book and Manuscript Library, Yale U.

Mandel, Charlotte. "Garbo/Helen: The Self-Projection of Beauty by H.D." *Women's Studies* 7.1/2 (1980): 127-35.

———. "H.D.'s 'Projector II' and *Chang*, a Film of the Jungle." *H.D. Newsletter* 1.2 (1987): 42-45.

———. "Magical Lenses." *H.D.: Woman and Poet*. Ed. Michael King. Orono: National Poetry Foundation, 1986. 301-17.

———. "The Redirected Image: Cinematic Dynamics in the Style of H.D. (Hilda Doolittle)." *Literature/Film Quarterly* 9.1 (1983): 36-45.

Marks, Elaine, and Isabelle de Courtivron, eds. *New French Feminisms*. New York: Schocken, 1981.

Martin, Taffy. *Marianne Moore: Subversive Modernist*. Austin: U of Texas P, 1986.

Massa, Ann. "Ezra Pound to Harriet Monroe: Two Unpublished Letters." *Paideuma* 16.1/2 (1987): 33-47.

McAlmon, Robert. *Being Geniuses Together, 1920-1930*. Revised and with Supplementary Chapters by Kay Boyle. 1938. San Francisco: North Point, 1984.

McMillan, Dougald. Transition: *The History of a Literary Era, 1927-1938*. New York: Braziller, 1976.

Mellow, James R. *Charmed Circle: Gertrude Stein and Company*. New York: Avon, 1974.

Mizener, Arthur. *The Saddest Story: A Biography of Ford Madox Ford*. New York: World Publishing, 1971.

Molesworth, Charles. *Marianne Moore: A Literary Life*. New York: Atheneum, 1990.

Monro, Harold. "The Imagists Discussed." *Egoist* 2.5 (1915): 77-80.

Monroe, Harriet. "As It Was." *Poetry* 1.1 (1912): 19-22.

———. "Its Inner Meaning." *Poetry* 6.6 (1915): 302-5.

———. "James Whitcomb Riley." *Poetry* 8.6 (1916): 305-7.

———. Letters to Alice Corbin Henderson. 3 April 1917; 9 April 1917; 3 July 1917; 7 September 1918; 21 November 1918; 4 March 1921; 14 June 1921; 5 August 1921; 16 October 1921; 26 October 1921; 30 December 1921; 3 February 1922; April 1922; 23 May 1922; 5 August 1922. Alice Corbin Henderson Papers. Harry Ransom Humanities Research Center, U of Texas at Austin.

———. Letter to Ezra Pound [draft]. 3 July 1917. Alice Corbin Henderson Papers. Harry Ransom Humanities Research Center, U of Texas at Austin.

———. Letters to George Platt Brett [carbon and draft]. 2 February 1921, 14 June 1921. Alice Corbin Henderson Papers. Harry Ransom Humanities Research Center, U of Texas at Austin.

———. "Lindsay's Poems." *Poetry* 3.5 (1914): 182-83.

———. "Moody's Poems." *Poetry* 1.2 (1912): 54-57.

———. "The Motive of the Magazine." *Poetry* 1.1 (1912): 26-28.

———. "A Nation-Wide Art." *Poetry* 7.2 (1915): 84-88.

———. "The New Beauty." *Poetry* 2.1 (1913): 22-25.

———. "The Open Door." *Poetry* 1.2 (1912): 62-64.

———. *A Poet's Life*. New York: Macmillan, 1938.

———. Rev. of *The Adventures of Young Maverick*, by Hervey White. *Poetry* 1.3 (1912): 95-96.

———. Rev. of *The Lyric Year*, by Mitchell Kennerley. *Poetry* 1.4 (1912): 128-31.

———. "Rhythms of English Verse II." *Poetry* 3.3 (1913): 100-111.

———. "'That Mass of Dolts.'" *Poetry* 1.5 (1913): 168-70.

———. "Tradition." *Poetry* 2.2 (1913): 67-68.

Monroe, Harriet, and Alice Corbin Henderson, eds. *The New Poetry: An Anthology.* New York: Macmillan, 1917.

———. *The New Poetry: An Anthology.* 1917. Rev. ed. New York: Macmillan, 1923.

Moore, Marianne. "The Accented Syllable." *Egoist* 3.10 (1916): 151-52.

———. *The Complete Prose of Marianne Moore.* Ed. Patricia C. Willis. New York: Viking, 1986.

———. "*The Dial*: A Retrospect." *Life and Letters To-Day* 27.3 (1940): 175-83.

———. "*The Dial*: A Retrospect." *Life and Letters To-Day* 28.1 (1941): 3-9.

———. "*The Dial*: A Retrospect." *Partisan Review* 9.1 (1942): 52-58.

———. Letters to Alyse Gregory. 13 May 1924; 11 July 1924; 14 March 1925. *Dial* Papers. Beinecke Rare Book and Manuscript Library, Yale U.

———. Letters to Bryher. 29 November 1920; 13 December 1920; 28 March 1921; 3 May 1921; 27 March 1926; 28 June 1929. Bryher Papers. Beinecke Rare Book and Manuscript Library, Yale U.

———. Letter to Dorothy Elise De Pollier. 7 March 1925. *Dial* Papers. Beinecke Rare Book and Manuscript Library, Yale U.

———. Letters to Ezra Pound. 8 December 1925; 26 April 1927; 9 February 1928 [damaged]; February or March 1928 [damaged]; 28 August 1928; 19 December 1932; 2 March 1933. Ezra Pound Papers. Beinecke Rare Book and Manuscript Library, Yale U.

———. Letters to Gertrude Stein. 13 July 1926; 4 March 1927; 5 April 1927; 24 February 1928. Gertrude Stein Papers. Beinecke Rare Book and Manuscript Library, Yale U.

———. Letters to H.D. 17 April 1924; 26 October 1924. H.D. Papers. Beinecke Rare Book and Manuscript Library, Yale U.

———. Letters to J. Sibley Watson. 13 October 1925 [carbon]; [1925, draft]; 21 December 1925 [carbon]; 14 January 1926 [carbon] (V:75:02); 12 April 1926 [carbon]; 29 April 1926 [carbon] (V:75:03). Marianne Moore Papers. The Rosenbach Museum and Library, Philadelphia.

———. Letters to Scofield Thayer. 8 June 1921; 2 March 1925; 15 May 1925; 29 June 1925; 7 September 1925; 11 September 1925; 15 October 1925; 10 December 1925; 28 December 1925; 12 March 1926; 23 April 1926. *Dial* Papers. Beinecke Rare Book and Manuscript Library, Yale U.

———. *A Marianne Moore Reader.* 1961. New York: Viking, 1965.

———. *Predilections.* New York: Viking, 1955.

Parisi, Joseph, ed. *Marianne Moore: The Art of a Modernist.* Ann Arbor: UMI P, 1990.

Pearce, T. M. *Alice Corbin Henderson.* Southwest Writers Series. Austin: Steck-Vaughn, 1969.

Platt, Susan Noyes. "*The Little Review*: Early Years and Avant-Garde Ideas." *The Old Guard and the Avant Garde: Modernism in Chicago, 1910-1940.* Ed. Sue Ann Prince. Chicago: U of Chicago P, 1990. 139-54.

———. "Modernism, Formalism, and Politics: The 'Cubism and Abstract Art' Exhibition of 1936 at The Museum of Modern Art." *Art Journal* 47.4 (1988): 284-95.

———. *Modernism in the 1920s: Interpretations of Modern Art in New York from Expressionism to Constructivism.* Ann Arbor: UMI Research P, 1985.

———. "Mysticism in the Machine Age: Jane Heap and *The Little Review*." *Twenty One/Art and Culture* 1.1 (1989): 18-44.

Poli, Bernard J. *Ford Madox Ford and* The Transatlantic Review. Syracuse: Syracuse UP, 1967.

Pollak, Felix. "Margaret Anderson's Saga of Perpetual Emotion." *Carleton Miscellany* 11.4 (1971): 85-93.

Pondrom, Cyrena N. "H.D. and the Origins of Imagism." *Signets: Reading H.D.* Ed. Susan Stanford Friedman and Rachel Blau DuPlessis. Madison: U of Wisconsin P, 1990. 85-109.

———. "Marianne Moore and H.D.: Female Community and Poetic Achievement." *Marianne Moore: Woman and Poet.* Ed. Patricia C. Willis. Orono: National Poetry Foundation, 1990. 371-402.

———, ed. "Selected Letters from H.D. to F. S. Flint: A Commentary on the Imagist Period." *Contemporary Literature* 10.4 (1969): 557-86.

Pound, Ezra. "Cooperation (A Note on the Volume Completed)." *Little Review* 5.3 (1918): 54-56.

———. "Das Schone Papier Vergeudet." *Little Review* 3.7 (1916): 16-17.

———. "Date Line." *Make It New. Essays by Ezra Pound.* New Haven: Yale UP, 1935. 3-19.

———. *Ezra Pound's Poetry and Prose: Contributions to Periodicals.* Ed. Lea Baechler, A. Walton Litz, and James Longenbach. 11 vols. New York: Garland, 1991.

———. *The Letters of Ezra Pound, 1907-1941.* Ed. D. D. Paige. New York: Harcourt, Brace, 1950.

———. *The Letters of Ezra Pound to Alice Corbin Henderson.* Ed. Ira B. Nadel. Austin: U of Texas P, 1993.

———. Letters to Amy Lowell. 1 August 1914; 12 August 1914. Amy Lowell Papers. Houghton Library, Harvard U.

———. Letter to F. S. Flint. 30 January 1921. F. S. Flint Papers. Harry

Ransom Humanities Research Center, U of Texas at Austin.

———. *Pound*/The Little Review: *The Letters of Ezra Pound to Margaret Anderson: The Little Review Correspondence.* Ed. Thomas L. Scott, Melvin J. Friedman, and Jackson R. Bryer. New York: New Directions, 1988.

———. "Small Magazines." *English Journal* 19.9 (1930): 689-704.

———. "The Tradition." *Poetry* 3.4 (1914): 137-41.

Pound, Ezra, and Ford Madox Ford. *Pound/Ford: The Story of a Literary Friendship.* Ed. Brita Lindberg-Seyersted. New York: New Directions, 1982.

Pound, Ezra, and James Joyce. *Pound/Joyce.* Ed. Forrest Read. New York: New Directions, 1970.

Pound, Ezra, and Wyndham Lewis. *Pound/Lewis.* Ed. Timothy Materer. New York: New Directions, 1985.

"Q.K." "Mr. Powys' Book." *New Republic* 7.88 (1916): 256.

Rich, Adrienne. "Compulsory Heterosexuality and Lesbian Existence." *Blood, Bread, and Poetry: Selected Prose, 1979-1985.* New York: Norton, 1986. 23-75.

Ridley, Hugh. "Tretjakov in Berlin." *Culture and Society in the Weimar Republic.* Ed. Keith Bullivant. Manchester: Manchester UP, 1977.

Schulman, Grace. *Marianne Moore: The Poetry of Engagement.* Urbana: U of Illinois P, 1986.

Scott, Bonnie Kime, ed. *The Gender of Modernism.* Bloomington: Indiana UP, 1990.

Shakespear, O[livia]. "The Poetry of D. H. Lawrence." *Egoist* 2.5 (1915): 81.

Slatin, John M. *The Savage's Romance: The Poetry of Marianne Moore.* University Park: Pennsylvania State UP, 1986.

Smoller, Sanford J. *Adrift Among Geniuses: Robert McAlmon, Writer and Publisher of the Twenties.* University Park: Pennsylvania State UP, 1975.

Sochen, June. *The New Woman in Greenwich Village, 1910-1920.* New York: Quadrangle/New York Times Book Co., 1972.

Spender, Dale. *The Writing or the Sex? Or Why You Don't Have to Read Women's Writing to Know It's No Good.* New York: Pergamon, 1989.

Stapleton, Laurence. *Marianne Moore: The Poet's Advance.* Princeton: Princeton UP, 1978.

Stein, Gertrude. "Bundles for Them." *Little Review* 9.3 (1923): 8-9.

Stock, Noel. *The Life of Ezra Pound.* London: Routledge and Kegan Paul, 1970.

Sutton, Walter, ed. *Pound, Thayer, Watson and* The Dial: *A Story in Letters.* Gainesville: UP of Florida, 1994.

Thayer, Scofield. Letters to J. Sibley Watson. 20 March 1923; 27 March 1923. *Dial* Papers. Beinecke Rare Book and Manuscript Library, Yale U.
———. Letter to Marianne Moore. 6 December 1925 (V:65:04). Marianne Moore Papers. The Rosenbach Museum and Library, Philadelphia.
Vendler, Helen. "Marianne Moore." *Marianne Moore*. Ed. Harold Bloom. New York: Chelsea House, 1987. 73-88.
Voss, Norine. "'Saying the Unsayable': An Introduction to Women's Autobiography." *Gender Studies: New Directions in Feminist Criticism*. Ed. Judith Spector. Bowling Green: Bowling Green SU Popular P, 1986. 218-33.
Walker, Cheryl. *Masks Outrageous and Austere: Culture, Psyche, and Persona in Modern Women Poets*. Bloomington: Indiana UP, 1991.
Wasserstrom, William. "Marianne Moore, *The Dial*, and Kenneth Burke." *Western Humanities Review* 17.3 (1963): 249-62.
———. *The Time of* The Dial. Syracuse: Syracuse UP, 1963.
Watson, J. Sibley. Letters to Marianne Moore. 29 August 1925; 7 October 1925; 10 October 1925; 30 November 1925; 24 January 1926 (V:75:02); May 1926; 1 June 1926; 29 January 1927 (V:75:03). Marianne Moore Papers. The Rosenbach Museum and Library, Philadelphia.
———. Letters to Scofield Thayer. 15 March 1923; 10 May 1923; 14 August 1924. *Dial* Papers. Beinecke Rare Book and Manuscript Library, Yale U.
Willett, John. *Art and Politics in the Weimar Period: The New Sobriety, 1917-1933*. New York: Pantheon, 1978.
Williams, Ellen. *Harriet Monroe and the Poetry Renaissance: The First Ten Years of* Poetry, *1912-1922*. Urbana: U of Illinois P, 1977.
Williams, William Carlos. "Prologue: The Return of the Sun." *Little Review* 5.11 (1919): 1-10.
Willis, Patricia. "American Modern: Scofield Thayer, Marianne Moore, and *The Dial*." *Yale Review* 78.2 (1989): 301-17.
———. "William Carlos Williams, Marianne Moore, and *The Dial*." *Sagetrieb* 3.2 (1984): 49-59.
Wright, Frank Lloyd. "A Word from Real Art." *Little Review* 3.6 (1916): 26.
Zilboorg, Caroline. "H.D.'s Influence on Richard Aldington." *Richard Aldington: Reappraisals*. Ed. Charles Doyle. English Literary Studies. Victoria, B.C.: U of Victoria, 1990. 26-44.
———, ed. *Richard Aldington and H.D.: The Early Years in Letters*. Bloomington: Indiana UP, 1992.
Zingman, Barbara. The Dial: *An Author Index*. Troy: Whitston, 1975.

INDEX

DATE DUE

FEB 1 8 1997			
AUG 2 3 2000			
NOV 0 2 2004			